U0130252

How to
Master Skills for the
TOEFL iBT

新托福考试专项进阶

——初级阅读

Reading

Basic

Timothy Hall | Arthur H. Milch | Denise McCormack | E2K

蔡青，刘洋 译

群言出版社
QUNYAN PRESS
· 北京 ·

图书在版编目(CIP)数据

新托福考试专项进阶. 初级阅读 / (美) 霍尔 (Hall,
T.), (美) 米尔奇 (Milch, A. H.), (美) 麦考马克
(McCormack, D.) 编著; 蔡青, 刘洋译. —北京: 群
言出版社, 2009 (2021.3重印)
ISBN 978-7-80080-975-0

Ⅰ. ①新⋯ Ⅱ. ①霍⋯ ②米⋯ ③麦⋯ ④蔡⋯ ⑤刘⋯ Ⅲ. ①英
语—阅读教学—高等教育—自学参考资料 Ⅳ. ①H310.41

中国版本图书馆CIP数据核字 (2009) 第027386号

版权登记: 图字01—2019—4788号

How to Master Skills for the TOEFL iBT Reading Basic
Copyright © 2007, Darakwon Press
Chinese language translation rights © 2009
by Qunyan Press
Chinese language translation rights arranged with Darakwon Press

责任编辑: 刘　波
封面设计: 大愚设计

出版发行: 群言出版社
地　　址: 北京市东城区东厂胡同北巷1号 (100006)
网　　址: www.qypublish.com (官网书城)
电子信箱: dywh@xdf.cn　qunyancbs@126.com
联系电话: 010-62418641　65267783　65263836
经　　销: 全国新华书店

印　　刷: 三河市良远印务有限公司
版　　次: 2009年8月第1版　2021年3月第25次印刷
开　　本: 880mm×1230mm　1/16
印　　张: 19
字　　数: 286千字
书　　号: ISBN 978-7-80080-975-0
定　　价: 58.00元

Contents

Contents (Answer Book)

Introduction

A. Information on the TOEFL® iBT

1. The Format of the TOEFL® iBT

Section	Number of Questions	Timing	Score
Reading	**• 3~4 Passages** 　- approximately 700 words each 　- 10 questions per passage	54~72 min.	30 points
Listening	**• 2~3 Conversations** 　- 12~25 exchanges each (3 min.) 　- 5 questions per conversation **• 3~4 Lectures** 　- 500~750 words each (4~5 min.) 　- 6 questions per lecture	41~57 min.	30 points
BREAK		10 min.	
Speaking	**• 1 Independent Task** (preparation: 15 sec. / response: 45 sec.) ❶ 1 paired choice **• 2 Integrated Tasks:** Read-Listen-Speak (preparation: 30 sec. / response: 60 sec.) ❶ 1 campus situation topic 　- reading: 80~110 words (45 sec.) 　- conversation: 150~180 words (60~80 sec.) ❷ 1 academic course topic 　- reading: 80~110 words (45 sec.) 　- lecture: 150~220 words (60~90 sec.) **• 1 Integrated Task:** Listen-Speak (preparation: 20 sec. / response: 60 sec.) ❶ 1 academic course topic 　- lecture: 230~280 words (90~120 sec.)	17 min.	30 points
Writing	**• 1 Integrated Task:** Read-Listen-Write (20 min.) 　- reading: 250~300 words (3 min.) 　- lecture: 250~320 words (2 min.) 　- a summary of 150~225 words **• 1 Independent Task** (30 min.) 　- a minimum 300-word essay	50 min.	30 points

2. What Is New about the TOEFL® iBT?

(1) The TOEFL® iBT is delivered through the Internet in secure test centers around the world at the same time.

(2) It tests all four language skills and is taken in the order of Reading, Listening, Speaking, and Writing, with a 10-minute break in the middle.

(3) The test is 3 hours long, and all of the four test sections will be completed in one day.

(4) Note-taking is allowed throughout the entire test, including the Reading section. At the end of the test, all notes are collected and destroyed at the test center.

(5) In the Listening section, one lecture may be spoken with a British or Australian accent.

(6) There are integrated tasks requiring test takers to combine more than one language skill in the Speaking and Writing sections.

(7) In the Speaking section, test takers wear headphones and speak into a microphone when they respond. The responses are recorded and transmitted to ETS's Online Scoring Network.

(8) In the Writing section, test takers must type their responses. Handwriting is not possible.

(9) Official scores are reported both online and by mail. All score reports sent after August 1, 2019 automatically include *MyBest*™ scores along with the traditional scores from your selected test date. This new feature combines your best scores for each section from all of your valid scores in the last two years to give you a way to show your best overall test performance.

B. Information on the Reading Section

The Reading section of the TOEFL® iBT measures test takers' ability to understand university-level academic texts. This section has 3~4 passages, and the length of each passage is about 700 words. Some passages may have underlined words or phrases in shade. Test takers can click on them to see a definition or explanation. Test takers have to answer 10 questions per passage. 54~72 minutes are given to complete this section, including the time spent reading the passages and answering the questions.

1. Types of Reading Passages

(1) Exposition – Material that provides an explanation of a topic

(2) Argumentation – Material that presents a point of view about a topic and provides evidence to support it

(3) Historical narrative – An account of a past event or of a person's life, narrated or written by someone else

(1) Vocabulary (1~2 questions per set)
 _ This type of question asks you to identify the meanings of words and phrases in the reading passage.

(2) Reference (0~2 questions per set)
 _ This type of question asks you to identify the referential relationship between the words in the passage.

(3) Factual Information (2~5 questions per set)
 _ This type of question asks you to identify specific information that is explicitly stated in the passage.

(4) Negative Factual Information (0~2 questions per set)
 _ This type of question asks you to check what information is NOT mentioned in the passage.

(5) Sentence Simplification (0~1 question per set)
 _ This type of question asks you to choose the sentence that best paraphrases the essential information in the highlighted sentence.

(6) Inference Questions (1~2 questions per set)
 _ This type of question asks you to identify an idea that is not explicitly stated in the passage.

(7) Rhetorical Purpose Questions (1~2 questions per set)
 _ This type of question asks you why the author uses particular words, phrases, or sentences.

(8) Insert Text Questions (1 question per set)
 _ This type of question provides an example sentence and asks you to decide where the best place for that sentence would be in the passage.

(9) Prose Summary (1 question per set)
 _ This type of question asks you to complete a summary chart with major ideas from the passage.
 _ This question is worth up to 2 points, and partial credit is given.
 _ This type of question does not occur with a Fill in a Table question in a same passage.

(10) Fill in a Table (1 question per set)

　　_ This type of question asks you to identify and organize the major ideas of the passage into table categories.

　　_ his question is worth up to 2 points for tables with 4 correct answers and 3 points for tables with 5 correct answers. Partial credit is given.

　　_ This type of question does not occur with a Prose Summary question in one passage.

2. Question Formats

There are three question formats in the Reading section:

(1) Four-choice questions with a single answer in traditional multiple-choice format

(2) Four-choice questions with a single answer that ask test takers to insert a sentence where it fits best in a passage

(3) "Reading to learn" questions with more than four choices and more than one answer

How to Use This Book

How to Master Skills for the TOEFL® iBT Reading Basic is designed to be used either as a textbook for a TOEFL® iBT reading preparation course or as a tool for individual learners who are preparing for the TOEFL® test on their own. With a total of 10 units, this book is organized to prepare you for the test with a comprehensive understanding of the test and thorough analysis of every question type. Each unit consists of 7 parts and provides a step-by-step program that provides question-solving strategies and the development of test-taking abilities. Here is a description of each unit.

❶ Overview

This part is designed to prepare you for the type of question the unit covers. You will be given a full description of the question type and its application in the passage. You also will be given some useful tips as well as an illustrated introduction and sample.

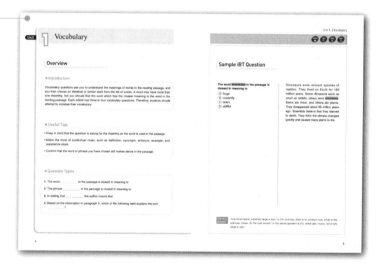

❷ Skill & Drill

The purpose of this section is to ensure that you understand the new types of questions that are described in the overview. You will be given a chance to confirm your understanding in brief texts before starting on the practice exercises. You will read some simple passages and answer the questions of a particular type. This part will help you learn how to deal with each type of question on the Reading section of the TOEFL® iBT.

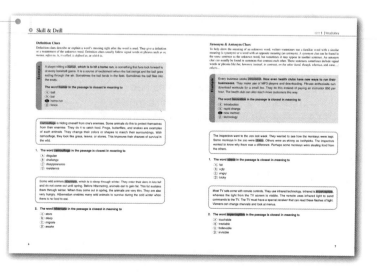

❸ Practice with Short Passages

This section is the first of the practice exercises in each unit. It is a halfway step before practicing with the long passages. Four short passages are offered, and a time limit is given for reading each passage. After reading each passage, you will solve some general comprehension questions as well as other questions of the type that is dealt with in the unit. Definitions of difficult words are offered to help you understand the material better.

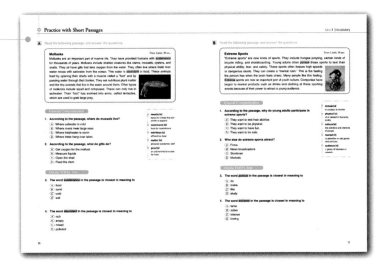

❹ Practice with Long Passages

This section is the second of the practice exercises in each unit. Four long passages are provided, and a time limit is also given for reading each passage. You first read the passage within a time limit and then solve the question or questions of the type that is mainly dealt with in the unit. Important words are also listed to help increase your understanding. Besides, a graphic organizer is provided to help you grasp the overall organization of each passage and understand important points.

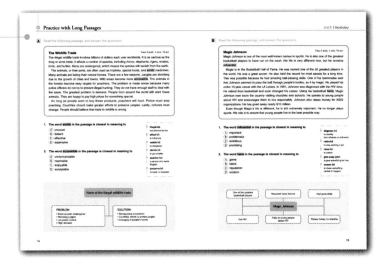

❺ Building Summary Skills

The purpose of this part is for you to understand the previous long passages thoroughly by completing the summaries of them. This will also help you enhance your ability of paraphrasing skills that are strongly recommended to those who are preparing for the TOEFL® iBT test.

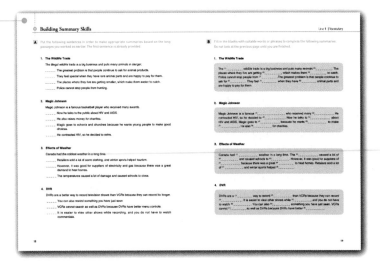

❻ Mini TOEFL iBT

This part gives you a chance to experience an actual TOEFL® iBT test in a shortened form. You will be given two passages with 6 questions each. The topics are similar to those on the actual TOEFL® test, as are the questions.

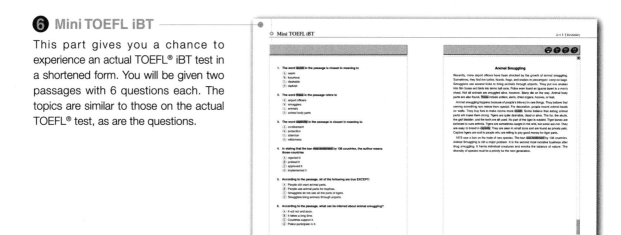

❼ Vocabulary Review

This part offers you a chance to review some of the words you need to remember after finishing each unit. Vocabulary words for each unit are also provided at the back of the book to help you prepare for each unit.

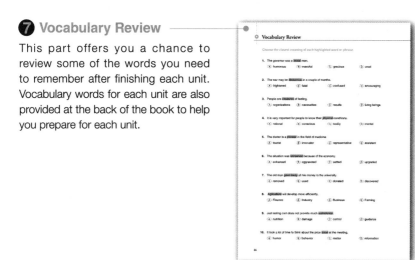

PART 1

Basic Comprehension

In this part, the reading comprehension questions include: vocabulary, reference, factual information, negative factual information, and sentence simplification. The learning objectives of these reading comprehension questions are to identify individual words, referential relations between the words in the passage, factual information, and essential sentences.

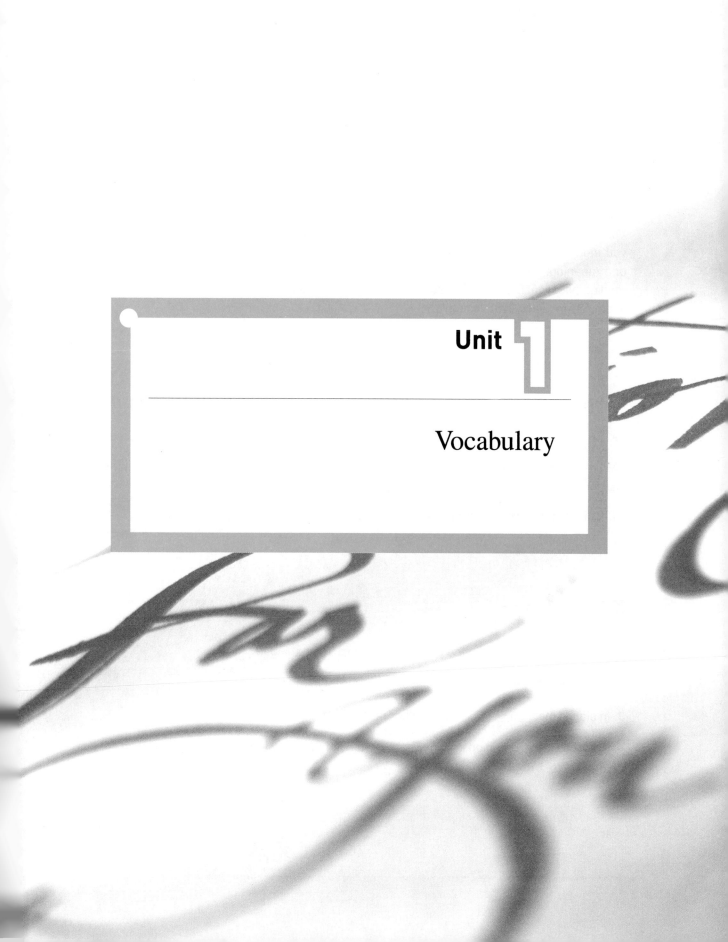

Unit 1

Vocabulary

1 Vocabulary

Overview

■Introduction

Vocabulary questions ask you to understand the meanings of words in the reading passage, and you then choose an identical or similar word from the list of words. A word may have more than one meaning, but you should find the word which has the closest meaning to the word in the reading passage. Each article has three to five vocabulary questions. Therefore, students should attempt to increase their vocabulary.

■Useful Tips

• Keep in mind that the question is asking for the meaning as the word is used in the passage.

• Make the most of contextual clues, such as definition, synonym, antonym, example, and experience clues.

• Confirm that the word or phrase you have chosen still makes sense in the passage.

■Question Types

1. The word _____ in the passage is closest in meaning to

2. The phrase _____ in the passage is closest in meaning to

3. In stating that _____, the author means that

4. Based on the information in paragraph X, which of the following best explains the term _____?

Sample iBT Question

The word enormous in the passage is closest in meaning to

Ⓐ huge
Ⓑ cowardly
Ⓒ scary
Ⓓ skillful

Dinosaurs were ancient species of reptiles. They lived on Earth for 160 million years. Some dinosaurs were as small as rabbits; others were enormous. Some ate meat, and others ate plants. They disappeared about 65 million years ago. Scientists believe that they starved to death. They think the climate changed quickly and caused many plants to die.

Enormous means 'extremely large in size.' In this example, there is an antonym clue, *small*, in the previous clause. So the best answer for the above question is (A), which also means 'extremely large in size.'

5

Skill & Drill

Definition Clues

Definition clues describe or explain a word's meaning right after the word is used. They give a definition or a restatement of the unknown word. Definition clues usually follow signal words or phrases such as *or, means, refers to, is, is called, is defined as*, or *which is*.

Camouflage is hiding oneself from one's enemies. Some animals do this to protect themselves from their enemies. They do it to catch food. Frogs, butterflies, and snakes are examples of such animals. They change their colors or shapes to match their surroundings. With camouflage, they look like grass, leaves, or stones. This improves their chances of survival in the wild.

1. The word camouflage in the passage is closest in meaning to

- (A) disguise
- (B) challenge
- (C) disappearance
- (D) resistence

Some wild animals hibernate, which is to sleep through winter. They enter their dens in late fall and do not come out until spring. Before hibernating, animals eat to gain fat. This fat sustains them through winter. When they come out in spring, the animals are very thin. They are also very hungry. Hibernation enables many wild animals to survive during the cold winter when there is no food to eat.

2. The word hibernate in the passage is closest in meaning to

- (A) store
- (B) sleep
- (C) migrate
- (D) awake

Synonym & Antonym Clues

To help show the meaning of an unknown word, writers sometimes use a familiar word with a similar meaning (a synonym) or a word with an opposite meaning (an antonym). A synonym clue can be found in the same sentence as the unknown word, but sometimes it may appear in another sentence. An antonym clue can usually be found in sentences that contrast each other. These sentences sometimes include signal words or phrases like *but, however, instead, in contrast, on the other hand, though, whereas,* and *some…; others…*

Example

Every business seeks innovation. **Now even health clubs have new ways to run their businesses.** They make use of MP3 players and downloading. Fitness enthusiasts can download workouts for a small fee. They do this instead of paying an instructor $50 per hour. The health club can also reach more customers this way.

The word innovation in the passage is closest in meaning to

ⓐ introduction
ⓑ rapid change
🅒 new method
ⓓ technology

The inspectors went to the zoo last week. They wanted to see how the monkeys were kept. Some monkeys in the zoo were obese. Others were as skinny as toothpicks. The inspectors wanted to know why there was a difference. Perhaps some monkeys were stealing food from the others.

1. **The word obese in the passage is closest in meaning to**

ⓐ fat
ⓑ ugly
ⓒ angry
ⓓ tricky

Most TV sets come with remote controls. They use infrared technology. Infrared is imperceptible, whereas the light from the TV screen is visible. The remote uses infrared light to send commands to the TV. The TV must have a special receiver that can read these flashes of light. Viewers can change channels and look at menus.

2. **The word imperceptible in the passage is closest in meaning to**

ⓐ touchable
ⓑ treatable
ⓒ believable
ⓓ invisible

Example Clues

Example clues provide examples of the unknown word. The unknown word and its examples have a part-whole relationship, so the unknown word is usually a more general word which can represent its examples. The clue may be introduced, but not always, by signal words such as *include, for example, for instance, such as*, and *like*. The clues are not always in the same sentence.

> **Example**
>
> In spring, many people suffer from **coughing, itching, sneezing, runny noses, and watery eyes**. People may think these are indications of a cold. If these symptoms last for a long time, they should see a doctor. It could be an allergy caused by dust, mold, or pollen. These can cause a lot of irritation.
>
> **The word symptoms in the passage is closest in meaning to**
>
> Ⓐ signs
> Ⓑ symbols
> Ⓒ patterns
> Ⓓ phenomena

> The northeast part of the United States gets the most forms of precipitation. The region is subject to rain, snow, and sleet. Some years, there is so much that it may damage crops. This causes many farmers to borrow money from the bank to pay for their expenses. It can also cause damage to buildings.

1. **The word precipitation in the passage is closest in meaning to**

    Ⓐ changes in temperature
    Ⓑ water from the sky
    Ⓒ dust in the air
    Ⓓ clouds above mountains

> The wolverine is a hardy animal. It is strong, and it can live in cold temperatures. It is able to catch large animals. It lives in the forests of Canada and the United States. The wolverine is able to walk up to 100 miles per day while hunting for food. It is strong and aggressive enough even to steal food from bears.

2. **The word hardy in the passage is closest in meaning to**

    Ⓐ horrible
    Ⓑ angry
    Ⓒ tough
    Ⓓ greedy

Experience Clues

Experience clues rely on your own knowledge or experience to understand an unknown word. Many times, the text will mention something you know about, but it will not directly tell you what the word means. So you need to use your logic and reasoning skills based on your experience and common knowledge.

Example

Digital dictionaries are very effective learning tools. They check spelling and word meanings. They also give synonyms. Even better, they show the words in a sentence. This helps students learn about the grammar of the word. Students can learn to use words with fewer mistakes. They become better writers this way.

The word effective in the passage is closest in meaning to

(A) impressive
(B) handy
(C) **useful**
(D) valid

Soccer has been slow to catch on in the U.S. This is because most people prefer to watch baseball, basketball, and football. These are American inventions. Many of them think that soccer is a sport for Europeans or South Americans. It is not a part of the USA's identity. They also do not like how the games have low scores.

1. **The phrase catch on in the passage is closest in meaning to**

(A) get popular
(B) be entertained
(C) get rooted
(D) be confusing

Clouds form when air near the ground is heated by the sun. The hot air rises in the atmosphere because it is less dense than the air around it. Eventually, the rising air cools. The water, at first in vapor form, condenses. It forms visible droplets. At this point, you can see the cloud.

2. **The word dense in the passage is closest in meaning to**

(A) thick
(B) hot
(C) cold
(D) light

A Read the following passage, and answer the questions.

Mollusks

Time Limit: 30 sec.

Mollusks are an important part of marine life. They have provided humans with sustenance for thousands of years. Mollusks include shelled creatures like clams, mussels, oysters, and snails. They all have gills that take oxygen from the water. They often live where fresh river water mixes with saltwater from the ocean. This water is abundant in food. These animals feed by opening their shells with a muscle called a "foot" and by passing water through their bodies. They eat nutritious plant matter and the tiny animals that live in the water around them. Other types of mollusks include squid and octopuses. These can only live in saltwater. Their "foot" has evolved into arms, called tentacles, which are used to grab large prey.

General Comprehension

1. **According to the passage, where do mussels live?**

   Ⓐ Where saltwater is cold
   Ⓑ Where rivers meet large seas
   Ⓒ Where freshwater is warm
   Ⓓ Where trees hang over lakes

2. **According to the passage, what do gills do?**

   Ⓐ Get oxygen for the mollusk
   Ⓑ Measure liquids
   Ⓒ Open the shell
   Ⓓ Feed the clam

○ **sustenance (n)**
food for nourishment

○ **muscle (n)**
tissue in a body that can shrink or expand

○ **nutritious (a)**
efficient as food

○ **matter (n)**
physical substance; stuff

○ **prey (n)**
an animal that is hunted for food

On the TOEFL Test

3. **The word sustenance in the passage is closest in meaning to**

   Ⓐ cold
   Ⓑ sand
   Ⓒ food
   Ⓓ salt

4. **The word abundant in the passage is closest in meaning to**

   Ⓐ rich
   Ⓑ empty
   Ⓒ mixed
   Ⓓ polluted

B Read the following passage, and answer the questions.

Extreme Sports

Time Limit: 30 sec.

"Extreme sports" are new kinds of sports. They include bungee jumping, certain kinds of bicycle riding, and skateboarding. Young adults often pursue these sports to test their physical ability, fear, and safety. These sports often feature high speeds or dangerous stunts. They can create a "mental rush." This is the feeling the person has when the brain feels stress. Many people like this feeling. Extreme sports are now an important part of youth culture. Companies have begun to market products such as drinks and clothing at these sporting events because of their power to attract a young audience.

General Comprehension

1. **According to the passage, why do young adults participate in extreme sports?**

    Ⓐ They want to test their abilities.
    Ⓑ They want to be physical.
    Ⓒ They want to have fun.
    Ⓓ They want to be safe.

2. **Who else do extreme sports attract?**

    Ⓐ Markets
    Ⓑ News broadcasters
    Ⓒ Stuntmen
    Ⓓ Firms

On the TOEFL Test

3. **The word pursue in the passage is closest in meaning to**

    Ⓐ do
    Ⓑ make
    Ⓒ like
    Ⓓ study

4. **The word extreme in the passage is closest in meaning to**

    Ⓐ tame
    Ⓑ sober
    Ⓒ intense
    Ⓓ boring

○ **include (v)**
to contain; to involve

○ **physical (a)**
of or related to the body; bodily

○ **culture (n)**
the activities and interests of people

○ **market (v)**
to advertise or sell goods and services

○ **audience (n)**
a group of listeners or viewers

Read the following passage, and answer the questions.

Disasters in Quebec

Time Limit: 30 sec.

The year 2003 was brutal for Quebec. The reason is fires. It was the most disastrous fire season in recent times. It was also the most expensive year for natural disasters in this region of Canada. The harshness of the fires was explained by 3 years of bad weather. Some places had their worst droughts in 100 years. The land was very dry. Over 2,400 forest fires burned vast areas of land. It cost nearly $500 million to fight these fires. Insurance companies paid out $250 million in claims. Three firemen lost their lives. It will take a long time to repair the damage. The year 2003 was the worst in a decade.

General Comprehension

1. **According to the passage, what caused a lot of damage in Quebec?**

   (A) storms
   (B) floods
   (C) snow
   (D) fire

2. **What was remarkable about the year 2003?**

   (A) It was the most expensive year for disasters.
   (B) Insurance companies made money.
   (C) Three mechanics lost their lives.
   (D) It was the worst in 5 years.

On the TOEFL Test

3. **The word harshness in the passage is closest in meaning to**

   (A) ease
   (B) worry
   (C) severity
   (D) discipline

4. **The word decade in the passage is closest in meaning to**

   (A) 10 years
   (B) 50 years
   (C) 100 years
   (D) 1,000 years

brutal (a)
very punishing

disastrous (a)
like a disaster

recent (a)
not long ago

burn (v)
to ruin with fire

lose (v)
to no longer have

repair (v)
to fix

D Read the following passage, and answer the questions.

The Brain and Computers

Time Limit: 30 sec.

One day, we will be able to control computers by thinking. We will not need a keyboard or a mouse. Scientists are developing ways to control computers with brainwaves. Korean researchers have made software that measures brain activity. When a person is relaxed, the brain is less active. The computer detects this. It then changes the graphics on a screen. Engineers call this a computer-brain interface. This is a direct link between the brain and the computer. Another researcher at MIT uses monkeys to map brain signals. For a monkey to grab food, its brain sends out electric signals to the arm. The researcher uses these signals to control a robotic arm. The robotic arm grabs for the food before the monkey does.

General Comprehension

1. **How will we control computers in the future?**

   (A) With a key
   (B) With our brains
   (C) With our eyes
   (D) With our hands

2. **What is a computer-brain interface?**

   (A) A way of looking at computers
   (B) A screen that has a brain in its center
   (C) A connection between the brain and the computer
   (D) An electric signal that moves robot arms in a circle

On the TOEFL Test

3. **The word detects in the passage is closest in meaning to**

   (A) calls
   (B) helps
   (C) drives
   (D) notices

4. **The word grabs in the passage is closest in meaning to**

   (A) throws
   (B) snatches
   (C) attacks
   (D) steals

- **brainwave (n)**
  electric signal in your brain
- **researcher (n)**
  someone who studies something deeply
- **graphics (n)**
  the visual aspect of computers
- **link (n)**
  connection; association; bond
- **map (v)**
  to locate something in space
- **robotic (a)**
  related to robots

Practice with Long Passages

A Read the following passage, and answer the questions.

The Wildlife Trade

Time Limit: 1 min. 30 sec.

The illegal wildlife trade involves billions of dollars each year worldwide. It is as serious as the drug or arms trade. It affects a number of species, including rhinos, elephants, tigers, snakes, birds, and turtles. Many are endangered, which means the species will vanish from the earth.

The animals, or their parts, are often used as trophies, special foods, and exotic medicines. Many animals are losing their natural homes. There are a few reasons. Jungles are shrinking due to the growth of cities and towns. Wild areas become more accessible. The animals in the forests become easy targets for poachers. The problem is made worse because many police officers do not try to prevent illegal hunting. They do not have enough staff to deal with the issue. The greatest problem is demand. People from around the world still want these animals. They are happy to pay high prices for something special.

As long as people want to buy these products, poachers will hunt. Police must stop poaching. Countries should make greater efforts to preserve jungles. Lastly, cultures must change. People should believe that trade in wildlife is wrong.

1. The word exotic in the passage is closest in meaning to

- (A) unusual
- (B) distant
- (C) effective
- (D) expensive

2. The word accessible in the passage is closest in meaning to

- (A) understandable
- (B) reachable
- (C) enjoyable
- (D) acceptable

illegal (a)
not allowed by law

affect (v)
to influence

vanish (v)
to disappear

shrink (v)
to get smaller

poacher (n)
a person who hunts illegally

preserve (v)
to keep; to maintain

Harm of the Illegal Wildlife Trade

PROBLEM:
- Many species endangered
- Shrinking jungles
- Lax police control
- High demand

SOLUTION:
- Strong police crackdown
- Countries' efforts to protect jungles
- Changing of people's minds

B Read the following passage, and answer the questions.

Magic Johnson

Time Limit: 1 min. 50 sec.

Magic Johnson is one of the most well-known names in sports. He is also one of the greatest basketball players to have run on the court. His life is very different now, but he remains influential.

Magic is in the Basketball Hall of Fame. He was named one of the 50 greatest players in the world. He was a great scorer. He also held the record for most assists for a long time. This was possible because he had amazing ball-passing skills. One of his teammates said that Johnson seemed to pass the ball through people's bodies, as if by magic. He played his entire 13-year career with the LA Lakers. In 1991, Johnson was diagnosed with the HIV virus. He retired from basketball and soon changed his career. Using his basketball fame, Magic Johnson now tours the country visiting churches and schools. He speaks to young people about HIV and encourages them to live responsibly. Johnson also raises money for AIDS organizations. He has given away nearly $10 million.

Even though Magic's life is different, he is still extremely important. He no longer plays sports. His role is to ensure that young people live in the best possible way.

1. **The word influential in the passage is closest in meaning to**

    (A) important
    (B) problematic
    (C) ambitious
    (D) promising

2. **The word fame in the passage is closest in meaning to**

    (A) game
    (B) talent
    (C) reputation
    (D) wisdom

diagnose (v)
to identify
(as a disease or sickness)

retire (v)
to stop working a job

raise (v)
to collect

give away (phr)
to give something for free

ensure (v)
to make something
certain to happen

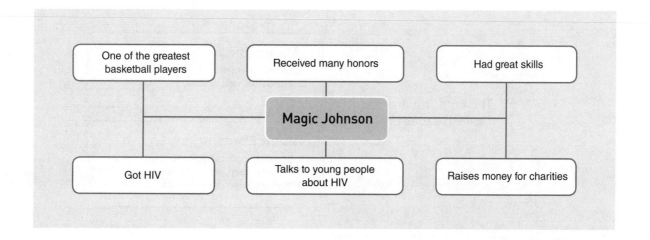

One of the greatest basketball players

Received many honors

Had great skills

Magic Johnson

Got HIV

Talks to young people about HIV

Raises money for charities

Read the following passage, and answer the questions.

The Effects of Weather

Time Limit: 1 min. 20 sec.

It was a brutal winter in eastern Canada this year. It comes as a surprise because last winter was so mild. The cold was bad for many people but good for some.

This year saw record low temperatures for long periods of time. There were nearly 25 days below −20˚C. This was worsened by the wind. It made temperatures feel even lower. Snow days, when schools close because of snow, actually became "cold days." A few schools had to close because the weather froze pipes and disabled heating systems. The cold also impacted agriculture. Forty percent of the grapevines had to be replaced in a few areas.

The cold was good for some people, however. Energy suppliers increased sales to match the heating demand. Clothing suppliers were quick to see opportunities also. They were able to sell lots of winter clothing. The cold weather also created ideal conditions for winter sports. This helped tourism and helped people appreciate the cold. Despite its negative effects, people were able to find the upside.

1. **The phrase record low in the passage is closest in meaning to**

   Ⓐ the lowest ever
   Ⓑ much lower
   Ⓒ the least low
   Ⓓ very low

2. **The word appreciate in the passage is closest in meaning to**

   Ⓐ thank
   Ⓑ overcome
   Ⓒ value
   Ⓓ improve

brutal (a)
harsh; severe

worsen (v)
to make worse

disabled (a)
not working

impact (v)
to hit or strike

replace (v)
to be or provide a substitute for

upside (n)
positive side

Negative Effects:
1. Schools were closed.
2. Agriculture was affected.

The Cold Weather in Eastern Canada

Positive Effects:
1. Energy suppliers made money.
2. Clothing suppliers made money.
3. Winter sports helped tourism.

D Read the following passage, and answer the questions.

DVR

Time Limit: 1 min. 20 sec.

Digital video recorders (DVRs) are changing the way people watch TV. They are expensive. However, they offer a number of advantages over the old ways of watching and recording TV shows.

DVRs are basically hard drives that can hold up to 30 hours of recorded shows. People can also watch one show while another is recording. Viewers do not have to watch commercials anymore. They can fast-forward to the next part of their show and skip the ads. They can even press pause in real time, rewind, and replay the segment they just saw. Meanwhile, the DVR records the program to the end.

VCRs, which use cassettes, are less convenient. First, you have to buy 15 cassettes to match a DVR's capacity. It requires a lot of storage space. Second, you cannot search through recordings as quickly or as easily as you can with a DVR. VCRs do not have the same menu options. Some DVRs also have great search functions. These allow viewers to search by title, director, and even topic.

1. The word advantages in the passage is closest in meaning to

   (A) developments

   (B) drawbacks

   (C) chances

   (D) benefits

2. The word capacity in the passage is closest in meaning to

   (A) suitability

   (B) ability

   (C) facility

   (D) durability

offer (v)
to provide or present

commercial (n)
advertisement

segment (n)
piece, section, division

match (v)
to equal

require (v)
to need or demand

option (n)
a choice

DVRs are a better way to record than VCRs.

DVRs
- Do not need cassettes
- Can view and record at the same time
- Can rewind while recording
- Are easy to search through

VCRs
- Need cassettes
- Cannot view and record at the same time
- Cannot rewind while recording
- Are not easy to search through

Building Summary Skills

A Put the following sentences in order to make appropriate summaries based on the long passages you worked on earlier. The first sentence is already provided.

1. The Wildlife Trade

The illegal wildlife trade is a big business and puts many animals in danger.

_____ The greatest problem is that people continue to ask for animal products.

_____ They feel special when they have rare animal parts and are happy to pay for them.

_____ The places where they live are getting smaller, which make them easier to catch.

_____ Police cannot stop people from hunting.

2. Magic Johnson

Magic Johnson is a famous basketball player who received many awards.

_____ Now he talks to the public about HIV and AIDS.

_____ He also raises money for charities.

_____ Magic goes to schools and churches because he wants young people to make good choices.

_____ He contracted HIV, so he decided to retire.

3. Effects of Weather

Canada had the coldest weather in a long time.

_____ Retailers sold a lot of warm clothing, and winter sports helped tourism.

_____ However, it was good for suppliers of electricity and gas because there was a great demand to heat homes.

_____ The temperatures caused a lot of damage and caused schools to close.

4. DVR

DVRs are a better way to record television shows than VCRs because they can record for longer.

_____ You can also rewind something you have just seen.

_____ VCRs cannot search as well as DVRs because DVRs have better menu controls.

_____ It is easier to view other shows while recording, and you do not have to watch commercials.

B Fill in the blanks with suitable words or phrases to complete the following summaries. Do not look at the previous page until you are finished.

1. The Wildlife Trade

The (1)_____ wildlife trade is a big business and puts many animals (2)_____. The places where they live are getting (3)_____, which makes them (4)_____ to catch. Police cannot stop people from (5)_____.The greatest problem is that people continue to ask for (6)_____. They feel (7)_____ when they have (8)_____ animal parts and are happy to pay for them.

2. Magic Johnson

Magic Johnson is a famous (1)_____ who received many (2)_____. He contracted HIV, so he decided to (3)_____. Now he talks to (4)_____ about HIV and AIDS. Magic goes to (5)_____ because he wants (6)_____ to make (7)_____. He also (8)_____ for charities.

3. Effects of Weather

Canada had (1)_____ weather in a long time. The (2)_____ caused a lot of (3)_____ and caused schools to (4)_____. However, it was good for suppliers of (5)_____ because there was a great (6)_____ to heat homes. Retailers sold a lot of (7)_____, and winter sports helped (8)_____.

4. DVR

DVRs are a (1)_____ way to record (2)_____ than VCRs because they can record (3)_____. It is easier to view other shows while (4)_____, and you do not have to watch (5)_____. You can also (6)_____ something you have just seen. VCRs cannot (7)_____ as well as DVRs because DVRs have better (8)_____.

1. **The word lavish in the passage is closest in meaning to**

   - (A) warm
   - (B) luxurious
   - (C) desirable
   - (D) darkish

2. **The word these in the passage refers to**

   - (A) airport officers
   - (B) smugglers
   - (C) animals
   - (D) animal body parts

3. **The word captivity in the passage is closest in meaning to**

   - (A) confinement
   - (B) protection
   - (C) attention
   - (D) wilderness

4. **In stating that the ban was endorsed by 136 countries, the author means those countries**

   - (A) rejected it
   - (B) praised it
   - (C) approved it
   - (D) implemented it

5. **According to the passage, all of the following are true EXCEPT:**

   - (A) People still want animal parts.
   - (B) People use animal parts for trophies.
   - (C) Smugglers do not use all the parts of tigers.
   - (D) Smugglers bring animals through airports.

6. **According to the passage, what can be inferred about animal smuggling?**

   - (A) It will not end soon.
   - (B) It takes a long time.
   - (C) Countries support it.
   - (D) Police participate in it.

Animal Smuggling

Recently, more airport officers have been shocked by the growth of animal smuggling. Sometimes, they find live turtles, lizards, frogs, and snakes in passengers' carry-on bags. Smugglers use several tricks to bring animals through airports. They put live snakes into film boxes and birds into tennis ball cans. Police even found an iguana taped to a man's chest. Not all animals are smuggled alive, however. Many die on the way. Animal body parts are also found. These include antlers, skins, dried organs, hooves, or feet.

Animal smuggling happens because of people's interest in rare things. They believe that owning something rare makes them special. For decoration, people mount animal heads on walls. They buy furs to make rooms more lavish. Some believe that eating animal parts will make them strong. Tigers are quite desirable, dead or alive. The fur, the skulls, the gall bladder, and the teeth are all used. No part of the tiger is wasted. Tiger bones are believed to cure arthritis. Tigers are sometimes caught in the wild, but some are not. They are easy to breed in captivity. They are seen in small zoos and are found as private pets. Captive tigers are sold to people who are willing to pay good money for tiger parts.

1975 saw a ban on the trade of rare species. The ban was endorsed by 136 countries. Animal smuggling is still a major problem. It is the second most lucrative business after drug smuggling. It harms individual creatures and wrecks the balance of nature. The diversity of species must be a priority for the next generation.

7. The word **pioneers** in the passage is closest in meaning to

   (A) diehards
   (B) innovators
   (C) ancestors
   (D) pilots

8. The word **prototype** in the passage is closest in meaning to

   (A) product
   (B) model
   (C) engine
   (D) form

9. The phrase **each other** in the passage refers to

   (A) problems
   (B) roads
   (C) people
   (D) airplanes

10. The word **issue** in the passage is closest in meaning to

    (A) concern
    (B) belief
    (C) distribution
    (D) possibility

11. According to the passage, all of the following are true EXCEPT:

    (A) Technology is advancing.
    (B) The car does not get good mileage.
    (C) Flying cars will be used in five years.
    (D) Flying cars cost a lot of money right now.

12. Based on the information in the passage, what can be inferred about flying cars?

    (A) They offer a number of advantages over normal cars.
    (B) Famous people will buy them.
    (C) They cost a lot of money.
    (D) They do not have gears.

The Flying Car

Have you ever dreamed about flying in the sky in your own flying car? It would be wonderful to fly at will. You would not need to spend hours in traffic everyday. You could also travel large distances very quickly. Since the Wright brothers built their airplane in 1903, several pioneers have worked to invent a flying car. According to car industry experts, the dream of flying cars will soon be real.

A talented engineer named Paul Moller recently invented such a car. Moller has spent almost 40 years and millions of dollars developing his prototype. The car has room for four people. It is designed to take off and land in small spaces and can fly as high as 10,000 meters. It uses four external engines to move up, down, and sideways. The car, unfortunately, is not fuel-efficient. It does not get good mileage. Moller's car is guided by computers and satellite systems. In case of a crash, it has airbags and parachutes. He showed that a car could be built to fly.

A flying car society has many problems to solve. The first concerns safety. If there are no roads, what will stop people from crashing into each other? It is easy for a single car to travel, but what happens when there are thousands? Another issue is cost. At the moment, it costs several million dollars for one car. How can people afford to buy them? The third issue is fuel. There needs to be enough fuel to supply these cars. The fuel also needs to be less polluting than the kind we use now. Still, technology is advancing. It is likely that these problems will be solved in a few years. Then, dreams of quick and easy flight will be realities.

Vocabulary Review

Choose the closest meaning of each highlighted word or phrase.

1. The governor was a brutal man.

   (A) humorous   (B) merciful   (C) gracious   (D) cruel

2. The war may be disastrous in a couple of months.

   (A) frightened   (B) fatal   (C) confused   (D) encouraging

3. People are creatures of feeling.

   (A) organizations   (B) necessities   (C) results   (D) living beings

4. It is very important for people to know their physical conditions.

   (A) rational   (B) conscious   (C) bodily   (D) mental

5. The doctor is a pioneer in the field of medicine.

   (A) tourist   (B) innovator   (C) representative   (D) assistant

6. The situation was worsened because of the economy.

   (A) enhanced   (B) aggravated   (C) settled   (D) upgraded

7. The old man gave away all his money to the university.

   (A) removed   (B) used   (C) donated   (D) discovered

8. Agriculture will develop more efficiently.

   (A) Finance   (B) Industry   (C) Business   (D) Farming

9. Just eating corn does not provide much sustenance.

   (A) nutrition   (B) damage   (C) control   (D) guidance

10. It took a lot of time to think about the price issue at the meeting.

    (A) humor   (B) behavior   (C) matter   (D) information

Unit 2

Reference

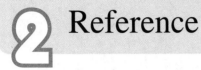

Reference

Overview

■Introduction

Reference questions ask you to understand the relationship between the words in the passage. Usually, the relationship is between a pronoun and the word to which the pronoun refers. When you find a referring word or pronoun in the passage, you should find out whether the word is singular or plural and if it is male or female.

■Useful Tips

• The word to which a pronoun refers often appears before the pronoun in the same clause.

• Substitute your answer for the highlighted word or phrase in the passage.

• Make sure that your answer is the same number (singular or plural) and case (first, second, or third person) as the highlighted pronoun.

■Question Types

1. The word _____ in the passage refers to

2. The phrase _____ in the passage refers to

Sample iBT Question

The word their in the passage refers to

- (A) crustaceans
- (B) humans
- (C) countries
- (D) dishes

Crustaceans, such as crabs, lobsters, and shrimp, live in water and on land. They are easy to catch and even to raise. This has allowed humans to use them as food. Countries along the sea use crustaceans as part of their traditional dishes. They are nutritious and easy to cook. They are also very tasty.

 The highlighted word *their* refers to the word *countries*, which is mentioned earlier in the same sentence. So the correct answer is (C).

Personal Pronouns

Personal pronouns are a set of words which refer back to someone (or sometimes something) previously mentioned in the passage. They are made up of *I, you, he, she, it, we, they*, and their derived forms (e.g. *me, yours, his, her, its, them*, etc.). On the TOEFL® iBT, third-person pronouns such as *it, its, they, their*, and *them* are especially frequently asked.

Example

An **auction** is a popular way of buying and selling. It is a useful way of deciding the value of things. E-Bay is a good example. On the Internet, buyers bid against one another to buy the item they want. Sellers can sell items at the highest price that buyers will pay.

The word it in the passage refers to

Ⓐ theory
Ⓑ price
Ⓒ process
Ⓓ auction

Anne Frank was a victim of World War II. She wrote a diary while hiding in a room from the Nazis. She was there for two years. It shows how miserable life under the Nazis was. After she died, her father published Anne's diary, and **it** became one of the most widely-read books in the world.

1. The word it in the passage refers to

Ⓐ victim
Ⓑ World War II
Ⓒ Anne
Ⓓ diary

In the 1920's, jazz was not well known to white people. Louis Armstrong was a musician who made jazz known to **them**. At the age of 14, Louis learned to play the trumpet. He soon got jobs in nightclubs. His unique voice and brilliant trumpet playing attracted black and white fans. Jazz became famous to all audiences soon after.

2. The word them in the passage refers to

Ⓐ white people
Ⓑ nightclubs
Ⓒ fans
Ⓓ audiences

Demonstratives

Demonstratives are pronouns or adjectives that point out which item is being referred to. In English, they include *this, that, these,* and *those. This* and *these* refer to something or someone near to the speaker/writer. *That* and *those* refer to something or someone distant from the speaker/writer. Sometimes *the former* and *the latter* are also asked on the TOEFL® iBT.

Example

It was a difficult time. **The southern states wanted to separate from the Union.** President Abraham Lincoln was not happy. This would divide his country in two. He needed to find a way to make the states agree upon the issue of slavery. The president promised that he would reunite the country.

The word this in the passage refers to

Ⓐ a difficult time
🅱 the southern states wanting to separate from the Union
Ⓒ the president's unhappiness
Ⓓ the issue of slavery

One day, Isaac Newton was sitting under a tree. He was thinking about how objects in the world were related to one another. This was nothing new. Newton often reflected upon these things. He was a physicist. Suddenly, the wind blew. An apple fell from the tree branch above him and hit him on the head. It shocked him into a series of thoughts that soon became the theory of gravity.

1. **The phrase these things in the passage refers to**

    Ⓐ sitting under a tree
    Ⓑ relationships between objects
    Ⓒ apples falling from the tree
    Ⓓ a series of thoughts

October 29, 1929, was a day when stock prices dropped. Investors panicked. They sold their stocks quickly. That was the first time in 30 years that America's economy had problems. People were afraid of losing money. Even worse, investing banks also lost all their money. Rich people became poor overnight.

2. **The word that in the passage refers to**

    Ⓐ a day when stock prices dropped
    Ⓑ investors' panicking
    Ⓒ losing money
    Ⓓ becoming poor suddenly

Relative Pronouns

Relative pronouns introduce a clause which modifies the noun right before them. The relative pronouns *which, that,* and *who* are frequently asked on the TOEFL® iBT. *Who* refers to people and *which* to things; *that* refers to both. Sometimes, however, *which* can refer to the entire previous clause.

Example

Scientists have been looking for energy sources to replace oil. They have studied wind, ethanol, and nuclear energy. They have also started to look at coal again. **Coal**, which is the cheapest energy source, is found in many parts of the world. However, it is dangerous to mine. It also pollutes the environment.

The word which in the passage refers to

- Ⓐ nuclear energy
- Ⓑ ethanol
- Ⓒ wind
- **Ⓓ coal**

The guitar, which is also known as the poor man's piano, has been cherished by many cultures. Spain made the guitar great. This country is responsible for many classical pieces. Brazil is also famous for guitar music. It developed the style of Bossa Nova. This style blends classical and jazz styles.

1. **The word which in the passage refers to**

- Ⓐ piano
- Ⓑ guitar
- Ⓒ Spain
- Ⓓ Brazil

Taxes are a necessary part of society. They help fund schools and build roads. Last year, taxes, which were levied at the rate of 25%, caused the citizens to complain. The people felt taxes were too high. The citizens wanted to be able to put more money into savings. They believed the government was not efficient.

2. **The word which in the passage refers to**

- Ⓐ schools
- Ⓑ society
- Ⓒ taxes
- Ⓓ roads

Indefinite Pronouns

Indefinite pronouns refer to an unknown or undetermined person, place, or thing. Indefinite pronouns include words with *some, any, every,* or *no* (e.g. *someone, anyone, everyone,* and *no one*) and *one, another, some, others, each,* and *none*.

Example

There are many **members** in an orchestra. Each has his or her own part to play. The first violins often play the basic melody. The cellos and violas play the harmony. Of course, the bass and tuba play the low notes. Clarinets and flutes often play the incidental parts of the music. Together, the musicians make beautiful sounds.

The word each in the passage refers to

Ⓐ members
Ⓑ orchestra
Ⓒ cello
Ⓓ tuba

The crisis at Three Mile Island was almost a huge nuclear disaster. This power plant provided electricity for thousands of people in Pennsylvania. One day, a valve failed to close. The core heated up for three days. It nearly exploded. The area around the plant was in great danger. Most within 20 miles would have died. It would have involved thousands of people.

1. **The word most in the passage refers to**

Ⓐ people in Pennsylvania
Ⓑ people who did not close the valve
Ⓒ people living around the plant
Ⓓ people who died

The Wizard of Oz is a famous movie. Its music is great. Millions of people grew up watching this movie on TV every year. Of course, many of them can sing the songs. The most memorable song begins with the very simple phrase "Somewhere over the rainbow." Many Americans can finish the rest of the verse. Even though some cannot sing the rest of the verse, it is part of the fabric of culture in the U.S.

2. **The word some in this passage means**

Ⓐ people in the movie
Ⓑ people in America
Ⓒ people who write songs
Ⓓ people from many different countries

Practice with Short Passages

A Read the following passage, and answer the questions.

A Laser Pointer Is Not a Toy

Time Limit: 40 sec.

A middle school student in Texas had to appear in front of a judge. A few weeks ago, the student aimed a laser pointer at his teacher's eyes in science class. The angry teacher asked him to stop, but the student persisted. As a result, the teacher suffered from eye problems. He took the student to court.

It is generally believed that looking directly into a laser is as dangerous as looking into the sun. The light can harm the retina, which is the back portion of the eye. The teacher made the student aware of this at the time. The student knew he could be hurting the teacher. The judge replied, "Laser pointers are not toys. They can be harmful." The student was fined for knowingly hurting the teacher.

General Comprehension

1. **Why did the teacher take the student to court?**

   (A) The student had a laser pointer.
   (B) The student hurt the teacher on purpose.
   (C) The teacher was angry at the student's parents.
   (D) The teacher wanted to continue with his lesson.

2. **Laser pointers are dangerous because**

   (A) they can melt plastic and glass
   (B) they can distract the teacher
   (C) they come in different colors
   (D) they can damage one's sight

On the TOEFL Test

3. **The word him in the passage refers to**

   (A) the student
   (B) the judge
   (C) the teacher
   (D) the student's father

4. **The word they in the passage refers to**

   (A) eyes
   (B) students
   (C) laser pointers
   (D) toys

aim (v)
to point or direct something at

persist (v)
to continue

aware of (phr)
conscious of

fine (v)
to be charged money by a judge

knowingly (ad)
on purpose; deliberately; intentionally

B Read the following passage, and answer the questions.

"Hey Jude" Time Limit: 30 sec.

According to the *Billboard* chart, "Hey Jude" was the number one song between 1960 and 1969. It was released in 1968 and topped the *Billboard* chart for nine weeks. It sold more than 4 million copies. It was recorded as one of the best-selling singles of the 1960s. It was also one of the Beatles' most successful songs.

Paul McCartney wrote the song during a long car ride. He wrote it for John Lennon's son, Julian. He was depressed because of his parent's divorce. Paul tried to send a hopeful message to cheer him up. The song started with "Hey Jude, don't make it bad, take a sad song, and make it better." Julian recalled that in many ways he was closer to Paul than to his father.

General Comprehension

1. **Why did Paul McCartney write the song "Hey Jude"?**

   Ⓐ To comfort a sad boy
   Ⓑ To set a world record
   Ⓒ To make a lot of money
   Ⓓ To give it to his wife

2. **According to the passage, what can you tell about Paul McCartney?**

   Ⓐ He was popular only between 1960 and 1969.
   Ⓑ He created the *Billboard* charts.
   Ⓒ He started writing songs in 1968.
   Ⓓ He was a talented song writer.

On the TOEFL Test

3. **The word one in the passage refers to**

   Ⓐ the *Billboard* chart
   Ⓑ song
   Ⓒ single
   Ⓓ a long car ride

4. **The word his in the passage refers to**

   Ⓐ Paul McCartney
   Ⓑ Julian Lennon
   Ⓒ John Lennon
   Ⓓ Paul McCartney's son

○ **release (v)**
to give to the public

○ **depressed (a)**
sad; unhappy

○ **divorce (n)**
the legal termination of marriage

○ **recall (v)**
to remember

Read the following passage, and answer the questions.

The New Deal
Time Limit: 40 sec.

The New Deal was designed by President Roosevelt in the 1930s. He wanted to help people who suffered in the Great Depression. Millions of people were poor. The banking system was not reliable. Roosevelt wanted to help the poor. He also wanted to improve the economy. Most of all, he wanted to prevent future problems.

The New Deal included work programs. It gave people jobs in cities and in the country. It also included social security. This insurance gave poor people money when they were too old to work. If a worker lost his job, he got unemployment insurance. To make banks safe, the New Deal provided deposit insurance. People received money from the government if the bank lost their money. These steps put people on their feet again.

General Comprehension

1. What is the New Deal?

(A) A series of government programs to help the economy
(B) A series of taxes to make the government rich
(C) A way to make insurance companies rich
(D) A way to make a business deal with banks

2. How did the New Deal help poor people?

(A) By giving them insurance money if they lost their jobs
(B) By giving them a chance to buy food stamps
(C) By giving them new shoes
(D) By giving them houses

reliable (a)
dependable; trustworthy

economy (n)
the system of buying and selling

include (v)
to contain

unemployment (n)
a time when you have no work

put someone on his feet (phr)
to give someone the ability to support himself

On the TOEFL Test

3. The word he in the passage refers to

(A) the poor
(B) Roosevelt
(C) a worker
(D) a person

4. The phrase this insurance in the passage refers to

(A) suffering in the Great Depression
(B) improving the economy
(C) social security
(D) deposit insurance

D   Read the following passage, and answer the questions.

Mystery Shoppers

Time Limit: 30 sec.

A few weeks ago, Kate met her friend Jean by chance at the shopping mall. Jean said that she enjoyed her new job. "I make money by going shopping, watching movies, and dining in fancy restaurants." It sounded like a joke.

Soon after, Kate learned what Jean meant. Jean is a mystery shopper. She is like a secret agent at the mall. Business owners hire her to check the quality of customer service. Mystery shoppers visit different stores, restaurants, hotels, and movie theaters. They act like normal customers. However, they collect information for the owners. This helps companies maintain high levels of service for their customers.

General Comprehension

1. Which of the following best explains the term "mystery shoppers"?

Ⓐ Shoppers who make a lot of money

Ⓑ Shoppers who are satisfied with their jobs

Ⓒ Shoppers who watch spy movies regularly in the movie theater

Ⓓ Shoppers who get paid for collecting information about services

2. Many companies want to employ mystery shoppers in order to

Ⓐ lose a lot of money

Ⓑ hire more employees

Ⓒ improve the quality of their service

Ⓓ give customers funny memories

On the TOEFL Test

3. The word her in the passage refers to

Ⓐ Kate

Ⓑ Jean

Ⓒ a secret agent

Ⓓ a normal customer

4. The word this in the passage refers to

Ⓐ collecting information

Ⓑ running a business

Ⓒ dining in restaurants

Ⓓ helping customers

○ **dine (v)**
to eat dinner

○ **mystery (n)**
a secret

○ **hire (v)**
to employ

○ **customer (n)**
a person who buys
products or services

○ **maintain (v)**
to keep at the same level

A Read the following passage, and answer the questions.

The Laser

Time Limit: 1 min. 40 sec.

The laser is one of the major achievements of the 20th century. It was invented in 1958. It was made possible by the theories developed by Albert Einstein. It is used in most sectors of society and is one of the most useful technologies.

Laser light is very different from normal light bulbs. It works by sending out a single color of light in one direction. Light bulbs send out light in a wide spectrum in all directions. The beam from a small laser pointer is much brighter than that of the light bulb. This intense energy has many uses.

Millions of lasers are sold each year. They are used in fiber optics to send information. They are used to record DVDs and CDs. They are found in computer CD/DVD-ROM drives. Lasers are also used for cutting and burning. Doctors use them to correct vision. Industries use them to cut metal. Builders use them to measure and create level surfaces. Police use lasers to clock how fast people drive. Lastly, lasers are used as visual effects in concerts. Lasers have influenced the way we live, work, and play. They remain a promising technology for the future.

1. **The word one in the passage refers to**

   (A) an achievement
   (B) a theory
   (C) a sector
   (D) technology

2. **The word that in the passage refers to**

   (A) laser light
   (B) a wide spectrum
   (C) the beam
   (D) energy

major (a)
significant; important

sector (n)
a division of society

spectrum (n)
range; distribution

intense (a)
strong; concentrated

measure (v)
to assess; to calculate

level (a)
flat

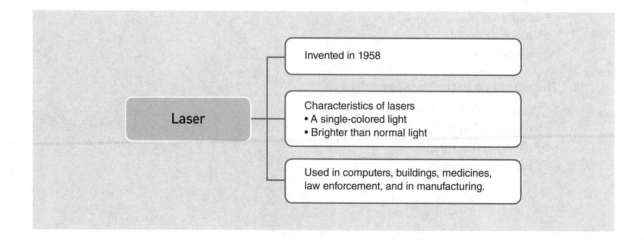

Laser
- Invented in 1958
- Characteristics of lasers
  - A single-colored light
  - Brighter than normal light
- Used in computers, buildings, medicines, law enforcement, and in manufacturing.

B Read the following passage, and answer the questions.

***Billboard* Magazine**

Time Limit: 1 min. 20 sec.

Billboard is a famous music magazine. It is highly influential. It collects sales data from music stores and radio stations. It then writes charts of the most popular music sales. It publishes these charts every week.

Billboard magazine appeared in 1894. It was eight pages long and sold for 10 cents. At first, it was not about music. It was used to promote local shows and events. The articles now inform music professionals. However, the charts are used by everyone. The *Billboard Hot 100* has been around since 1958. It is the most famous chart. People can find the top 100 songs in the United States. This list provides the news about hit songs, video releases, and music trends.

The company covers many aspects of music. It deals with CD and DVD sales. It also sells Internet music downloads. A few years ago, it started *Billboard Hot Ringtones*. This allows phone users to download any song on the *Billboard* charts. The magazine is aware of trends. It keeps finding ways to modernize itself and remain successful.

1. **The word it in the passage refers to**

   Ⓐ sales data
   Ⓑ *Billboard* magazine
   Ⓒ music
   Ⓓ *Billboard Hot 100*

2. **The word this in the passage refers to**

   Ⓐ a company
   Ⓑ *Billboard Hot Ringtones*
   Ⓒ any song
   Ⓓ the magazine

○ **influential (a)**
powerful; important

○ **publish (v)**
to print for public reading

○ **cover (v)**
to address; to investigate

○ **trend (n)**
a fashion or current style

○ **modernize (v)**
to become useful in the present time

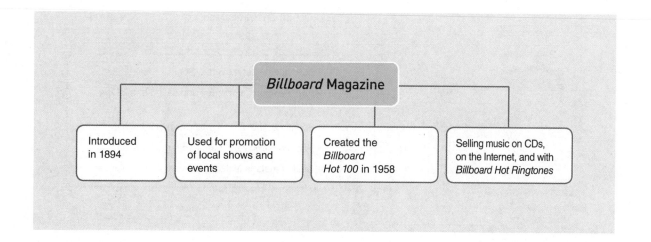

37

Read the following passage, and answer the questions.

Amerigo Vespucci

Time Limit: 50 sec.

Everyone knows that Christopher Columbus discovered America. However, he believed that he had reached a part of India. Of course, this was not the case. Amerigo Vespucci was the first European who asserted that this land was not India. For this reason, America was named after Vespucci.

Amerigo was born in Italy in 1454. He spent half of his life as a businessman. In his forties, he moved to Spain. He became the director of a shipping company. He helped Columbus prepare for his second voyage to the New World. This gave Amerigo Vespucci the opportunity to voyage to "The New World."

In 1502, Vespucci discovered land. He believed it was a new continent, not a part of Asia. In 1507, a mapmaker suggested calling the newly discovered lands "America" in honor of Amerigo. His name was given to both North and South America. Amerigo died of malaria in 1512. However, his legacy remains.

1. The word this land in the passage refers to

(A) America
(B) India
(C) Spain
(D) Asia

2. The word it in the passage refers to

(A) Vespucci
(B) land
(C) North America
(D) South America

assert (v)
to share one's opinion

spend (v)
to pass the time

in one's forties (phr)
between the ages of 40~49

voyage (n)(v)
a long journey on a ship; to travel

continent (n)
a large land mass

Amerigo Vespucci —
- Born in Italy but moved to Spain
- Ran a shipping company and sailed to the New World
- Found out that the new land was not India in 1502
- Had the New World named after him in 1507
- Died of malaria in 1512

D Read the following passage, and answer the questions.

Starting Your Own Business

Time Limit: 1 min. 40 sec.

Starting your own business is not easy. It requires hard work and long hours. It requires personal sacrifice like time away from your family. But to many, it is worthwhile. They like being their own boss. They like following their own ideas. The most important part of starting a business is to have a plan.

The first step is to come up with a concept, a unique idea. Will you create a new product or service that helps people in a new way? Or will you copy other people, only do it better? Developing a concept helps you focus your energy and money in crucial areas of your business. The second step is to decide what role in the company you would be happiest doing. Do you like people? Or do you prefer working with numbers? Or perhaps you like working with the product? Remember, you will spend a lot of time doing this work. It is important to enjoy it as much as you can. The third step is to have a financial plan. You need to get loans for your business. You also need to know how long the money you have will last until your company has started running.

1. **The word they in the passage refers to**
   - (A) long hours
   - (B) family
   - (C) many
   - (D) ideas

2. **The word it in the passage refers to**
   - (A) a product
   - (B) time
   - (C) a financial plan
   - (D) work

○ **sacrifice (n)**
giving something up for a higher cause

○ **concept (n)**
a principle or idea

○ **crucial (a)**
necessary; important

○ **financial (a)**
having to do with money and budgets

○ **loan (n)**
an act of borrowing or lending money

Starting Your Own Business

- Takes dedication
- Needs a core concept
- Needs to know the owner's role
- Needs a financial plan

A Put the following sentences in order to make appropriate summaries based on the long passages you worked on earlier. The first sentence is already provided.

1. The Laser

Albert Einstein's theories made the laser possible.

_____ It is used in computer drives, in factories, in doctors' offices, and in police departments for measuring.

_____ It is also used for visual effects in shows.

_____ Lasers are different from light bulbs because laser light only goes one way with only one color.

_____ The laser has many applications.

2. *Billboard* Magazine

Billboard magazine writes charts about music sales, and it posts the most popular songs in the United States.

_____ Even now, the company continues to modernize, and it sells music downloads.

_____ The magazine started in 1894, but it just advertised shows and events.

_____ Also, it started a new feature, *Hot Ringtones*, so your phone can sound like your favorite song.

_____ Then it started writing about music.

3. Amerigo Vespucci

North and South America were named after Amerigo Vespucci because he learned that this land was not India.

_____ Even though Amerigo died in 1512, his name is remembered forever.

_____ A mapmaker suggested calling the New World "America."

_____ This was to honor Vespucci's efforts.

_____ Amerigo moved to Spain to work for a shipping company, and he decided to sail to the New World.

4. Starting Your Own Business

It is difficult to start your own business.

_____ You have to decide what work you want to do, and you also need a plan on how to budget your money.

_____ It will also make your company efficient.

_____ You must work a lot, and sometimes you cannot spend time with your family.

_____ You need a plan to do this, and you need a good concept that will make your company interesting.

B Fill in the blanks with suitable words or phrases to complete the following summaries. Do not look at the previous page until you are finished.

1. The Laser

(1)_____ theories made the laser possible. Lasers are different from (2)_____ because laser light only goes (3)_____ with only (4)_____. The laser has many (5)_____. It is used in (6)_____, in factories, in doctors' offices, and in police departments for (7)_____. It is also used for (8)_____ in shows.

2. *Billboard* Magazine

Billboard magazine writes charts about (1)_____, and it posts the (2)_____ songs in the United States. The magazine started in (3)_____, but it just (4)_____ shows and events. Then it started (5)_____ about music. Even now, the company continues to (6)_____, and it sells (7)_____. Also, it started a new feature, *Hot Ringtones*, so your (8)_____ can sound like your favorite song.

3. Amerigo Vespucci

North and South America were (1)_____ after Amerigo Vespucci because he learned that this land was not (2)_____. Amerigo moved to (3)_____ to work for a (4)_____, and he decided to sail to the (5)_____. A mapmaker suggested calling the New World (6) "_____." This was to (7)_____ Vespucci's efforts. Even though Amerigo died in (8)_____, his name is remembered forever.

4. Starting Your Own Business

It is difficult to start your own (1)_____. You must (2)_____ a lot, and sometimes you cannot spend time with your (3)_____. You need a (4)_____ to do this, and you need a (5)_____ that will make your company interesting. It will also make your company (6)_____. You have to decide what (7)_____ you want to do, and you also need a plan on how to (8)_____ your money.

1. **The word ancient in the passage is closest in meaning to**
   - (A) friendly
   - (B) anxious
   - (C) peaceful
   - (D) old

2. **The word these in the passage refers to**
   - (A) thinkers
   - (B) colonies
   - (C) France, Spain, North Africa, and Italy
   - (D) city-states

3. **The word conquered in the passage is closest in meaning to**
   - (A) befriended
   - (B) defeated
   - (C) copied
   - (D) attacked

4. **According to the passage, all of the following are true EXCEPT:**
   - (A) Greece is in Europe.
   - (B) Greek culture was studied.
   - (C) Democracy is a Roman term.
   - (D) The Romans conquered Greece in 146 BC.

5. **According to the passage, what can be inferred about the Romans?**
   - (A) Without them, the Greek influence would not have been as strong today.
   - (B) The Greeks relied on them for the strength they gave to their country.
   - (C) The Greeks needed to give them ideas on art.
   - (D) They had a very powerful military.

6. **Why does the author mention that today, most countries in Europe are democracies?**
   - (A) To change the subject of the passage
   - (B) To tie Greece's past to current issues
   - (C) To tell us that modern countries are like Greece
   - (D) To help us forget that the Romans were very influential

The History of Greek Influence

Greece is a beautiful country in the south of Europe. It used to be called Hellas in ancient times. Greece is believed to be the birthplace of European civilization. Its culture has had a great influence on Europe and the Middle East.

Greece's past stretches back over thousands of years. Greek culture started in Crete in 3,000 BC. The culture's Golden Age lasted from 600 to 400 BC. Many famous thinkers lived during that time, including Socrates and Plato. Greece had great power. It had colonies all over the Mediterranean Sea. These were found in southern France, Spain, North Africa, and Italy.

From 500 to 336 BC, Greece was made up of 300 small city-states. Athens and Sparta were two of the most powerful. Their governments were similar, but their ways of life were very different. Sparta was very focused on war but was happy to keep to itself. Athens was focused on art and education but wanted to rule the entire country. Of course, this led to many wars, especially against Sparta. In the end, Sparta won the battles.

After that, Roman armies and Greek armies often fought. In 146 BC, the Romans conquered Greece. This allowed the Greeks to change Roman life. They influenced Roman art and ideas. This mix of cultures eventually became the basis of European cultures. When Romans moved through Europe, they brought Greek culture with them. A thousand years later, Greek ideas were revisited in Europe. This was a time when artists and thinkers studied Greek and Roman ideas. Architecture was one topic. Literature and art were others. Politics was also studied. The term "democracy" comes from Greek. It meant power to the people. Today, most countries in Europe are democracies. It is a powerful political system thanks to the Greeks.

7. **The word debated in the passage is closest in meaning to**

   Ⓐ welcomed
   Ⓑ opposed
   Ⓒ discussed
   Ⓓ persuaded

8. **The word managed in the passage is closest in meaning to**

   Ⓐ produced
   Ⓑ controlled
   Ⓒ used
   Ⓓ designed

9. **The word it in the passage refers to**

   Ⓐ the ESCB
   Ⓑ the Euro
   Ⓒ England
   Ⓓ their unity

10. **According to the passage, all of the following are true EXCEPT:**

    Ⓐ The banknotes have the same design on one side.
    Ⓑ Coins have national symbols on one side.
    Ⓒ The Euro gives economic leverage.
    Ⓓ All countries participated.

11. **According to the passage, what can be inferred about the Euro?**

    Ⓐ It mostly has support.
    Ⓑ It has very little support.
    Ⓒ Only rich countries support it.
    Ⓓ Only southern European countries support it.

12. **Why does the author mention that their unity gives them enough economic power to compete with larger countries?**

    Ⓐ To show that the Euro is outdated
    Ⓑ To show that the Euro has a great purpose
    Ⓒ To show that the Euro is useless to most people
    Ⓓ To show that the Euro has a lot of supporters in all of Europe

The Euro: a Common Currency

The Euro was highly debated in Europe. Should all these countries use the same currency? Common money is a symbol of common culture. Many Europeans did not agree with this. They were concerned about a loss of national identity. They were also worried that one country's economy would affect another's. Would inflation in Italy affect the French economy?

In 1999, twelve European countries united under the Euro. It benefits citizens and companies. When citizens travel within the Euro area, they do not need to change money. They are able to compare prices more easily. They also do not need to worry about exchange rates. The united currency helps business trade grow. It plays an important role in forming a European single market. In this way, Europeans can compete with the USA and Asian countries.

The Euro is managed by the European System of Central Banks (ESCB). The ESCB produces the banknotes and coins. All banknotes have the same design regardless of country. Only a country code is printed on one side of the banknotes. Each coin has one common side and the other a national side. The national side of the coins is designed by each member country using a unique national symbol. Their designs were chosen through a public survey.

The Euro was adopted on January 1, 2002. Belgium, Germany, Greece, Italy, Spain, France, Ireland, Luxembourg, the Netherlands, Austria, Portugal, and Finland ratified it. England chose not to participate. Now, the Euro is a part of the daily lives of 300 million Europeans. Their unity gives them enough economic power to compete with larger countries.

Vocabulary Review

Choose the word with the closest meaning to each underlined word or phrase.

1. The company is facing some financial problems.

   (A) hostile   (B) monetary   (C) polluted   (D) discharged

2. It is very important to know about customer satisfaction in business.

   (A) performer   (B) amateur   (C) participant   (D) client

3. The price of the goods includes shipping and handling.

   (A) contains   (B) accepts   (C) mentions   (D) occurs

4. A powerful earthquake caused many buildings to crumble last night.

   (A) colorful   (B) vulnerable   (C) exhausted   (D) forceful

5. Humidity is the measuring of moisture in the atmosphere.

   (A) concluding   (B) refusing   (C) estimating   (D) decreasing

6. The van travels at a maximum of 140 kilometers an hour.

   (A) saves   (B) goes   (C) catches   (D) communicates

7. The new edition of this book will be published soon.

   (A) expended   (B) separated   (C) printed   (D) operated

8. The students knowingly had to guess the answers because they didn't know the correct ones.

   (A) respectively   (B) intentionally   (C) especially   (D) immediately

9. The old movie was creative and unique.

   (A) uncommon   (B) regular   (C) fair   (D) complete

10. The country stretches for almost 3 million square kilometers.

    (A) removes   (B) settles   (C) drops   (D) extends

Unit 3

Factual Information

3 Factual Information

Overview

■Introduction

Factual Information questions ask you to identify specific information that is clearly mentioned in the passage. This is one of the most frequent question types. You need to find the right spot in the passage that has the information about which the question asks within a short time period.

■Useful Tips

- Read the questions first to know what exactly is being asked.

- Scan the passage to find out where the relevant specific information is in the passage.

- Remove the choices that are not relevant to the passage.

- Do not choose an answer just because it is mentioned in the passage.

■Question Types

1. According to the passage, which of the following is true of _____?

2. According to paragraph X, who [when, where, what, how, why] _____?

3. In paragraph X, the author states that _____?

Sample iBT Question

According to the passage, which of the following is true of Tolstoy?

(A) He was in the army for a while.
(B) He was an idealist.
(C) He explained how the poor behave.
(D) He spent his time helping rich people.

Tolstoy was a realist. He felt it was his duty to write about the social and political issues of his time. Many of his books do just that. He describes how the Russian nobles behave towards the poor people around them. In many cases, Tolstoy used examples from his own life. He was also a rich noble. He was also able to write sharp descriptions of war. He served in the army for some time. In his heart, he wanted to help the poor people of his country and stop war.

Correct Answer
The question is about Tolstoy. You need to find out what specific information is mentioned about him in the passage. Then remove choices that give information that is not true. So the correct answer is (A). The passage doesn't mention the rest of the choices.

Skill & Drill

Factual Information questions ask you to identify facts, details, or other information that are explicitly mentioned in the passage. The information is usually found in just one or two sentences of the text. So you can find the correct answer even without reading the whole passage. The correct answer is paraphrased in one of sentences in the passage.

Example

Meteoroids are large bodies that float in space. These bodies are larger than dust but smaller than 10 meters across. **When a meteoroid enters the Earth's atmosphere, it heats up. The gas all around it starts to glow.** We see this on Earth and call it a shooting star. Scientists say that from 1,000 tons to more than 10,000 tons of meteoroids fall on the Earth everyday.

According to the passage, which of the following is true of meteoroids?

Ⓐ Meteoroids are the same as space dust.
Ⓑ Meteoroids are too tiny to be seen.
● Meteoroids burn up when they hit Earth's atmosphere.
Ⓓ Meteoroids never fall on Earth.

Read the questions first. Use the key words highlighted in each question to scan for the answer in the passage.

The people of ancient Egypt believed that a dead person moved on to another world. So, they wanted to prepare the dead for their next life. They tried to use various methods to make dead bodies last for a long time. One way was to make a mummy. The Egyptians dried out the dead body and wrapped it with cloth. This stopped bacteria and fungi from growing.

1. Why did the ancient Egyptians create mummies?

Ⓐ To prepare the dead for the next world
Ⓑ To show off their wrapping ability
Ⓒ To follow the wills of dead people
Ⓓ To save time and money

Franz Schubert, an Austrian composer, was a musical genius. He was a master of writing short pieces. He began composing when he was only 13. Some of his most famous works were written in his teens. He died at the age of 31, but he left over six hundred beautiful pieces. In life, he received little recognition. Schubert remained poor while he was alive.

2. Which of the following is true of Franz Schubert?

Ⓐ He began composing at the age of 31.
Ⓑ He was good at composing short pieces.
Ⓒ He wrote over six hundred works in his teens.
Ⓓ He gained great popularity during his life.

Galileo was an Italian astronomer. He was also a physicist and philosopher. He loved to watch the night sky. He was the first person to make a telescope. He designed more than sixty of them. The first ones had little power. It was difficult to see through them. He always wanted to make them stronger and clearer. His invention greatly helped our understanding of the heavens.

3. **Why did Galileo make many telescopes?**

   (A) To give them as gifts
   (B) To improve them
   (C) To break the world record
   (D) To help people understand science

Asia is the largest land mass on Earth. It contains one-third of the world's land. Much of the land is uninhabited. But Asia holds more than 60% of the world's people. It has 48 different countries, including China and India. They are the most populous countries in the world. Asia is also the birthplace of the world's five major religions. They are Hinduism, Buddhism, Judaism, Christianity, and Islam.

4. **Which of the following is true of Asia?**

   (A) It is the largest continent on Earth.
   (B) One-third of the world's population lives there.
   (C) It takes up 60% of the world's land mass.
   (D) It is the home of 48 different religions.

The modern world began with the Renaissance. It means "rebirth" in French. It started in Italy in the 14th century. It was a time of great cultural and intellectual change. Thinkers took old ideas from the Greeks and Romans and modernized them. It changed many people's beliefs. The ideas were expressed through art, literature, and architecture.

5. **According to the passage, what did the Renaissance accomplish?**

   (A) It made modern society come to an end.
   (B) It caused a rebirth of ideas.
   (C) It made people move to Italy.
   (D) It prevented the chance of intellectual growth.

A Read the following passage, and answer the questions.

Holocaust Survivor   Time Limit: 50 sec.

The auditorium at the University of Michigan was full. Students gathered to listen to the story of a Holocaust survivor. He was a 74-year-old Jewish man. He worked as a volunteer at the Jewish center. He started to recount his sad memories. "After I was in Nazi work camps, I have always felt it is my duty to tell the truth about the Holocaust to people. I was the only survivor out of my six family members. It causes me great sorrow." When his story was finished, a German student came up to him. He was a foreign exchange student. He wanted to apologize for what the Germans did to the Jews. However, the Jewish man said, "You need to know what your ancestors did to millions of innocent people. But you do not need to feel guilty about what they did."

General Comprehension

1. **The word recount in the passage is closest in meaning to**

   Ⓐ remind
   Ⓑ describe
   Ⓒ suppress
   Ⓓ consider

2. **According to the passage, what can be inferred about the Holocaust?**

   Ⓐ It was done by the Jews.
   Ⓑ It happened 74 years ago.
   Ⓒ It involved the killing of millions of Nazis.
   Ⓓ It resulted in the death of many innocent people.

On the TOEFL Test

3. **According to the passage, which of the following is true of the Jewish man?**

   Ⓐ He did not want to forgive the German student.
   Ⓑ He lived in America with his family.
   Ⓒ He spent 74 years in Nazi camps.
   Ⓓ He lost his family in the Holocaust.

4. **According to the passage, how did the German student feel about the Holocaust?**

   Ⓐ Ashamed
   Ⓑ Flattered
   Ⓒ Satisfied
   Ⓓ Indifferent

auditorium (n)
a large room or building where people gather for a performance

volunteer (n)
a person who offers to work or help without pay

apologize (v)
to say one is sorry

ancestor (n)
a forefather; a forebear

innocent (a)
free from guilt or blame

guilty (a)
feeling ashamed and regretful

B Read the following passage, and answer the questions.

A Robotic Astronaut

Time Limit: 40 sec.

Robots are replacing people in many jobs. They are used in the car industry. People complain that they take needed jobs away from people. But there is one place where robots are welcome to do work.

A robot astronaut was developed by NASA. It is called Robonaut. Robonauts look like humans. However, they have more flexible arms and hands than humans. They can do some of the more difficult work in space. Robonauts are expected to work with human astronauts in future missions. They need no spacesuits, oxygen, and meals to survive in space. Humans need air to breathe and protection from extreme temperature changes. Most importantly, Robonauts will be sent where astronauts cannot go yet because the risks are too high.

General Comprehension

1. **How do people feel about robots?**

   Ⓐ They do not like how robots take jobs.
   Ⓑ They do not want Robonauts to hurt astronauts.
   Ⓒ They think robots are of great help.
   Ⓓ They want robots to replace astronauts.

2. **The word extreme in the passage is closest in meaning to**

   Ⓐ various
   Ⓑ distant
   Ⓒ radical
   Ⓓ unreasonable

- **replace (v)**
  to take the place of
- **complain (v)**
  to say one is unhappy
- **flexible (a)**
  able to bend
- **survive (v)**
  to continue to live
- **protection (n)**
  defense; safety
- **risk (n)**
  danger

On the TOEFL Test

3. **According to the passage, where is the one place robots are welcome to do work?**

   Ⓐ At NASA
   Ⓑ In space
   Ⓒ On the sun
   Ⓓ On Earth

4. **According to the passage, what is one advantage of Robonauts?**

   Ⓐ They do not need food or oxygen to survive in space.
   Ⓑ They do not need extra fuel to keep working in space.
   Ⓒ They resemble humans in appearance.
   Ⓓ They were developed by NASA, which ensures their quality.

Read the following passage, and answer the questions.

Making Prints

Time Limit: 50 sec.

There were two popular techniques to make prints in the 1600s. They were engraving and etching. Engraving was an older method. It involved cutting lines on to a copper plate with a tool called a burin. It was a steel rod with a sharp end. Little slivers of metal would rise from the plate and have to be carefully removed. Then, the plate would be inked and paper set down on top to make the print. The resulting print had neat lines. Etching was different. First, the copper plate was coated with resin or wax. Then, the artist scratched the picture into the resin with a needle. This exposed the copper only in the scratches. Finally, the plate was given an acid bath, which ate at the metal, causing a more irregular line. The plate would then be inked for the print.

General Comprehension

1. **The word it in the passage refers to**

   (A) engraving
   (B) etching
   (C) copper plate
   (D) burin

2. **The phrase ate at in the passage is closest in meaning to**

   (A) dissolved
   (B) bent
   (C) thinned
   (D) corroded

method (n)
a systematic way of doing things

sliver (n)
thin piece

remove (v)
to get rid of

resin (n)
a sticky substance found in some plants

expose (v)
to uncover

On the TOEFL Test

3. **According to the passage, what were two printing techniques in the 1600s?**

   (A) Inking and pressing
   (B) Coating and waxing
   (C) Engraving and etching
   (D) Etching and scratching

4. **According to the passage, what is used for etching?**

   (A) A steel rod
   (B) A silver stick
   (C) Resin and wax
   (D) A metal burin

D   Read the following passage, and answer the questions.

A Missing Girl
Time Limit: 50 sec.

Kentucky police asked for the public's help in finding a missing 11-year-old girl. She was one of twenty middle school students who went exploring in Mammoth Cave National Park. It is a popular destination. She was last seen at the entrance of Mammoth Cave in the morning of the first day. The teacher said, "I asked the students to split up into two groups. A few hours later, the two groups met again. Then we realized the girl was missing." The teacher immediately reported it to a park ranger. She was wearing a green short-sleeved shirt, a yellow cap, and white sneakers and was carrying a backpack. The parents asked that everything possible be done in the search for their missing daughter. The park spokesman said, "She may now be in the park. But the park is so huge, so we need the public's help." They searched for three days with no luck.

General Comprehension

1.   According to the passage, what can you tell about Mammoth Cave?

   (A) It draws many tourists.
   (B) It is located in the center of a middle school.
   (C) It has no paths or trails for travelers.
   (D) It is the home of many animals.

2.   The missing girl was wearing all of the following EXCEPT:

   (A) Sneakers
   (B) A green shirt
   (C) Glasses
   (D) A cap

---

public (n)
people; citizens

explore (v)
to travel through a place in order to learn about it

destination (n)
where someone is going; a journey's end

split up (phr)
to divide

spokesman (n)
a person who communicates the ideas and opinions of another person or group

search for (phr)
to look for

On the TOEFL Test

3.   According to the passage, which of the following is true of the missing girl?

   (A) She was last seen by her parents.
   (B) She was missing along with her teacher.
   (C) She stayed with the rescue team.
   (D) She was never found at Mammoth Cave.

4.   According to the passage, why did the missing girl go to the national park?

   (A) She was on a class trip.
   (B) She was a member of the Girl Scouts.
   (C) She wanted to search for fossils.
   (D) She was supposed to meet a friend's parents.

Practice with Long Passages

A Read the following passage, and answer the questions.

> **The Holocaust**
> Time Limit: 1 min. 50 sec.
>
> During the Holocaust, millions of Jews were murdered by the Nazis. It was one of the most terrible incidents in world history. When Adolf Hitler came to power in 1933, he planned to rid Europe of all Jews. He secretly built death camps. By the end of the war, around 6 million Jewish people had been killed.
>
> Many people have tried to address the tragedy of the Holocaust through art, literature, and cinema. Prisoners often tried to express themselves through art. In many cases, they risked their lives in doing so. They would have to hide their writings and sketches from the guards. They were not allowed to record the horrors they saw. They were not allowed to express their own humanity. Now people create diaries, poetry, and novels. The Holocaust has also been chosen as a subject of movies. "Schindler's List" and "Life Is Beautiful" are the most famous.
>
> It is important to remember this tragedy. This should never happen again. Many museums have been built throughout the world. They serve to remind future generations of this tragic past. Many European countries have made January 27 "Holocaust Memorial Day." This date in 1945 is the day that Auschwitz, a famous death camp, was liberated.

1. **According to the passage, which of the following is true of Holocaust artists?**

   Ⓐ They were liberated in 1946.
   Ⓑ They could not express themselves.
   Ⓒ They could not remember the Holocaust.
   Ⓓ They were always the subject of movies.

2. **According to the passage, what have Europeans done as a tribute to the tragedy?**

   Ⓐ They have made movies.
   Ⓑ They have class trips.
   Ⓒ They have built museums.
   Ⓓ They have adopted a holiday.

incident (n)
an event that happened

address (v)
to discuss; to deal with

generation (n)
all the people who are born around the same time

liberate (v)
to set free

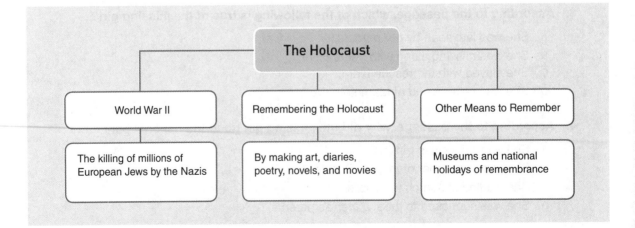

The Holocaust

World War II	Remembering the Holocaust	Other Means to Remember
The killing of millions of European Jews by the Nazis	By making art, diaries, poetry, novels, and movies	Museums and national holidays of remembrance

B Read the following passage, and answer the questions.

> ### NASA
> Time Limit: 1 min. 30 sec.
>
> Since 1958, NASA has made a number of great gains in science and technology. It is the leader in aerospace research. It has provided us with new ways to view Earth and space.
>
> In 1961, President Kennedy announced that America should land a man on the moon and return him safely to Earth. He wanted to beat the Russians to the honor. NASA accomplished Kennedy's mandate with Apollo 11. It was a famous rocket flight. On July 20, 1969, NASA put men on the moon. The first man to step on the moon's surface was Neil Armstrong. It was a great moment. His first words were, "That's one small step for man, one giant leap for mankind."
>
> In the 1980s, the space shuttle became a new public interest. NASA launched the first space shuttle in 1981. They developed the shuttle to be a reusable craft. Rockets could be used only once. NASA also had many unmanned missions. Robots were used. Spacecraft made flights toward other planets such as Jupiter, Saturn, Uranus, and Neptune. They sent back scientific data and color images.

1. **According to the passage, why did Kennedy want to put a man on the moon?**

   Ⓐ Because NASA was established to explore the moon
   Ⓑ Because NASA was doing research on space
   Ⓒ Because he did not want the Russians to get to the moon first
   Ⓓ Because he wanted to leave an achievement of lasting memory

2. **According to the passage, when was the first space shuttle launched?**

   Ⓐ 1958
   Ⓑ 1961
   Ⓒ 1969
   Ⓓ 1981

- **announce (v)**
  to say to the public
- **mandate (n)**
  a written order or command
- **launch (v)**
  to send up into the air
- **unmanned (a)**
  without an operator or pilot

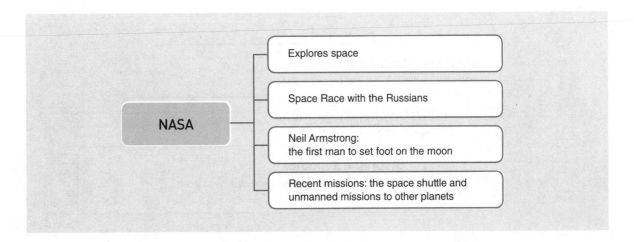

NASA
- Explores space
- Space Race with the Russians
- Neil Armstrong: the first man to set foot on the moon
- Recent missions: the space shuttle and unmanned missions to other planets

Read the following passage, and answer the questions.

The Art Thief and His Mother

Time Limit: 2 min.

A French art thief went to jail in 2002. He stole from over 170 museums across Europe. His entire collection was worth $2.5 billion dollars. The police caught the thief. Unfortunately, the police failed to recover all of the stolen goods. The thief's mother disposed of them in a permanent way.

There were musical instruments, weapons, and vases in his apartment. There were also 60 paintings. The thief, Stephane, and his girlfriend, Anne, stole art and precious objects every weekend. He loved art, but he also enjoyed the thrill of stealing. They often went to museums with relaxed security. She would keep a look out while he cut the paintings from their frames.

The police discovered this, and arrested Stephane. Anne ran to his home to tell his mother. The mother was furious that her son was in trouble. She threw all of the items except the paintings into the river. She then cut the 60 paintings up into small pieces and put them in the garbage disposal. These precious paintings from the 17th and 18th centuries were destroyed forever. The mother did not want the police to find the evidence. She was afraid that she would lose her job because the paintings were kept in her apartment. At her age, she said, she would not be able to find another job. It is a great shame that so much history was lost for a petty reason.

1. **How did the couple steal precious objects?**

   (A) Stephane looked for items while Anne stole them.
   (B) Anne watched Stephane, who carried a large backpack.
   (C) Stephane talked to the guards while Anne put the objects in a bag.
   (D) Anne watched for people while Stephane swiped the objects.

2. **Why couldn't the police recover all of the stolen items?**

   (A) The thief's mother hid them all.
   (B) The thief's mother sold them all.
   (C) The thief's mother gave them away.
   (D) The thief's mother threw them away.

dispose of (phr)
to throw something away

keep a look out (phr)
to watch

furious (a)
very angry

evidence (n)
a clue to a crime; proof

petty (a)
not important

Stephane: the art thief
— Stole $2.5 billion of art and precious objects

Anne: Stephane's girlfriend
— Helped him steal

Stephane's mother
— Threw all the objects away and destroyed them

D Read the following passage, and answer the questions.

Mammoth Cave

Time Limit: 1 min. 50 sec.

With more than 579km of tunnels, Mammoth Cave is the world's longest cave. The word "mammoth" refers to its size. The cave is very famous because of its length and rich history.

Mammoth Cave is a limestone cave. It is hidden under the forests and hills of central Kentucky. The cave is made up of a series of chambers beneath the earth. It has at least five levels. There are many passages and tunnels that are not open to the public. The process of forming this cave was very slow. It started with the sea. Over millions of years, the shells and bones of animals became thick layers on the sea bottom. The layers became limestone formed in the water. Then, the sea disappeared. Rainwater passed through the rock and slowly dissolved it. It took almost 250 million years for Mammoth Cave to form.

On July 1, 1941, the cave became a national park. This would ensure that the cave was protected against real estate developers. The land is not the only thing that is important. The park is home to thousands of species of plants and animals. It became a World Heritage Site in 1981. Mammoth Cave is a treasure for all the people in the world.

1. **According to the passage, what does "mammoth" refer to?**

   Ⓐ An insect that flies around lights
   Ⓑ The mammoths that are buried there
   Ⓒ The immensity of the cave
   Ⓓ The shape of the cave system

2. **According to the passage, what is the layout of the cave?**

   Ⓐ A series of chambers and levels
   Ⓑ One large hole in the ground
   Ⓒ Two rooms side by side
   Ⓓ A simple hollow

be made up of (phr)
to consist of

chamber (n)
a large room; a hollow place

layer (n)
a thickness, usually one of several

dissolve (v)
to mix with a liquid and disappear

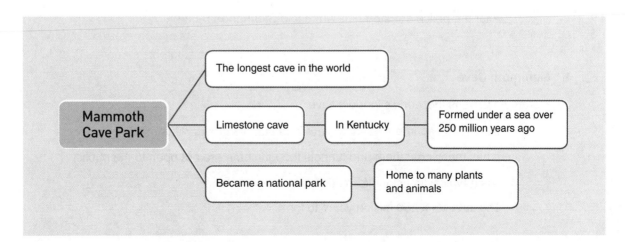

59

Building Summary Skills

A Put the following sentences in order to make appropriate summaries based on the long passages you worked on earlier. The first sentence is already provided.

1. **The Holocaust**

   The Holocaust resulted in the death of approximately 6 million Jews in Europe.

   _____ There are also museums and national holidays in Europe to pay tribute to those who died.

   _____ In the camps and ghettos, Jews tried to express themselves through art and writing.

   _____ There have been books and films about the Holocaust.

   _____ In many cases, this was dangerous because they were not permitted to show their humanity.

2. **NASA**

   NASA is an organization that explores space.

   _____ They were the first human beings to go there.

   _____ It helps with scientific discoveries.

   _____ Now, NASA has a space shuttle program and robot missions to other planets.

   _____ It was responsible for putting Neil Armstrong and other men on the moon.

3. **The Art Thief and His Mother**

   A French art thief went to jail for stealing 2.5 billion dollars in art.

   _____ He loved art, but he also loved stealing.

   _____ His girlfriend, Anne, watched for guards and people while he was taking the precious objects in the museums.

   _____ The mother then threw the big objects in the river and the paintings down the drain.

   _____ After the police arrested him, Anne told Stephane's mother.

4. **Mammoth Cave**

   Mammoth Cave is the world's longest cave.

   _____ In 1941, it became a national park to ensure its preservation.

   _____ It has many chambers and tunnels though some are not open to the public.

   _____ It is a typical limestone formation.

   _____ The cave took 250 million years to form.

B Fill in the blanks with suitable words or phrases to complete the following summaries. Do not look at the previous page until you are finished.

1. The Holocaust

The (1)_____ resulted in the death of approximately (2)_____ Jews in Europe. In the camps and ghettos, Jews tried to express themselves through (3)_____. In many cases, this was (4)_____ because they were not permitted to show their (5)_____. There have been (6)_____ about the Holocaust. There are also (7)_____ and (8)_____ in Europe to pay tribute to those who died.

2. NASA

NASA is an (1)_____ that explores (2)_____. It helps with (3)_____. It was (4)_____ for putting Neil Armstrong and other men on the (5)_____. They were the (6)_____ human beings to go there. Now, NASA has a (7)_____ program and (8)_____ to other planets.

3. The Art Thief and His Mother

A (1)_____ art thief went to jail for stealing (2)_____ dollars in art. His girlfriend, Anne, watched for (3)_____ and people while he was taking the precious objects in the (4)_____. He loved art, but he also loved (5)_____. After the police (6)_____ him, Anne told Stephane's mother. The mother then threw the big objects in the (7)_____ and the paintings down the (8)_____.

4. Mammoth Cave

Mammoth Cave is the world's (1)_____ cave. It has many (2)_____ and (3)_____ though some are (4)_____ to the public. The cave took (5)_____ years to form. It is a typical (6)_____ formation. In (7)_____, it became a (8)_____ to ensure its preservation.

1. **The word permission in the passage is closest in meaning to**

   Ⓐ protection
   Ⓑ prohibition
   Ⓒ contribution
   Ⓓ approval

2. **The word select in the passage is closest in meaning to**

   Ⓐ privileged
   Ⓑ elected
   Ⓒ needed
   Ⓓ talented

3. **The word they in the passage refers to**

   Ⓐ ideas
   Ⓑ areas of creative work
   Ⓒ written work, designs, and music
   Ⓓ copyrights

4. **According to the passage, all of the following are true EXCEPT:**

   Ⓐ Copyright is protected by law.
   Ⓑ Copying an author's work without his or her permission is against the law.
   Ⓒ Copyright law only protects literary works and movies.
   Ⓓ A copyright may be noted by a specific mark.

5. **According to paragraph 4, what can be inferred about the writer's attitude toward copyrights?**

   Ⓐ He supports copyrights.
   Ⓑ He is ambivalent about copyrights.
   Ⓒ He is happy to see works get copied.
   Ⓓ He believes copyright laws are out of date.

6. **Why does the author introduce ©, the copyright mark?**

   Ⓐ To show how the history of copyright symbols has changed
   Ⓑ To provide an example of how a copyright is indicated
   Ⓒ To maximize the importance of copyrights
   Ⓓ To introduce a new copy machine

Copyright

A copyright is a way to control the use of ideas. You cannot use other people's ideas. It is illegal to print, copy, sell, or distribute someone else's work. You may not change, translate, record, or perform any part of an author's work. This requires permission. Also, it may be illegal to copy and paste other people's e-mail messages. Copying without permission equals theft.

Copyright deals with more than ideas. It also deals with the way something is expressed. Copyrights exist in wide areas of creative work. These include written work, designs, and music. They also include paintings, photographs, and TV broadcasts. A copyright may be marked by © in the work. However, even if there is no symbol, the work is immediately protected by law as soon as the work is created.

The Statute of Anne was the first copyright law. It was passed in England in 1710. Before the statute, the power of creation was held in the hands of select people and guilds. The statute applied to the general public, not just a privileged few. It protected the author of a work, not his guild. Also, it put a time limit on the copyright. A person had sole rights for 21 years.

There is no doubt that copyright plays an important role in creativity. If writers have control over their own work, they feel safe to produce more. For most creators, the work and the legal right to the work are of equal concern. Such legal protection aids economic, cultural, and social development.

7. The word similarity in the passage is closest in meaning to

- (A) difficulty
- (B) difference
- (C) sameness
- (D) strength

8. According to the passage, all of the following are true EXCEPT:

- (A) Romanesque is the name of a building style in the 11th and 12th centuries.
- (B) Romanesque walls had to be thick to support the roof.
- (C) Romanesque ideas were spread through printed books.
- (D) Romanesque buildings use stone materials.

9. The word achievement in the passage is closest in meaning to

- (A) accomplishment
- (B) symbol
- (C) performance
- (D) monument

10. According to paragraph 3, what was the result of the thick walls?

- (A) The insides of buildings were very dark.
- (B) The windows of Romanesque buildings were relatively big.
- (C) The inside of a Romanesque church was very bright.
- (D) The insides of buildings could be kept warm.

11. Why does the author claim that Romanesque was a pan-European style?

- (A) Because it influenced the Gothic style
- (B) Because it had a stone vaulted roof
- (C) Because it used relatively small windows
- (D) Because it could be found in many European countries

12. Based on the information in the passage, what can we infer about the Gothic style?

- (A) Before the Romanesque period, people were very rich.
- (B) The Gothic style is very different from Romanesque style.
- (C) Romanesque architects were not smart enough to solve structural problems.
- (D) Romanesque buildings were relatively light compared with pre-Romanesque ones.

Romanesque Architecture

The term "Romanesque" refers to the architectural period in 11th and 12th century Europe. It shared a similarity of forms and materials used by the ancient Romans. Romanesque means "in the manner of the Romans." Before the 11th century, people were busy fighting each other. They rarely had enough to eat. People had no time or energy to build big and fancy buildings. Around 975, Europe society began to calm down. By 1050, kings began to order the building of large, stone structures.

The stone vaulted building was a major achievement of Romanesque architects. Curved ceilings replaced wooden roofs. Wood was likely to catch on fire. Vaulted stone posed building problems for builders. What shapes worked? How was the weight of stone to be supported?

Builders invented some solutions, which included domes and rounded points. To support the heavy stone, they used thick walls and piers. Windows had to be small to keep the strength of the wall. This resulted in churches with dark interiors. This did not change until the Gothic design was used some centuries later.

Romanesque was the first pan-European building style since Roman times. The spreading of the style can be explained in this way: people at this time traveled for religious purposes. They would see great buildings and bring home ideas on how they were built. Romanesque buildings can be seen all over France, England, Italy, Germany, and northern Spain.

Vocabulary Review

Choose the word with the closest meaning to each underlined word or phrase.

1. The sign should be immediately removed from public.

   (A) kept   (B) hesitated   (C) lasted   (D) taken out

2. People call the thin outer layer of the skin the "epidermis."

   (A) routine   (B) class   (C) origin   (D) sheet

3. The man recounted his point of view on the economy.

   (A) offered   (B) stated   (C) repaired   (D) resigned

4. The auditorium was getting crowded with students and parents.

   (A) hall   (B) cave   (C) plain   (D) chamber

5. The company spokesman said that the company would hire more people.

   (A) interviewer   (B) mouthpiece   (C) patron   (D) employee

6. The old man complained about the cold temperature in the theater.

   (A) admired   (B) violated   (C) grumbled   (D) praised

7. Buying first class seats on airplanes is the most expensive method of travel.

   (A) means   (B) note   (C) visit   (D) prevention

8. It is useless to argue about such petty matters in the meeting.

   (A) important   (B) huge   (C) appropriate   (D) insignificant

9. People addressed him as "the chairman of the committee."

   (A) returned   (B) called   (C) reached   (D) surrendered

10. The government launched a new business in the small town.

    (A) ruined   (B) involved   (C) commenced   (D) consumed

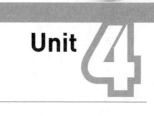

Unit 4

Negative Factual Information

Negative Factual Information

Overview

■Introduction

Negative Factual Information questions ask you to find wrong information that is not mentioned in the passage. Like Factual Information questions, the key is to find the right spot in the passage in which the answer to the question can be found within a short time period. You will probably need more time to answer this type of question than a Factual Information question because you have to scan more of the passage to make sure that your choice is not mentioned.

■Useful Tips

• Make use of the keywords in the question and answer choices to spot relevant information in the passage.

• Don't forget that necessary information may be spread out over an entire paragraph or several paragraphs.

• Make sure that your answer is NOT mentioned in the passage or contradicts the passage.

■Question Types

1. According to the passage, which of the following is NOT true of _____ ?

2. All of the following are mentioned in the paragraph X as _____ EXCEPT:

3. The author's description of _____ mentions all of the following EXCEPT:

4. Which of the following is NOT mentioned in the passage?

Sample iBT Question

According to the passage, which of the following is NOT true?

Ⓐ The human body tries to maintain a normal temperature.

Ⓑ Drinking enough water helps the body perspire.

Ⓒ Tight clothing keeps sweat from the air.

Ⓓ If there is a lot of humidity, water on the skin dries out easily.

The human body does not like hot weather. It must work hard to keep a normal temperature. The body needs to sweat to stay cool. Sweating is slowed in a few ways. First, the body may not have enough water, so it is important to drink water. Next, tight clothing prevents sweat from going into the air. Sweat usually takes heat with it and cools the body. Clothes stop air from passing over the skin. Humidity also causes problems. If there is a lot of water in the air, water on the skin does not evaporate easily.

Correct Answer Check and make sure which choice is not mentioned in the text. A lot of humidity prevents water on the skin from drying out easily. So the correct answer is (D).

Negative Factual Information questions ask you to check what information is NOT mentioned in the passage. You should decide which of the four answer choices is not discussed in the passage or does not agree with one or more statements in the passage.

Example

At the end of the 19th century, an Australian began using women's names for cyclones. They wished that they would not have strong winds to damage people and houses. From 1979, men's names have also been used. There is one interesting thing when people name storms. If a tropical storm causes a lot of damage to people and buildings, its name is never used again in the future. However, if it does not, its name is used over again. Hurricane Katrina killed thousands of people in the USA. That name will never be used again. Storms are mostly horrible, but they can be good to people because strong storms clean dirty air and bring us clean air.

According to the passage, all of the following are true EXCEPT:

(A) A strong storm gives good things to people.
(B) An American began naming hurricanes with women's names in the 19th century.
(C) Hurricane Katrina damaged a lot of people and many buildings.
(D) Men's names are also used for naming storms.

Read the questions and answer choices first. Then scan for the information you need to answer the questions. Try to eliminate obviously wrong answer choices.

Atoms are the basic building blocks of the physical world. Yet they are so small that they can only be seen with a strong microscope. An atom is made up of three parts: protons, neutrons, and electrons. The neutrons and protons are at the center of the atom. This is called the nucleus. Protons have positive charges. Neutrons have no charge. Electrons, which orbit the nucleus, have negative charges.

1. **According to the passage, which of the following is NOT true of atoms?**
   (A) They are made up of three parts.
   (B) They can be seen with a telescope.
   (C) They have electrons which orbit the center.
   (D) They have protons which have positive charges.

Culture is defined as the way groups of people give meaning to their world. Culture achieves this in a systematic way. It affects how we dress, how we act, and even how we think. In one culture, people may look at each other in the eye. They may think this is friendly. In another culture, looking someone in the eye is a sign of disrespect. With these belief systems in place, people will regularly behave accordingly.

2. **According to the passage, which of the following is NOT true of culture?**

   (A) It influences how we find meaning.

   (B) It affects how we dress and behave.

   (C) It influences our notions of respect.

   (D) It affects nothing in a systematic way.

Charlie Chaplin was the most famous star in silent pictures. He was born in London. He was the director, producer, and writer of his comic films. Of course, he was also an actor. His stardom began in 1914 when he first appeared as "The Little Tramp." His look included a jacket that was too small and pants that were too large. Many people called him the funniest man in the world.

---

3. **According to the passage, which of the following is NOT true of Charlie Chaplin?**

   (A) He was good at making comic films.

   (B) He produced some silent movies.

   (C) He appeared in his movies himself.

   (D) He was the funniest composer in the world.

Gravity is the natural force that pulls other objects toward each other. Earth's gravity keeps our feet on the ground. Because of this force, we do not float above the earth. It is the result of the great size of our planet. Gravity also holds the solar system together. It makes the moon circle the earth and Earth orbit the sun.

---

4. **All of the following are mentioned in the passage EXCEPT:**

   (A) the nature of gravity

   (B) the effect of gravity on Earth

   (C) the effect of gravity on flight

   (D) the effect of gravity outside Earth

Galaxies are made up of stars, dust, and gas. All of this matter orbits a center of gravity. Our own galaxy, the Milky Way, is huge. It contains three hundred billion stars. These stars are spread out long distances apart. The distances are so huge that they must be expressed in terms of time and the speed of light. It takes thousands of years for light to travel across our galaxy.

---

5. **All of the following are mentioned in the passage EXCEPT:**

   (A) how we can see galaxies

   (B) what galaxies are made of

   (C) the distances across a galaxy

   (D) the way to measure distance

A Read the following passage, and answer the questions.

Sea Gypsy Children

Time Limit: 30 sec.

Small groups of nomads called sea-gypsies live on the west coast of Thailand. They have lived there for hundreds of years. Their language, culture, and lifestyle are totally different from the rest of Thai society. Because their life is based on the sea, these nomad children are experts at swimming. They can stay submerged for long periods of time. They also have a great ability to see underwater. They can spot small things underwater without goggles. Their heightened abilities have much to do with their reliance on the ocean. Their eyes have become used to the underwater environment. Also, they have a great knowledge of marine life. During the great tsunami of 2004, sea-gypsies could survive thanks to their understanding of the sea.

General Comprehension

1. **The word reliance in the passage is closest in meaning to**

   (A) ignorance
   (B) confidence
   (C) dependence
   (D) residence

2. **Which of the following is true of the lifestyle of sea-gypsies?**

   (A) It is tightly connected with the ocean.
   (B) It is similar to that of mainland people.
   (C) It is highly civilized.
   (D) It has changed since 2004.

On the TOEFL Test

3. **According to the passage, which of the following is NOT true of sea-gypsy children?**

   (A) They are good at diving.
   (B) They rarely use goggles.
   (C) Their eyesight is better than that of normal children.
   (D) They learn swimming at school.

4. **All of the following are mentioned in the passage EXCEPT:**

   (A) Sea-gypsy culture is unique in Thailand.
   (B) Most Thai people can see things clearly in water.
   (C) Goggles are useful tools in the water.
   (D) Sea-gypsies are in touch with sea.

---

nomad (n)
a member of a group of people who move from place to place without a fixed home

expert (n)
a master at something; an authority on something

submerged (a)
under water

goggles (n)
special glasses worn to protect the eyes from water

heightened (a)
strengthened, increased, or improved

marine (a)
related to the sea

B Read the following passage, and answer the questions.

The Red Planet

Time Limit: 50 sec.

We know that there is no life on Mars. The Viking robot missions to the Red Planet proved that. The missions were due to one man for the most part. Percival Lowell, a rich American businessman, suggested that Mars contained life. He was fascinated by Mars. He spent 23 years studying it. He was so deeply involved in the search for Martian life that he built his own laboratory. It housed a huge telescope. At 7,000 feet (2.13km) above sea level in a dry climate, it was the perfect site to view Mars. Lowell believed that he saw a network of lines crossing Mars. He also thought that the lines were built by intelligent life. There was also the chance that water was on the planet. He drew many maps in his notebooks. His idea drew the public's attention. People soon believed that life on Mars could exist.

General Comprehension

1. **The word it in the passage refers to**

   Ⓐ Mars
   Ⓑ life
   Ⓒ telescope
   Ⓓ climate

2. **According to the passage, what can be inferred about the Viking?**

   Ⓐ It is a kind of telescope.
   Ⓑ It is a group of astronauts.
   Ⓒ It is involved in searching Mars.
   Ⓓ It is Percival Lowell's observatory.

On the TOEFL Test

3. **According to the passage, Percival Lowell did all of the following EXCEPT:**

   Ⓐ landing on the surface of Mars
   Ⓑ establishing a laboratory for Mars
   Ⓒ spending more than 20 years studying Mars
   Ⓓ sketching the surface of Mars

4. **According to the passage, which of the following is NOT true of Percival Lowell?**

   Ⓐ He showed extraordinary enthusiasm about Mars.
   Ⓑ He was wealthy enough to build his own laboratory.
   Ⓒ He is one of the celebrated people in the exploration of Mars.
   Ⓓ He denied the possibility of life on the Mars.

○ **planet (n)**
a large body in outer space that circles the sun or another star

○ **mission (n)**
a trip with a purpose

○ **be involved in (phr)**
to give a lot of time, effort, or attention to something

○ **laboratory (n)**
a room or a building where scientific research is carried out

○ **huge (a)**
very large in size

○ **climate (n)**
general weather conditions of a particular place

C Read the following passage, and answer the questions.

Gone with the Wind

Time Limit: 30 sec.

Gone with the Wind is an American film classic. The story takes place during the American Civil War between the southern and northern states. It is the story of Scarlett O'Hara, a pretty woman who lives on a plantation in the south. She is in love with a man, Ashley. He will not marry her because he is engaged to another woman. Scarlett is angry. It takes war and the threat of his death to realize that she values their friendship. Scarlett hopes to protect her friend from the armies. While doing so, she falls in love with Rhett, a man who teases her but loves her. The movie is a great tale of love in the context of war. History makes the story possible and the characters' situations believable.

General Comprehension

1. **The phrase takes place in the passage is closest in meaning to**

   (A) happens
   (B) breaks
   (C) exists
   (D) shoots

2. **The word so in the passage refers to**

   (A) living on a plantation
   (B) falling in love with Ashley
   (C) being angry
   (D) protecting her friend

classic (n)
a piece of writing or a film with a high standard and lasting value

plantation (n)
a large farm on which crops are raised

engaged (a)
having a formal agreement to get married

threat (n)
a warning of harm; a menace

On the TOEFL Test

3. **According to the passage, which of the following is NOT true of *Gone with the Wind*?**

   (A) It is one of the great American films.
   (B) The setting is during the Second World War.
   (C) It is about a love affair.
   (D) It uses historical information.

4. **The author's description of *Gone with the Wind* mentions all of the following EXCEPT:**

   (A) war
   (B) friendship
   (C) hate
   (D) love

D Read the following passage, and answer the questions.

Gravity

Time Limit: 30 sec.

Gravity has been used for all kinds of mechanical purposes. For one, it was used to make round bullets called shot. Armies used this for hundreds of years. The method involved a shot tower, which was a very tall building. Liquid lead was taken to the top of the tower and poured through a metal grid. This would separate the liquid in a uniform way. As the lead drops fell through, they would form round balls and cool. They would then land in a pool of water to prevent flattening and ensure the lead was cool. Afterwards, the lead balls would be checked for shape and size. They were then ready for the guns.

General Comprehension

1. **The word one in the passage refers to**

   (A) a purpose
   (B) gravity
   (C) shot
   (D) a method

2. **The word separate in the passage is closest in meaning to**

   (A) shape
   (B) pour
   (C) stretch
   (D) divide

On the TOEFL Test

3. **According to the passage, which of the following is NOT true of making shot?**

   (A) It involves a tower.
   (B) It relies on gravity.
   (C) It creates lead.
   (D) It needs a grid.

4. **The author's description of a shot tower mentions all of the following EXCEPT:**

   (A) bricks
   (B) a grid
   (C) water
   (D) lead

---

purpose (n)
the reason for which something is made or done

liquid (n)
a substance which flows and can be poured, like water

grid (n)
a pattern or structure made from horizontal and vertical lines

flatten (v)
to make flat

ensure (v)
to make something certain to happen

check (v)
to examine

Practice with Long Passages

Read the following passage, and answer the questions.

The Gypsies

Time Limit: 1 min. 10 sec.

The Roma are people who live all over Europe, North Africa, and the Americas. They are often called Gypsies. People mistakenly believed they came from Egypt because they traditionally have dark skin and hair. This misunderstanding explains the origin of the word "Gypsy." In fact, they call themselves Roma. Their people came from northern India to Europe a thousand years ago. Their language, Romany, is an Indo-Aryan language, but they usually speak the language of their home country.

Sadly, they have never had good lives in their home countries. The Roma live with racism all the time. For example, in Hungary, they are often put in separate classrooms in schools. Sometimes they are put in classrooms with students who have learning problems. Consequently, many do not finish school. Less than one percent of Roma have college degrees. This makes them unable to find good work. As a result, many Roma live in poverty. They are marked by social problems and crime.

1. **According to the passage, which of the following is NOT true of the Roma people?**

   (A) They came from northern India.
   (B) They all speak Romany.
   (C) They have not been welcomed in Europe.
   (D) They are subject to social problems and crime.

2. **Which of the following is NOT mentioned in the passage?**

   (A) The customs of the Roma
   (B) The language of the Roma
   (C) The schooling of the Roma
   (D) The work of the Roma

mistakenly (ad)
not accurately

traditionally (ad)
historically

misunderstanding (n)
a false belief

consequently (ad)
as a result

be marked by (phr)
be characterized by

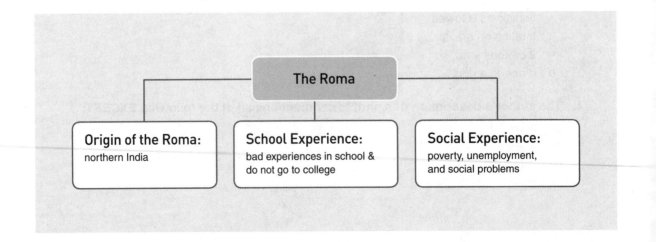

The Roma		
Origin of the Roma: northern India	**School Experience:** bad experiences in school & do not go to college	**Social Experience:** poverty, unemployment, and social problems

B Read the following passage, and answer the questions.

The Planet Mars

Time Limit: 1 min. 20 sec.

Mars is the fourth planet in the solar system. It is visible from Earth, which has made it a focus of study for centuries. It has some incredible geological features.

Mars is half the size of Earth, but its surface area is about the same as Earth's dry land. The reddish color of its surface comes from the presence of minerals like iron oxide (rust). The planet is less dense than our own. It has approximately one-tenth the mass. The northern part of the planet is distinct from the southern part. The north is quite flat from the amount of lava flows. There is a large, flat volcano called Olympus. It is the highest mountain in the solar system at 26km high.

The south has the largest canyon system, which is 4,000km long and 7km deep. Some of this was formed by meteors billions of years ago. It makes the Grand Canyon seem like a small sandbox in comparison. There is one huge crater called the Hellas Impact Basin. It was formed by a meteor. It is 2,100km wide.

1. **According to the passage, which of the following is NOT true of Mars?**

   (A) It looks reddish due to minerals.
   (B) It is one tenth of Earth's mass.
   (C) It never had any volcanic activity.
   (D) It has a big crater created by a meteor.

2. **All of the following are mentioned in the passage EXCEPT:**

   (A) the composition of the atmosphere of Mars
   (B) the topography of its surface
   (C) the differences between various areas
   (D) the effects of meteors on the surface

○ **feature (n)**
  a characteristic; a trait

○ **presence (n)**
  existence; appearance

○ **lava (n)**
  liquid rock that comes from a volcano

○ **impact (v)**
  to crash

○ **basin (n)**
  a particular region where the surface is lower than in other places

---

Geological Features of Mars

The Northern Part
• covered by a lava plane
• very flat
• has the highest volcano in the solar system.

The Southern Part
• pitted with craters and canyons
• has the largest canyon in the solar system
• has a huge impact crater

Read the following passage, and answer the questions.

Indies

Time Limit: 1 min. 50 sec.

The independent film industry is on the rise. Indies, as the films are called, are defined by the amount of money they receive from a big Hollywood studio. 50% of their budget is the limit in order to be independent. Part of the reason for the growth is content. Hollywood takes fewer risks than Indies. Another reason is the lower cost of technology.

Film viewers know the Hollywood formula. Many movies coming from the big studios have the same kinds of stories. The reasons are obvious: they make movies that customers want. And people always want the same sorts of things. However, this is not entirely true. Many viewers are tired of the same stories. They want to see films with refreshing plots and interesting perspectives. They want to see a film about unique topics. Indie films have the flexibility to do this.

The cost of cameras and editing equipment is on the decline. These necessary tools for filmmaking were once so costly that only Hollywood could afford them. Great video cameras are now affordable for most people. And now, most editing can be done on home computers. There are many programs for sale. There are even film editing programs for free on the Internet.

1. **According to the passage, which of the following is NOT true of Hollywood films?**

   Ⓐ They follow a formula.
   Ⓑ They come from large studios.
   Ⓒ They appeal to minorities.
   Ⓓ They take fewer risks.

2. **All of the following are mentioned in the passage as contributing to the growth of Indies EXCEPT:**

   Ⓐ interesting content
   Ⓑ good casting
   Ⓒ ability to change
   Ⓓ cheaper equipment

○ **on the rise (phr)**
   increasing
○ **formula (n)**
   a plan
○ **refreshing (a)**
   fresh and pleasing
○ **perspective (n)**
   points of view
○ **flexibility (n)**
   an ability to change

Hollywood Films
• Follow the same formula
• Have mass appeal

VS.

Indie Films
• Refreshing outlook
• Unique topics
• Made possible by the low cost of technology

D Read the following passage, and answer the questions.

Thermodynamics

Time Limit: 1 min. 20 sec.

Thermodynamics is essential to our understanding of science. The term *thermodynamic* came from Lord Kelvin in 1849. It comes from Greek and means "heat power." This theory states four laws, two of which are explained as follows:

When energy moves, we feel it. The first law says that all energy in a system can be accounted for. When it moves, it has to go somewhere. We cannot create or destroy energy. It only moves. An example of this is the difference between a normal light bulb and a fluorescent bulb. Fluorescent bulbs are more efficient because much of the energy is kept in the bulb to create light. In a normal bulb, some of the energy makes light, but much of it is lost in the form of heat.

The second law says that eventually differences in heat will balance out. When ice cubes melt, water warms to the temperature of the room. The air will cool when the river is cool. This degree of equalization is called entropy. All energy differences will seek to equalize over time.

1. **According to the passage, all of the following are true EXCEPT:**

   (A) Energy moves from place to place.
   (B) Heat can be used to create power.
   (C) Hot and cold try to balance.
   (D) Light is a form of heat.

2. **All of the following are mentioned in the passage EXCEPT:**

   (A) energy differences
   (B) the destruction of energy
   (C) steam engines
   (D) light bulbs

account for (phr)
to explain

fluorescent (a)
glowing from gas

efficient (a)
bright and glowing

eventually (ad)
sooner or later

equalize (v)
to become equal;
to balance out

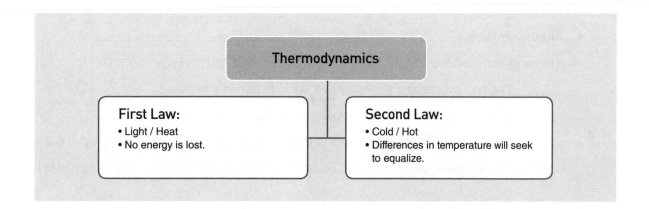

A Put the following sentences in order to make appropriate summaries based on the long passages you worked on earlier. The first sentence is already provided.

1. **The Gypsies**

   Gypsies originally came from northern India, not from Egypt.

   _____ Because they do not get well educated, they cannot find good jobs.

   _____ Some speak Romany, but most speak the language of their home country.

   _____ Their communities are often poor and have social problems and crime.

   _____ They have bad experiences in schools, like in Hungary for example.

2. **The Planet Mars**

   Mars, our neighboring planet, has some fascinating land features.

   _____ These were formed millions of years ago.

   _____ The north is characterized by large lava plains, and it also has the highest volcano in the solar system.

   _____ The south is characterized by canyons and craters.

   _____ One crater, the Hellas Impact Basin, is over 2,000km wide.

3. **Indies**

   The number of independent films is increasing, but Hollywood is funding films less and less.

   _____ The cost of cameras and other equipment is decreasing, which gives many people the power to make their own film.

   _____ This means that movies can be different from the Hollywood formula.

   _____ These films are flexible enough to address interesting or unpopular topics.

   _____ Many viewers are tired of the same stories and find Indie films refreshing.

4. **Thermodynamics**

   Thermodynamics describes the relationship between heat and power.

   _____ The first law states that energy in a system stays in a system.

   _____ The second law states that different temperatures try to equalize.

   _____ This means that hot temperatures "try" to cool down, and cold temperatures "try" to warm up.

   _____ It only moves, never to be lost. Efficient light bulbs do not allow energy to be lost in heat.

B   Fill in the blanks with suitable words or phrases to complete the following summaries.
Do not look at the previous page until you are finished.

1.   The Gypsies

(1)_____ originally came from (2)_____, not from Egypt. Some speak
(3)_____, but most speak the language of their (4)_____. They have
(5)_____ experiences in schools, like in Hungary for example. Because they do not get
well (6)_____, they cannot find good jobs. Their communities are often (7)_____ and
have social problems and (8)_____.

2.   The Planet Mars

Mars, our neighboring planet, has some fascinating (1)_____. The (2)_____ is
characterized by large (3)_____, and it also has the highest (4)_____ in the
solar system. The (5)_____ is characterized by (6)_____ and craters. These were
formed millions of years ago. One crater, the (7)_____, is over (8)_____ wide.

3.   Indies

The number of (1)_____ is increasing, but (2)_____ is funding films less
and less. This means that movies can be (3)_____ from the Hollywood formula. Many
viewers are (4)_____ of the same stories and find (5)_____ refreshing.
These films are (6)_____ enough to address interesting or unpopular topics. The
(7)_____ of cameras and other equipment is (8)_____, which gives many people the
power to make their own film.

4.   Thermodynamics

Thermodynamics describes the relationship between (1)_____. The first law
states that (2)_____ in a system (3)_____ in a system. It only moves (4)_____ to
be lost. Efficient (5)_____ do not allow energy to be lost in heat. The second law
states that different (6)_____ try to equalize. This means that hot temperatures "try" to
(7)_____ and cold temperatures "try" to (8)_____.

1. **The word advance in the passage is closest in meaning to**
   - Ⓐ development
   - Ⓑ procession
   - Ⓒ complication
   - Ⓓ usefulness

2. **What principle is the steam engine based on?**
   - Ⓐ Energy can be used for work.
   - Ⓑ Water can be boiled.
   - Ⓒ Man is not strong.
   - Ⓓ Machines need fuel.

3. **The word expanded in the passage is closest in meaning to**
   - Ⓐ stretched
   - Ⓑ grew
   - Ⓒ shrank
   - Ⓓ heated

4. **According to the passage, which of the following is NOT true of the steam engine?**
   - Ⓐ Its design is based on Boyle's Law.
   - Ⓑ It requires heated water.
   - Ⓒ It was used for mining.
   - Ⓓ It was used for airplanes.

5. **The word goods in the passage is closest in meaning to**
   - Ⓐ possessions
   - Ⓑ virtues
   - Ⓒ merchandise
   - Ⓓ vehicles

6. **According to paragraph 4, what can we infer about steam engines?**
   - Ⓐ Steam engines were used in trains.
   - Ⓑ Steam engines were only a little helpful.
   - Ⓒ Steam engines revolutionized the world.
   - Ⓓ Steam engines have moving parts.

The Steam Engine

The steam engine was a great advance for mankind. It made modern industry possible. Suddenly, the work of hundreds of men could be replaced by a machine. "Work" was to be accomplished by a new muscle: energy. It relied on basic principles of thermodynamics. In particular, it relied on Boyle's law.

Boyle's Law stated that the pressure of a gas is a function of its volume and its temperature. When a gas is heated in a balloon, it increases its volume and decreases its pressure. If the volume cannot change, the heat will cause the pressure to increase.

The steam engine basically took advantage of these facts. Energy, in the form of heat, could be changed into physical power. Energy could move things if controlled in the right way. Captured heat could be used for physical work. First, water was boiled to make steam. In this way, the water behaved like a gas. It could expand when heated. As the steam expanded, it moved into a tube called a cylinder. The bottom of the cylinder, called a piston, moved down as the gas expanded. The piston turned a metal arm which then could be used for all kinds of work.

The steam engine was used in textile mills, in farming, and in mining. It turned the great wheels of machines used for weaving. It was used to power machinery that separated cotton from the seed or grain from the stalk. The engine was used to pump water out of mines and lift coal and people up to the surface. Of course, it was used for the great trains that moved people and goods across continents.

7. **The word they in the passage refers to**

 (A) Russians
 (B) roller coasters
 (C) railway companies
 (D) passengers

8. **According to paragraph 2, what can we infer about roller coasters?**

 (A) They took a lot of effort to run.
 (B) They were not fun to ride.
 (C) They were reliant on ice.
 (D) They had lots of enthusiasts.

9. **The word employed in the passage is closest in meaning to**

 (A) followed
 (B) used
 (C) left
 (D) hired

10. **According to the passage, all of the following are true EXCEPT:**

 (A) The first roller coaster was created in the 17th century.
 (B) After the Second World War, more roller coasters were built than ever before.
 (C) Disneyland opened in 1955.
 (D) The 20th century saw great advances in roller coasters.

11. **All of the following are mentioned in the passage EXCEPT:**

 (A) the setup of amusement parks in America
 (B) Disney's adoption of wooden frame coasters
 (C) the rise in construction of coasters in the USA
 (D) the advantages of tubular steel construction

12. **Why does the author introduce Disney?**

 (A) Because it created the first American roller coaster
 (B) Because it opened many amusement parks in the U.S.
 (C) Because it created many coasters during World War II
 (D) Because it first introduced the steel roller coaster

The History of the Roller Coaster

The first roller coasters were created in Russia in the 17th century. However, they were not like modern ones. They were more like big sleds. People rode down steep ice slides. These sleds required very good navigation skills to slide down safely, and there were many accidents.

At the end of the 19th century, American railway companies introduced roller coasters. They set up amusement parks to make money on the weekends, when people rarely traveled. In 1884, the first real roller coaster appeared. It was a gravity-driven train. Passengers climbed flights of stairs to board the car. Then the car was pushed from the station to move down a hill and over a few bumps. At the bottom, passengers got out of the car and workers lifted the car to the second station.

During the early 20th century, there was great progress in roller coasters. Unlike previous coasters, the new ones employed mechanical tracks. The first was built in 1912. This was a great advance. It enabled people to enjoy greater speed and steeper hills but with much more safety than previous ones. Through the 1920s, many roller coasters were built, but after World War II, the number of roller coasters significantly decreased.

Disneyland, America's first theme park, opened in 1955. It opened a new era for amusement parks. Disney adopted the first tubular steel roller coaster in 1959. Before this, roller coasters always had been built on wooden frames. The steel track not only offered greater stability but also opened the door for loops and corkscrews.

Vocabulary Review

Choose the word with the closest meaning to each underlined word or phrase.

1. It is good to learn about different cultures by traveling.
   - (A) models
   - (B) events
   - (C) customs
   - (D) professions

2. The team equalized the game when it scored a goal.
   - (A) evened
   - (B) eliminated
   - (C) competed
   - (D) spread

3. People's gravity is always the same whether on a mountaintop or in a valley.
   - (A) movement
   - (B) figuration
   - (C) combination
   - (D) heaviness

4. The player accounted for losing too many games recently.
   - (A) regretted
   - (B) served
   - (C) explained
   - (D) fixed

5. There are many believable characters in the novel.
   - (A) extreme
   - (B) trustworthy
   - (C) moderate
   - (D) insulting

6. People at the meeting moved on to the subject of pollution.
   - (A) changed
   - (B) decreased
   - (C) outlined
   - (D) motivated

7. The family's old plantation has been operating for 100 years.
   - (A) neighbor
   - (B) society
   - (C) jungle
   - (D) farm

8. The country was marked by nature resources.
   - (A) originated
   - (B) scheduled
   - (C) characterized
   - (D) imagined

9. North America ranges from Newfoundland on the East Coast to Alaska on the West Coast.
   - (A) circle
   - (B) seaside
   - (C) nature
   - (D) curve

10. People will need a lot of endurance to climb the mountain.
   - (A) go up
   - (B) locate
   - (C) manage
   - (D) rebound

Unit 5

Sentence Simplification

Sentence Simplification

Overview

■Introduction

Sentence Simplification questions ask you to choose the sentence that best restates the essential meaning of the original sentence in the passage. The correct answer uses different vocabulary and different grammar to retell the original sentence in a simpler way. This type of question does not appear in every reading passage. Also, there is never more than one Sentence Simplification question in a passage.

■Useful Tips

• Figure out what the essential information is in the original sentence.

• Do not focus on minor information such as details and examples.

• Keep in mind that incorrect answers contradict something in the original sentence or leave out important information from it.

• Make sure that your answer agrees with the main argument of the paragraph or the passage as a whole.

■Question Type

Which of the following best expresses the essential information in the highlighted sentence? *Incorrect* answer choices change the meaning in important ways or leave out essential information.

Sample iBT Question

Which of the following best expresses the essential information in the highlighted sentence? *Incorrect* **answer choices change the meaning in important ways or leave out essential information.**

A) Poor people have loved the guitar.

B) The guitar is nicknamed the poor man's piano.

C) Various cultures have enjoyed the guitar.

D) The guitar has been played at cultural events.

The guitar, which is also known as the poor man's piano, has been cherished by many cultures. Spain made the guitar great. This country is responsible for many classical pieces. Brazil is also famous for guitar music. It developed the style of Bossa Nova. This style blends classical and jazz styles.

Correct Answer Choices (A) and (D) change the meaning of the highlighted sentence. Choice (B) focuses on minor details. Choice (C) is the best restatement of the original sentence.

Skill & Drill

Sentence Simplification questions ask for the same information stated in a different way. They ask you to choose the sentence that best paraphrases the essential information in the highlighted sentence.

There is great concern about global warming. There is evidence that temperatures are rising. For example, the North Pole has not seen such extreme melting in thousands of years. It was once possible to walk across certain parts of the Arctic Ocean on ice as polar bears do. Now, there open stretches of water.

Which of the following best expresses the essential information in the highlighted sentence?

- Ⓐ The North Pole experienced a thousand years of melting.
- Ⓑ The North Pole has not melted for thousands of years.
- ⬤ The North Pole has not melted to this extent in a long time.
- Ⓓ The thousands of years of melting were extreme for the North Pole.

Charles Darwin published *The Origin of Species*. He wrote that life forms change in response to their environments. His theory of natural selection caused a major change in science. But this challenged religious beliefs. His theory said that life evolved. God was not responsible for the life we see today.

1. **Which of the following best expresses the essential information in the highlighted sentence?**

    - Ⓐ According to Darwin, particular environments cause life forms to change.
    - Ⓑ Darwin wrote that life forms change the environments around them.
    - Ⓒ According to Darwin, change is the essence of life forms.
    - Ⓓ Darwin wrote that life forms change spontaneously.

Snowflakes have amazing shapes. No two are exactly the same. All snowflakes are usually flat and six-sided. They form when ice grows on a tiny piece of dust. The shape of snowflakes is determined by the temperature. The snowflake falls in the air and passes through different temperatures. This freezes the water in unique shapes. The biggest snowflake was over 28cm across.

2. **Which of the following best expresses the essential information in the highlighted sentence?**

    - Ⓐ The shape of snowflakes helps predict the temperature.
    - Ⓑ The temperature determines the size of snowflakes.
    - Ⓒ The shape of snowflakes depends on the temperature.
    - Ⓓ The temperature shapes snowflakes.

Meteorologists need data from around the world. They use many means to collect this data. One is to use satellites. They have changed the study of weather forever. The satellites check the earth's surface. They look at water vapor and heat. They send back data on weather conditions. By using this data, meteorologists can predict the weather with more accuracy.

3. **Which of the following best expresses the essential information in the highlighted sentence?**

    Ⓐ The accuracy of data is the most important factor in weather forecasts.
    Ⓑ Scientists need more accuracy in predicting the weather.
    Ⓒ Weather data enables scientists to forecast the weather more exactly.
    Ⓓ Meteorologists cannot predict the weather accurately even with satellite data.

Cells are the basic structural unit in the human body. We have about 100 million of them. They are not all the same types, however. They develop to have specific functions, forming organs, muscles, nerves, skin, and bones. Each body part has a special cell type. However, one type of cell, a stem cell, can grow into any of the other cell types.

4. **Which of the following best expresses the essential information in the highlighted sentence?**

    Ⓐ Cells form specific functions in specific body parts.
    Ⓑ Cells are formed by organs, muscles, and nerves.
    Ⓒ Cells take on specific functions to form body parts.
    Ⓓ Cells are specifically designed to grow into other cells.

Jeremy Bentham was an English philosopher. He proposed many legal and social reforms which were of great influence. He believed that the church and state should be separate. He argued for equal rights for women. He was a firm believer in free speech. He also argued for the end of slavery. Bentham also believed in health insurance for the rich and poor.

5. **Which of the following best expresses the essential information in the highlighted sentence?**

    Ⓐ Bentham's legal and social proposals had a great influence.
    Ⓑ Bentham influenced many proposals on social and legal reforms.
    Ⓒ Bentham proposed many legal and ethical reforms.
    Ⓓ Bentham was influenced by social and legal reforms.

Practice with Short Passages

A Read the following passage, and answer the questions.

Mutant Cells

Time Limit: 30 sec.

Cancer results from the mutation of one cell. The DNA of this cell changes. Only 10% of this DNA change is hereditary. This means that only 10% of cancers come from your family. Most of the changes are due to the environment. They may be caused by smoking or living in a polluted area. As we age, we grow more mutated cells. For this reason, cancer occurs most often as we get older. When the cell replicates, it copies the mutant DNA to the new cell. In the end, the cells change so much that they no longer follow the body's normal signals. They start growing, without control, into a tumor.

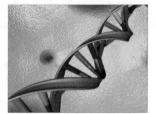

General Comprehension

1. **How do cells change to result in cancer?**

   (A) The DNA changes in one cell, and then the cells replicate.
   (B) The DNA forces cells to change, and then the cells replicate.
   (C) The cells change in the environment, and then they repeat.
   (D) The cells change to improve DNA mutants.

2. **What is the relationship between age and cancer?**

   (A) 10% of cancers are caused by environmental changes.
   (B) 90% of cancers are already present in our genetic code at birth.
   (C) As we get older, we get more mutant cells, which could form cancer.
   (D) As we get older, we change our environment, which causes all cancers.

mutation (n)
a change from the normal path

hereditary (a)
coming from one's parents

polluted (a)
dirty

replicate (v)
to copy itself

normal (a)
usual; ordinary; common

On the TOEFL Test

3. **Which of the following best expresses the essential information in the first highlighted sentence?**

   (A) DNA changes result from smoke or living near pollution.
   (B) Changes in DNA can be attributed to smoking and pollution.
   (C) Smoke causes pollution, which in turn forces DNA to change.
   (D) Pollution is a type of smoke that causes DNA to change.

4. **Which of the following best expresses the essential information in the second highlighted sentence?**

   (A) Mutant DNA is copied to the new cell during the process of replication.
   (B) The process of replication makes mutant DNA replication easy.
   (C) Cells only copy mutant DNA into the new cell during replication.
   (D) The cell replicates by copying mutant DNA into the new cell.

B Read the following passage, and answer the questions.

A Heroic Tornado Victim

Time Limit: 30 sec.

Sue, 18 years old, was not at her high school graduation. But the principal said she was present in the hearts of her classmates. She was seriously hurt by a category-4 tornado. Winds threw debris at over 400km per hour. Amazingly, Sue saved the lives of her two younger brothers. When she saw the twister near her house, she threw herself over her two little brothers. As the tornado passed, she kept them from getting hurt. She took the brunt of the injuries. Flying debris ripped through the house and hit her. Her two brothers were mostly unharmed, but she is now unconscious. Her courage touched her neighbors, friends, and family.

General Comprehension

1. **What is a category-4 tornado?**

    Ⓐ A strong tornado
    Ⓑ A weak tornado
    Ⓒ A speedy tornado
    Ⓓ A sudden tornado

2. **According to the passage, which of the following is true of Sue?**

    Ⓐ She was a selfish person.
    Ⓑ She was a high school graduate.
    Ⓒ She was a volunteer.
    Ⓓ She was a courageous person.

---

graduation (n)
a ceremony to celebrate the end of school

debris (n)
pieces of something that was destroyed

twister (n)
a spinning funnel of wind, a tornado

take the brunt of (phr)
to receive the worst part of something

On the TOEFL Test

3. **Which of the following best expresses the essential information in the first highlighted sentence?**

    Ⓐ Sue covered her brothers with her body as the tornado approached.
    Ⓑ The tornado's winds went so fast that Sue had to cover her brothers.
    Ⓒ The twister was near, and Sue had to look after her little brothers.
    Ⓓ Her brothers needed Sue to protect them from the approaching twister.

4. **Which of the following best expresses the essential information in the second highlighted sentence?**

    Ⓐ Sue is hurt, and her brothers were, too.
    Ⓑ Sue's brothers made her unconscious.
    Ⓒ Sue's brothers were not hurt, but she was.
    Ⓓ The tornado hurt Sue and her brothers.

C Read the following passage, and answer the questions.

Muir Woods

Time Limit: 45 sec.

The logging industry has had great political power for a long time. It uses this power to get at many of America's great forests. In the early part of the century, companies cut down much of the coastal forest of California. Many of the largest trees on earth grew here. The great redwoods and sequoias were used for lumber and paper. Most of these forests were reduced. A man called Kent saw what was happening, so he bought the land to preserve it. At first he thought the trees were saved. Then a water company wanted to flood the valley for electric power. The company took Kent to court. In order to save the wooded land, Kent donated it to the federal government. It became a national park. It was named Muir Woods after the famous naturalist John Muir. The valley was the first private donation to become a national park. It set the way for future forest preservation.

General Comprehension

1. **Why was the valley an attractive place for industries?**

   Ⓐ Logging and water companies saw great resources to exploit.
   Ⓑ The logging and water companies saw it as a beautiful place.
   Ⓒ The lumber could be used to reduce the forests.
   Ⓓ The beautiful land could be used to attract tourists.

2. **Why is this site important?**

   Ⓐ It began a trend of donating private lands for federal protection.
   Ⓑ It became a national park with thousands of visitors each year.
   Ⓒ It was donated by Kent, who was a famous politician.
   Ⓓ The trees are redwoods and sequoias, which are very big.

get at (phr)
to obtain something for one's use

lumber (n)
wood used for building

donate (v)
to give as a gift

set the way for (phr)
to prepare

preservation (n)
the act of saving for the future

On the TOEFL Test

3. **Which of the following best expresses the essential information in the first highlighted sentence?**

   Ⓐ There was a man who called Kent to see how to buy land.
   Ⓑ Kent was a man who did not like forests being grown in California.
   Ⓒ Kent monitored the situation to buy the land.
   Ⓓ Kent bought the land to prevent forest reduction.

4. **Which of the following best expresses the essential information in the second highlighted sentence?**

   Ⓐ The valley was first donated as a private park to the nation.
   Ⓑ The valley was the first national park to be privately donated.
   Ⓒ The valley was the first park to receive donations from the nation.
   Ⓓ The valley was the first park to be a national donation in private.

D Read the following passage, and answer the questions.

The Death Penalty

Time Limit: 30 sec.

The death penalty has been under debate for over a thousand years. This type of "justice" comes from the Hammurabi Codes. They were ancient laws that said, "An eye for an eye; a tooth for a tooth." Some believe that the death penalty is fair. A criminal who commits the worst crime should pay the highest price. The only way to keep society civil is to remove the bad elements. Some see the death penalty as a deterrent. If criminals know they will pay with their lives, they will not commit crimes. Others believe that the death penalty is a sign of a cruel society. They believe we have progressed so that crude punishment is not needed. There is no right reason for killing.

General Comprehension

1. **What does the phrase "An eye for an eye; a tooth for a tooth" mean?**

   (A) Always look at crime hard.
   (B) The punishment must fit the crime.
   (C) Punish people by removing their eyes.
   (D) Murder is the worst kind of offense.

2. **What is an objection to the death penalty?**

   (A) It is a barbaric form of punishment.
   (B) The crime is worth the punishment.
   (C) We should never punish criminals.
   (D) The philosophy of punishment is complex.

under debate (phr)
controversial

penalty (n)
punishment

criminal (n)
a person who commits a crime

remove (v)
to take out; to get rid of

deterrent (n)
a preventative idea

cruel (a)
very mean

On the TOEFL Test

3. **Which of the following best expresses the essential information in the first highlighted sentence?**

   (A) Civil society is keeping its bad elements away.
   (B) Removing criminals is the sole way to keep society healthy.
   (C) The way to organize society is by keeping bad people.
   (D) Civilization is best kept by bad people.

4. **Which of the following best expresses the essential information in the second highlighted sentence?**

   (A) There are some people who think the death penalty is cruel.
   (B) Some people believe the death penalty belongs in society.
   (C) Some people think a cruel society is one that has the death penalty.
   (D) The death penalty needs to belong to a cruel society, some think.

Practice with Long Passages

A Read the following passage, and answer the questions.

DNA

Time Limit: 1 min. 20 sec.

DNA is an important means of fighting crime. Detectives use it to catch criminals. They use DNA found at a crime scene to determine the real murderer. This method is one of the most reliable ways to identify criminals.

DNA is a molecule that contains the blueprint for life. It controls how the body develops as it grows. It transfers the genetic traits of parents to their offspring. DNA is found in each of the 100 trillion cells of the human body. Each person has a set of DNA that is completely unique.

Investigators often find some traces of DNA at the crime scene or on the victim. There may be a piece of hair, a drop of blood, or even skin. The police can collect these samples to analyze them. With luck, they find a match between the sample and the suspect. Some factors may prevent them from succeeding, however. DNA samples could be contaminated. The sample may be mixed with someone else's, or it may be partially destroyed, by heat for example.

1. **Which of the following best expresses the essential information in the highlighted sentence?** *Incorrect* **answer choices change the meaning in important ways or leave out essential information.**

   They use DNA found at a crime scene to determine the real murderer.

   (A) DNA is used to figure out who the real murderer is.
   (B) DNA from the murderer is collected and studied.
   (C) The murderer uses DNA to tip off the investigators.
   (D) The crime scene has details of who the murderer is.

2. **Which of the following best expresses the essential information in the highlighted sentence?** *Incorrect* **answer choices change the meaning in important ways or leave out essential information.**

   Each person has a set of DNA that is completely unique.

   (A) The DNA each person has is common.
   (B) People's DNA is unique to humans.
   (C) Every person has a unique set of DNA.
   (D) The DNA each person has is not unique.

reliable (a)
dependable; trustworthy

identify (v)
to recognize

transfer (v)
to move from one place to another

trait (n)
characteristic; quality; attribute

offspring (n)
children

suspect (n)
a person thought to have committed a crime

contaminate (v)
to spoil

3. **Which of the following best expresses the essential information in the highlighted sentence?** *Incorrect* **answer choices change the meaning in important ways or leave out essential information.**

    The sample may be mixed with someone else's, or it may be partially destroyed, by heat, for example.

    A Someone's DNA is useless if it is exposed to heat or mixed with someone else's.
    B Heat and mixing are two ways to destroy DNA for an investigation.
    C The sample can contain heat and someone else's DNA when mixed.
    D DNA can be mixed up with someone else's as a way to destroy it.

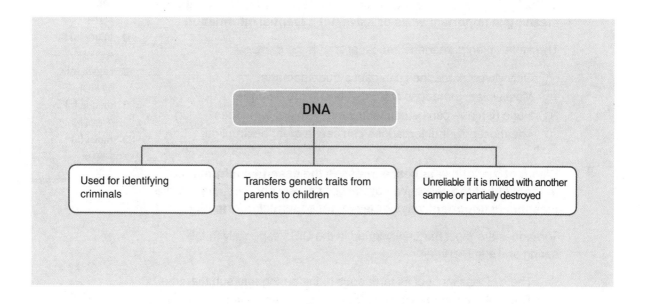

Read the following passage, and answer the questions.

Tornadoes

Time Limit: 1 min.

A tornado is a violent, rotating column of air. It reaches from a storm cloud to the ground. The most violent tornadoes are capable of huge damage. They can have wind speeds of 500km per hour. These twisters are very dangerous to life and property.

Tornadoes are most frequently found in the U.S., especially in the spring and summertime. Each year, 800 tornadoes are reported across the country. They result in 80 deaths and over 1,500 injuries. Paths of damage can be one mile wide and 50 miles long.

There is a region named "Tornado Alley." It is a zone from Ohio to Texas. Violent tornadoes develop more frequently here than anywhere else in the country. The place is unique because cold dry air comes from the Rocky Mountains. It meets warm, moist air from the Gulf of Mexico. These conditions are perfect for tornadoes.

1. **Which of the following best expresses the essential information in the highlighted sentence?** *Incorrect* **answer choices change the meaning in important ways or leave out essential information.**

   The most violent tornadoes are capable of huge damage.

   (A) Only violent tornadoes can cause huge damage.
   (B) Most violent tornadoes are capable of huge damage.
   (C) Huge damage can be caused by most violent tornadoes.
   (D) The most powerful tornadoes can cause great destruction.

2. **Which of the following best expresses the essential information in the highlighted sentence?** *Incorrect* **answer choices change the meaning in important ways or leave out essential information.**

   Tornadoes are most frequently found in the U.S., especially in the spring and summertime.

   (A) The U.S. has most of its tornadoes in the spring and summertime.
   (B) The U.S. has the most tornadoes, which usually happen in spring and summer.
   (C) The U.S. is frequently affected by tornadoes, especially in spring and summer.
   (D) The U.S. has the most tornadoes of all, though only in the spring and summertime.

rotate (v)
to spin

injury (n)
a casualty

region (n)
an area

unique (a)
distinctive

moist (a)
damp

3. **Which of the following best expresses the essential information in the highlighted sentence?** *Incorrect* **answer choices change the meaning in important ways or leave out essential information.**

Violent tornadoes develop more frequently here than anywhere else in the country.

(A) Violent tornadoes happen most frequently in the country.

(B) Tornado Alley gets violent tornadoes the most frequently of all the country.

(C) Tornado Alley gets tornadoes, some of which are violent, everywhere in its zone.

(D) Violent tornadoes occur more frequently in the country than in Tornado Alley.

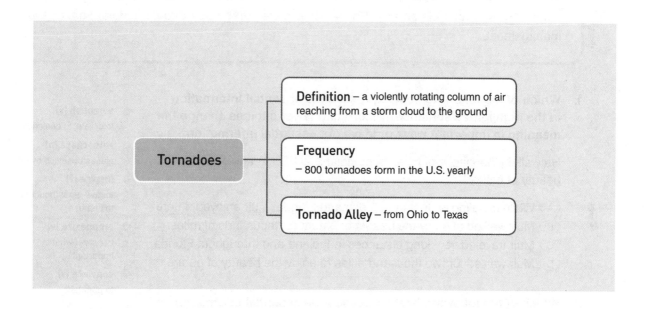

Tornadoes

Definition – a violently rotating column of air reaching from a storm cloud to the ground

Frequency
– 800 tornadoes form in the U.S. yearly

Tornado Alley – from Ohio to Texas

Read the following passage, and answer the questions.

John Muir Time Limit: 1 min. 20 sec.

John Muir helped establish one of the greatest national parks in the world. He was born in Scotland in 1838 and moved to the U.S. in 1849. Instead of graduating from a university, he got a job as an industrial engineer. Soon after, he decided to explore the wilderness. He walked thousands of miles from Indiana to Florida enjoying the beauty of nature. Muir had planned to journey to South America but was stopped by malaria. He went to California instead.

He arrived in San Francisco in 1868. He soon left for Yosemite, which he had only read about. He was inspired by his first sight of this great place. Muir wrote, "No temple made with hands can compare with Yosemite. Yosemite is the grandest of all special temples of Nature."

In 1903, President Roosevelt visited Yosemite Park with Muir. Muir told the president about the state's poor management of the valley. He emphasized the importance of protecting nature. He was able to convince Roosevelt to protect the valley through federal control and management.

1. **Which of the following best expresses the essential information in the highlighted sentence? *Incorrect* answer choices change the meaning in important ways or leave out essential information.**

He walked thousands of miles from Indiana to Florida enjoying the beauty of nature.

  Ⓐ While traveling on foot from Indiana to Florida, Muir enjoyed nature.
  Ⓑ Muir walked to enjoy the beauty of nature for thousands of miles.
  Ⓒ Muir traveled very long distances in Indiana and throughout Florida.
  Ⓓ Muir walked for two thousand miles to enjoy the beauty of nature.

2. **Which of the following best expresses the essential information in the highlighted sentence? *Incorrect* answer choices change the meaning in important ways or leave out essential information.**

He soon left for Yosemite, which he had only read about.

  Ⓐ Muir soon left Yosemite after he read about it.
  Ⓑ Muir soon went to Yosemite, about which he had only read.
  Ⓒ Muir soon left to go see Yosemite and read what he wanted.
  Ⓓ Muir went to Yosemite but left soon when he read about it.

establish (v)
to create; to designate

wilderness (n)
places unsettled by man

inspire (v)
to give great thoughts; to impress

emphasize (v)
to repeat what is important

convince (v)
to persuade

3. **Which of the following best expresses the essential information in the highlighted sentence? *Incorrect* answer choices change the meaning in important ways or leave out essential information.**

    He was able to convince Roosevelt to protect the valley through federal control and management.

    (A) Muir was so persuasive that he got Roosevelt to keep the valley safe under federal control.
    (B) Muir could only convince Roosevelt to protect the valley through federal control.
    (C) Muir persuaded Roosevelt to protect the federal management of the valley.
    (D) Muir could convince Roosevelt but only when protection of the valley became federal.

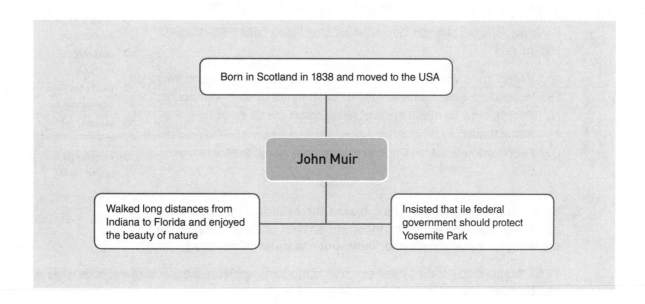

Read the following passage, and answer the questions.

The Code of Hammurabi

Time Limit: 1 min.

Hammurabi was the sixth king of Babylon. He was born in 1810 BC. He ruled over his empire from 1792 BC until his death in 1750 BC. He is perhaps best known for creating a set of laws called The Code of Hammurabi.

While the penalties of the law seem cruel to modern people, two aspects of the code were ahead of their time. First, he put the laws in writing. They were not just his words. Second, he tried to apply his laws systematically. This was an important step forward in the evolution of civilization. The idea of "innocent until proven guilty" comes from the code.

The laws were written on stone tablets and placed in a public place. People could see them, but not many people could read and understand them. The tablets were plundered a number of years later and removed to Elamite Susa. They were rediscovered there in 1901. Now the stone tablets stand in the Louvre Museum in France.

1. **Which of the following best expresses the essential information in the highlighted sentence?** *Incorrect* **answer choices change the meaning in important ways or leave out essential information.**

    He is perhaps best known for creating a set of laws called The Code of Hammurabi.

    (A) People know what he did best, which was creating codes and laws.
    (B) People know him best because he created the Code of Hammurabi.
    (C) People know he made the best laws, called the Code of Hammurabi.
    (D) People know what his Code of Hammurabi is and think it is the best.

2. **Which of the following best expresses the essential information in the highlighted sentence?** *Incorrect* **answer choices change the meaning in important ways or leave out essential information.**

    While the penalties of the law seem cruel to modern people, two aspects of the code were ahead of their time.

    (A) Two aspect of the code were advancing while modern people deemed the laws cruel.
    (B) While modern people were making cruel penalties, two aspects of the code were used.
    (C) Though the penalties seem cruel these days, two aspects were quite advanced.
    (D) Since the penalties were cruel, two aspects of the code were advanced by modern people.

- **aspect (n)**
  quality
- **evolution (n)**
  development
- **innocent (a)**
  not guilty
- **tablet (n)**
  a flat stone
- **plunder (v)**
  to rob
- **remove (v)**
  to take away

3. **Which of the following best expresses the essential information in the highlighted sentence?** *Incorrect* **answer choices change the meaning in important ways or leave out essential information.**

People could see them, but not many people could read and understand them.

- Ⓐ People who saw the rules could read and understand many of them.
- Ⓑ Few people could read the codes because they could not see them.
- Ⓒ Only people who could see the rules could understand them.
- Ⓓ Few could read and comprehend the rules despite their visibility.

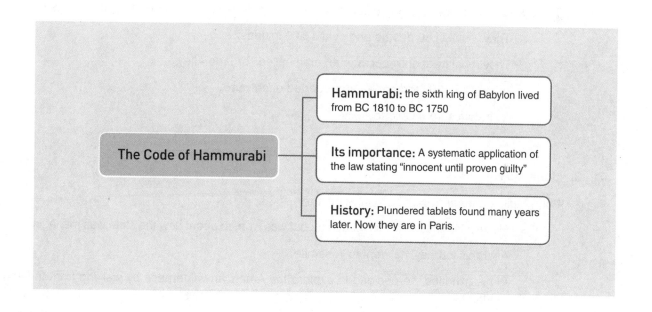

The Code of Hammurabi

Hammurabi: the sixth king of Babylon lived from BC 1810 to BC 1750

Its importance: A systematic application of the law stating "innocent until proven guilty"

History: Plundered tablets found many years later. Now they are in Paris.

Building Summary Skills

A   Put the following sentences in order to make appropriate summaries based on the long passages you worked on earlier. The first sentence is already provided.

1. DNA

DNA is used to catch criminals because it is a very reliable method.

_____ If the DNA in the sample matches the DNA of someone they know, police have identified the criminal.

_____ All of our cells contain DNA.

_____ DNA can be contaminated, however.

_____ When investigators find traces of a person, they analyze them.

2. Tornadoes

Tornadoes are violently rotating columns of air, and they usually occur during spring and summer.

_____ They result in 80 deaths and over 1,500 injuries.

_____ They most frequently occur in an area called Tornado Alley.

_____ In the U.S., 800 tornadoes are reported each year.

_____ It stretches from Ohio to Texas.

3. John Muir

John Muir, a naturalist, was born in Scotland in 1838.

_____ He was fascinated by this great park but was worried about how the state was managing it.

_____ After this journey, he went to Yosemite.

_____ In his twenties, he decided to explore the American wilderness by walking from Indiana to Florida.

_____ He asked the president of the U.S. to protect this beautiful place.

4. The Code of Hammurabi

Hammurabi was the sixth king of the Babylonian Dynasty.

_____ Another importance of this law is that the concept of "innocent until proven guilty" comes from the Code of Hammurabi.

_____ He created the Code of Hammurabi.

_____ These laws became famous because they were written down for the first time and publicly placed.

B Fill in the blanks with suitable words or phrases to complete the following summaries. Do not look at the previous page until you are finished.

1. DNA

DNA is used to (1)_____ because it is a very (2)_____ method. All of our cells contain (3)_____. When (4)_____ find traces of a person, they (5)_____ them. If the DNA in the sample (6)_____ the DNA of someone they know, police have (7)_____ the criminal. DNA can be (8)_____, however.

2. Tornadoes

Tornadoes are violently (1)_____ columns of air, and they usually occur during (2)_____. In the U.S., (3)_____ tornadoes are reported each year. They result in (4)_____ deaths and over (5)_____ injuries. They most frequently occur in an area called (6)_____. It stretches from (7)_____ to (8)_____.

3. John Muir

John Muir, a (1)_____, was born in (2)_____ in 1838. In his twenties, he decided to explore the (3)_____ by walking from Indiana to Florida. After this journey, he went to (4)_____. He was (5)_____ by this great park but was (6)_____ by how the state was managing it. He asked the (7)_____ of the U.S. to (8)_____ this beautiful place.

4. The Code of Hammurabi

(1)_____ was the (2)_____ king of the (3)_____. He created the Code of Hammurabi. These (4)_____ became famous because they were (5)_____ for the first time and (6)_____. Another importance of these laws was that the concept of " (7)_____ until proven (8)_____ " comes from the Code of Hammurabi.

1. **The word barren in the passage is closest in meaning to**

   Ⓐ rich
   Ⓑ poor
   Ⓒ damp
   Ⓓ sandy

2. **Why does the author mention flypaper traps in paragraph 2?**

   Ⓐ To challenge beliefs about plants
   Ⓑ To explain what Darwin studied
   Ⓒ To show an example of carnivorous plants
   Ⓓ To argue an important point

3. **The word they in the passage refers to**

   Ⓐ insects
   Ⓑ scientists
   Ⓒ basic structures
   Ⓓ various types

4. **The word release in the passage is closest in meaning to**

   Ⓐ discharge
   Ⓑ detache
   Ⓒ move
   Ⓓ stick

5. **According to the passage, all of the following are true EXCEPT:**

   Ⓐ About five hundred carnivorous plants exist.
   Ⓑ The first popular paper on carnivorous plant was introduced by Charles Darwin in 1875.
   Ⓒ There are carnivorous plants in swamps or bogs.
   Ⓓ Charles Darwin explained seven different types of traps.

6. **Which of the following best expresses the essential information in the highlighted sentence? *Incorrect* answer choices change the meaning in important ways or leave out essential information.**

   Ⓐ Scientists believe that these leaf types have evolved from a hairy leaf.
   Ⓑ Scientists cannot agree that these leaf types are mutations from a simple, hairy leaf.
   Ⓒ Scientists suggest leaving the types of mutations to a simple, hairy leaf.
   Ⓓ Scientists have all the leaf types from suggested mutations of leaves.

Carnivorous Plants

Carnivorous plants usually grow in places where the soil is barren. These places include swamps or bogs. They require very humid conditions and lots of sun. But they must get their nutrients by eating small animals or insects. These plants have clever ways of trapping their prey.

Charles Darwin wrote the first well-known paper on carnivorous plants in 1875. He describes five kinds of traps. Pitfall traps catch insects in a rolled leaf that has a pool of bacteria at the bottom. Flypaper traps catch insects using a sticky liquid. Snap traps catch insects with rapid leaf movements. Bladder traps suck in insects with a bladder that creates a vacuum. Finally, lobster-pot traps use inward pointing hairs to force insects towards the center of the plant. They cannot go backwards.

The changing of carnivorous plants over time is hard to study. There are few fossil records. For the most part, only seeds or pollen exist. However, we can learn much from the structure of current traps. Pitfall traps have clearly evolved from rolled leaves. Flypaper traps also show a simple change from sticky, non-lethal leaves to the deadly kind.

The Venus Fly Trap is an interesting plant. There are three hairs in the middle of each leaf. The insect must touch two hairs quickly for the leaf to fold shut. Then the plant may eat.

Scientists have suggested that all these leaf types are mutations from a simple, hairy leaf. It is able to collect drops of rainwater in which bacteria can breed. Insects land on the leaf and get caught in the water. They suffocate. The bacteria then begin to decay the insect and release the nutrients into the plant. There are around five hundred plants that are known to be carnivorous.

7. **The word normal in the passage is closest in meaning to**

  (A) ordinary

  (B) unusual

  (C) frequent

  (D) serious

8. **The word complex in the passage is closest in meaning to**

  (A) complicated

  (B) chewable

  (C) overwhelming

  (D) boring

9. **The phrase this condition in the passage refers to**

  (A) the Sahara Desert

  (B) desertification

  (C) Dust Bowl

  (D) the Great Plains

10. **According to paragraph 2, what has prevented the Dust Bowl from happening again?**

  (A) Better cattle breeds

  (B) Good farming practices

  (C) Better irrigation techniques

  (D) The Great Plains Preservation Plan

11. **According to the passage, which of the following is NOT true?**

  (A) Desertification is one of the political issues.

  (B) The Sahara Desert expands by 10km every other year.

  (C) Droughts are common in the desert.

  (D) The word desertification was introduced in the 1950s.

12. **Which of the following best expresses the essential information in the highlighted sentence? *Incorrect* answer choices change the meaning in important ways or leave out essential information.**

  (A) Land only recovers with the return of rains.

  (B) Rain helps the recovery of all managed land.

  (C) Rains support the recovery of well-managed lands only.

  (D) Droughts prevent land from recovering from poor management.

Desertification

The Sahara Desert is growing by 10km each year. The whole earth gets 600km² of desert area more every year. This process is called "desertification." This term started being used in the1950s.

The idea of desertification was first known in the 1930s. Much of the Great Plains grew very dry as a result of drought and poor farming techniques. It was called the "Dust Bowl." Millions were forced to leave their farms and their ways of life. Since then, there have been great improvements in farming practices in the Great Plains. These have prevented the "Dust Bowl" disaster from occurring again.

Grazing is one worry. Cows do two things to the soil. First, they eat grasses and plants that hold the soil in place. Second, their hooves break down the top layer of soil. The result is that the good soil can be blown away by the wind. The dirt left behind is not good for growing.

Some think that droughts cause this condition. In fact, it is mostly caused by people. It has become one of the most serious global problems. Droughts are normal in dry and semi-dry places. Well-managed lands can recover from droughts when the rains return. It is man's effect on nature that is the key. A five-year drought was worsened by poor land management in West Africa some years ago. It caused the deaths of more than 100,000 people and 12 million cattle.

Desertification is a common issue in politics. There are still many things that we do not know about it. The process is a very complex form of degradation. More research needs be done to understand it better.

Vocabulary Review

Choose the word with the closest meaning to each underlined word or phrase.

1. His good speech inspired me to become a politician.
   - (A) behaved
   - (B) accepted
   - (C) influenced
   - (D) acted

2. Japan is moister than Korea due to all the rain it gets.
   - (A) damper
   - (B) noisier
   - (C) drier
   - (D) lighter

3. He likes to think of himself as a normal person.
   - (A) harmful
   - (B) detailed
   - (C) ordinary
   - (D) final

4. People usually have many different aspects.
   - (A) influences
   - (B) features
   - (C) professions
   - (D) pieces

5. The last emperor was so cruel that he killed many innocent people.
   - (A) personal
   - (B) talented
   - (C) mean
   - (D) gentle

6. Bordeaux, France, is a very famous region for wine.
   - (A) border
   - (B) hometown
   - (C) area
   - (D) break

7. Yesterday, I got a fine from a cop because I missed a traffic sign.
   - (A) reason
   - (B) judgment
   - (C) gift
   - (D) punishment

8. What is the most frequently asked question from your customers?
   - (A) often
   - (B) widely
   - (C) correctly
   - (D) similarly

9. I work on a rotating system. This week, I work at night.
   - (A) loading
   - (B) changing
   - (C) confusing
   - (D) counting

10. Europeans plundered a lot of cultural properties from Egypt.
    - (A) charged
    - (B) experienced
    - (C) allowed
    - (D) robbed

PART 2

Making Inferences

In this part, the reading comprehension questions include: rhetorical purpose, inference, and insert text. The learning objectives of these reading comprehension questions are to understand the rhetorical function of a statement or paragraph, the logic of the passage, and strongly implied ideas in the text.

Unit 6

Rhetorical Purpose

Rhetorical Purpose

Overview

■Introduction

Rhetorical Purpose questions ask you to understand why and how the author uses a particular piece of information in the passage. Because this type of question usually focuses on the logical development of the passage, you need to figure out how one sentence or paragraph relates to another.

■Useful Tips

- Read the question first, and then recognize the author's purpose immediately by scanning the specific phrases or sentences.

- Focus on the logical links between sentences and paragraphs, not on the overall organization of the passage.

- Familiarize yourself with the words or phrases for rhetorical functions like *to illustrate, to criticize, to explain, to contrast, to compare, to note,* etc.

■Question Types

1. The author discusses _____ in paragraph X in order to ~

2. Why does the author mention _____?

3. The author uses X as an example of ~

4. Why does the author quote _____ in the passage?

5. In paragraph X, why does the author give details about _____?

6. In paragraph X, the author explains _____ by ~

7. How does the author explain the idea of _____ in paragraph X?

Sample iBT Question

Why does the author mention that they check spellings and word meanings?

- (A) To criticize the price of digital dictionaries
- (B) To explain why digital dictionaries are effective
- (C) To question who needs digital dictionaries
- (D) To define the meaning of the words *digital dictionaries*

Digital dictionaries are very effective learning tools. They check spellings and word meanings. They also give synonyms. Even better, they show the words in a sentence. This helps students learn about the grammar of the word. Students can learn to use words with fewer mistakes. They become better writers this way.

 If you look at the logical links between the sentences, you will find that the author presents several supporting details or examples in order to explain why digital dictionaries are useful for learning. Therefore, the correct answer is (B).

● Skill & Drill

Rhetorical Purpose questions ask you why the author uses particular words, phrases, or sentences. These words, phrases, or sentences can be used to argue, define, illustrate, or contrast ideas. So you need to look at the logical links between ideas rather than focusing on the overall organization of the whole passage.

Example

Fireflies are interesting insects. They use their light as a type of signal. They can turn their light on and off in a precise way. The flies do this to find a mate. In some species of flies, females prefer males who have a long flash. In other species, females prefer males that can flash quickly. Some species of firefly can produce two different colors of light, red and green.

Why does the author mention that females prefer males who have a long flash?

- (A) To define the idea of mating between species
- (B) To show how their lights are used to find a mate
- (C) To hide the truth about how fireflies find their mates
- (D) To question the need for the use of flashing lights

Avalanches are dangerous. When great sheets of ice and snow slide down the mountain, they destroy anything in their path. Snow that does not stick together is likely to slide. Skiers get hurt and even die. Scientists study snowflakes to learn more about avalanches. They look to see how ice crystals form. Certain shapes make sticky snow. Other shapes can make snow slide.

1. **The author uses they destroy anything in their path as an example of which of the following?**
   - (A) How avalanches hurt skiers and even kill them
   - (B) When avalanches develop sliding snow
   - (C) Why avalanches are great sheets of ice
   - (D) How avalanches are dangerous

The Maldives are a group of islands in the Indian Ocean. There are over one thousand small islands in this group. The islands are formed by coral that rests on the tops of underwater volcanoes. The coral often grows in a circular formation. When the coral reaches the surface, an island forms. Often there is a section in the middle where there is no coral. This forms a lake in the middle of the island that is fed by seawater.

2. **Why does the author mention that when the coral reaches the surface, an island forms?**
   - (A) To specify the shape of the island in the sea
   - (B) To contrast the formation of different islands
   - (C) To explain the formation of the Maldives
   - (D) To summarize the information in the passage

An eating disorder is a way of eating that harms your health. Some people overeat and gain weight. Others eat too little. Some do something called binge eating. They eat too much at one time to the point where they feel pain. They often feel embarrassed about eating, so they try to do this alone. One aspect of any eating disorder is that the people cannot control the way they eat.

3. **The author discusses binge eating in the passage in order to**

   (A) contrast overeating and not eating
   (B) explain what overeating and eating too little are
   (C) illustrate why people feel embarrassed
   (D) compare embarrassing ways of eating alone

Poverty is a major social issue. There are a number of causes. Certain groups of people may be denied basic rights. They are not given work because of their race or religion. A lack of freedom is another. Sometimes a leader prevents his people from living and working in the ways they want. He keeps all the money and power for himself. A third cause is war. It can ruin the basic economy of a country. People spend most of their energy surviving rather than improving their lives.

4. **The author discusses a number of causes in order to**

   (A) show why poverty is a major issue
   (B) introduce the details about how poverty occurs
   (C) explain what a social issue is about
   (D) define the meaning of poverty

Cherrapunji in India is the wettest place on earth. Sometimes it rains for two months without stopping. Strangely, the water does not stay in one place. The land used to be green with plants, but because of people, this is no longer true. They have destroyed the land. Now, when it rains, the water flows away over the hard earth. The dirt and plants are washed away.

5. **Why does the author mention that strangely, the water does not stay in one place?**

   (A) To say how the land used to be
   (B) To tell the reader about the rain
   (C) To show what is unusual about the area
   (D) To explain the difference in rainfall

Practice with Short Passages

A Read the following passage, and answer the questions.

Bugs Have the Answers

Time Limit: 30 sec.

Police must know the exact time and place when a person died. This can help answer questions about the way that person died. It may be either an accident or a crime. Crime experts can look to insects for these answers. Insects such as moths, mites, or beetles have different life cycles. They also have different eating habits. Some types of mites only eat flesh from dead bodies in the early stages of rot. Other mites feed on flesh at later stages. Beetles typically feed on flesh in late stages and in damp conditions. Moths eat flesh in dry conditions. Experts can look at which insect is present and when they have laid their eggs. This can help determine the time and place that a person died.

General Comprehension

1. **Why do police need to know the time and place a person died?**

   Ⓐ To learn how the person died
   Ⓑ To tell the family the news
   Ⓒ To learn about the insects on the body
   Ⓓ To check whether the place was damp or not

2. **How do bugs give the information police need?**

   Ⓐ They only eat in damp, dark conditions.
   Ⓑ They are always hungry for flesh and blood.
   Ⓒ They have predictable eating and living habits.
   Ⓓ They lay their eggs during the warm part of the day.

flesh (n)
the soft part of a person or animal's body between the bones and the skin

rot (n)
decay; decomposition

feed on (phr)
to eat

typically (ad)
normally; usually

damp (a)
wet

determine (v)
to identify

On the TOEFL Test

3. **The author uses some types of mites as an example of which of the following?**

   Ⓐ The different habits of insects
   Ⓑ The way mites feed on bodies
   Ⓒ The best-tasting flesh for bugs
   Ⓓ The only way to tell the time

4. **Why does the author mention when they have laid their eggs in the passage?**

   Ⓐ To contrast with the nesting habits of birds
   Ⓑ To see what kinds of people have been murdered
   Ⓒ To describe the best way to find bodies
   Ⓓ To show a way to tell the time of death

B Read the following passage, and answer the questions.

Anxiety Disorders

Time Limit: 30 sec.

Anxiety disorders stop people from doing what they want to do. Anxious people actually have physical symptoms of their feelings. Their heart might beat fast. They may start to sweat. They may even have a severe panic attack. People with this disorder cannot control their worries. They worry over simple things like appointments or cleaning their house. They may even worry if their desk is not in order. Doctors say people have this disorder if they spend more days than not worrying. They say such people always feel tired or annoyed because of their worries. They cannot sleep or eat sometimes. Basically, worries are at the center of their entire lives.

General Comprehension

1. **What is an example of a symptom of anxiety?**

   (A) A feeling of calm
   (B) A rapid heartbeat
   (C) A high temperature
   (D) A weak voice

2. **What is anxiety disorder?**

   (A) A type of appointment with the doctor
   (B) A time where you only get worried about messes
   (C) A condition where worrying is a regular part of life
   (D) The time when people worry the most in their lives

anxiety (n)
a feeling of nervousness or worry

disorder (n)
a problem or illness which affects someone's mind or body

severe (a)
intense; strong

annoyed (a)
in a bad mood; fairly angry about something

entire (a)
total; whole

On the TOEFL Test

3. **The author discusses a severe panic attack in order to**

   (A) give an example of a physical symptom
   (B) make people sweat to control their worries
   (C) explain how disorders work in the brain
   (D) show why we should exercise when we can

4. **The author mentions they cannot sleep or eat sometimes as an example of which of the following?**

   (A) What doctors say we should do
   (B) How the disorder affects people
   (C) Keeping appointments or cleaning
   (D) Panicking because of a fast heartbeat

Read the following passage, and answer the questions.

The Strait of Magellan

Time Limit: 30 sec.

At one time, travel from the Atlantic to the Pacific was dangerous. This was in a time before the Panama Canal. Ships had to go around the bottom of the world. Sometimes they would take the long trip below Africa. They could also take the Drake Passage. This was the stretch of water between the South Pole and America. The water and weather was very dangerous. Huge blocks of ice threatened to wreck ships. Magellan found another way in 1520. The passage was called the Strait of Magellan. It passed between the continent to the north and Tierra del Fuego, an island, to the south. This narrow strip of water was protected by land. It gave ships the safety they needed.

General Comprehension

1. **Why was it dangerous to travel between the Atlantic and Pacific Oceans?**

   Ⓐ The ships got frozen in the ice.
   Ⓑ There were pirates in these waters.
   Ⓒ The water and weather were not safe.
   Ⓓ The ships could hit land at any time.

2. **Why is the Strait of Magellan safe?**

   Ⓐ It has a lot of room for ships.
   Ⓑ It is protected by land on both sides.
   Ⓒ The blocks of ice do not fit there.
   Ⓓ The South Pole is not far away.

stretch (n)
a distance

block (n)
a chunk

threaten (v)
to menace; to bully;
to intimidate

wreck (v)
to destroy completely or
ruin

strip (n)
a thin piece

On the TOEFL Test

3. **Why does the author mention the time before the Panama Canal?**

   Ⓐ To give the reader a sense of the passage of time
   Ⓑ To show that the Strait of Magellan was not important at all
   Ⓒ To describe the need for a dangerous way around the oceans
   Ⓓ To confuse the reader about the focus of the passage

4. **The author mentions this narrow strip of water was protected by land in order to**

   Ⓐ contrast the sentence before it
   Ⓑ describe how deep the water was there
   Ⓒ explain why the strait was a good place
   Ⓓ refute the need for the Panama Canal

D Read the following passage, and answer the questions.

The Way We Speak
Time Limit: 50 sec.

The way we speak can tell others a lot about our backgrounds. We can guess if someone is from the northern part of our country or the southern. What happens if a child has a southern accent but uses northern words? We might guess that the child's family moved from the north to the south. The child has the accent of his friends but uses some words only used by his parents. Our social background also affects the way we speak. A famous sociolinguist, William Labov, tried to find a link between accent and social class. He went to three different shops in New York. The first was used by upper class people, the second by the middle class, and the third by the lower class. He found that in general, people in the upper class shop did not pronounce "R" in the same way as customers in the other shops.

General Comprehension

1. **How does the place we live affect the way we speak?**

   (A) We find links between our accents and social class.
   (B) We want to tell others about our background.
   (C) We cannot tell the difference between northerners and southerners.
   (D) We use certain words and have accents.

2. **How did William Labov identify social class in language?**

   (A) Customers used different shops for food.
   (B) People pronounced the letter "R" differently.
   (C) People liked to use the upper class shop in general.
   (D) There is a link between the words we use and accent.

background (n)
history

affect (v)
to influence

sociolinguist (n)
a person who studies language and society

accent (n)
a way of speaking

pronounce (v)
to say

On the TOEFL Test

3. **Why does the author mention the child who has a southern accent but uses northern words?**

   (A) To show how people use language differently
   (B) To contrast the meaning of accent versus vocabulary
   (C) To illustrate how southerners speak
   (D) To illustrate how children speak with adults

4. **The author discusses the link between accent and social class in order to**

   (A) find a link between accent, childhood, New York, and social class
   (B) support the idea that our background influences the way we think
   (C) show how accent will change our background if we are not careful
   (D) explain the difference between middle class and upper class shops

Practice with Long Passages

A Read the following passage, and answer the questions.

Time Limit: 1 min. 40 sec.

Forensic Science

Forensics is a branch of science used by the legal system. *Forensic* means "related to the courts." This field helps answer legal questions about our world around us.

A common use of forensics is in fighting crime. Police try to link the criminal to the crime. They look for fingerprints or shoeprints in the room. Police look for evidence in the form of bodily fluids. They can also look at scratch marks on skin or pieces of hair. They can even match bite marks to a suspect.

Police also study how poisons work on the body. Crime experts record how much of a chemical was used. They also guess how much time has passed since its use. They try to see what chemicals were present at the scene. Blood samples can expose the short-term use of a drug or poison. Hair samples can expose long-term use. Hair grows 1cm per month. This gives experts an idea of when drugs or poisons were used.

These are just a few of the areas that forensics looks at. The field is very broad. Science is very useful to the legal system. It can be used to help answer difficult questions.

1. **Why does the author mention a branch of science used by the legal system in paragraph 1?**

   - (A) To show the application of forensics
   - (B) To illustrate a few things that forensics looks at
   - (C) To explain that forensics is a difficult field of study
   - (D) To define what forensics is

2. **The author mentions fingerprints or shoeprints in paragraph 2 in order to**

   - (A) show how police use forensics
   - (B) show how police look for fluids
   - (C) show how police look at hair
   - (D) show how police analyze bites

3. **The author uses hair samples in paragraph 3 as an example of which of the following?**

   - (A) How poisons work in the body
   - (B) How poisons get into the body
   - (C) Why poisons are found in the body
   - (D) What drugs are used for hair care

legal (a)
related to the law

link (v)
to connect

fluid (n)
liquid

suspect (n)
a person who is thought to be a criminal

expose (v)
to show or demonstrate

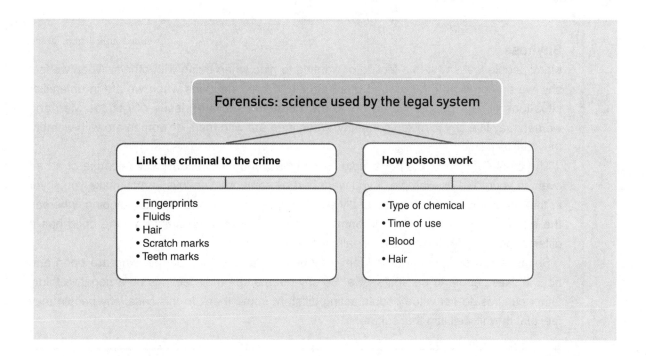

B   Read the following passage, and answer the questions.

Shyness

Time Limit: 1 min. 50 sec.

Many people feel shy. It is a feeling of wanting to hide when being with others. When we feel shy, we do not wish to be around other people. It often happens when we are in unfamiliar situations or with people we do not know. Sometimes it is an issue of gender. Men and women may feel shy in mixed company. When men are with men, or women are with women, they feel less shy.

The cause of shyness is not simple. Sometimes, you can become shy because of a bad event in your life. For example, if you were hurt by someone you love, it may make you shyer in the future. You can also be naturally shy. In some families, one child is outgoing, whereas the other is shy. The family environment is the same for both children. One child has a different personality. Scientists even talk of a shyness gene.

Shyness can be a cultural problem. American culture values people who are open and bold. It likes people to be aggressive. So shy people see their feelings as a negative thing. Other cultures do not value people acting different from others. In this case, shy people may feel that they fit well into that culture.

---

1.   **The author mentions gender in paragraph 1 in order to**

   (A) describe what shyness does to women rather than men
   (B) show that shyness happens in certain company
   (C) explain the difference between new situations and old ones
   (D) state that shyness only happens

2.   **The author discusses children in paragraph 2 in order to**

   (A) support an impossible idea
   (B) explain differences in feelings
   (C) describe how shyness is fake
   (D) show that people can be born shy

3.   **Why does the author mention American culture in paragraph 3?**

   (A) To exemplify a culture that does not value shyness
   (B) To tell how Americans feel about culture
   (C) To show what aggressive people do to shy people
   (D) To discuss different ways of being shy around others

gender (n)
the fact of being either male or female

in mixed company (phr)
when a man is with a woman or a woman is with a man

outgoing (a)
friendly and enjoys being with people; extroverted

whereas (conj)
in contrast with

personality (n)
the mental characteristics of a person

aggressive (a)
behaving in an angry or rude way

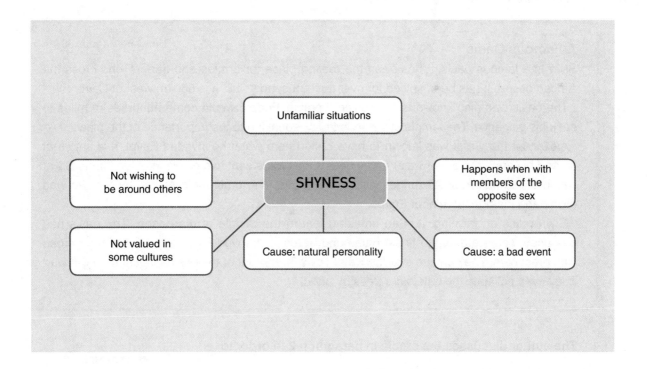

Read the following passage, and answer the questions.

A Famous Oasis

Time Limit: 1 min. 30 sec.

Siwa is a famous oasis. It has been the resting place for armies and traders who cross the African desert. It has been settled for over ten thousand years. It is 560km west of Cairo.

The oasis was also known for its powerful oracle. People would come hundreds of miles to seek his guidance. The temple still stands today, speaking to the importance of the place.

Alexander the Great was known to have rested here when he invaded Egypt. It is said that he and his army ran out of water in the desert. The gods sent two crows to guide him to Siwa, which saved his army. Alexander visited the oracle. The oracle told Alexander that he was divine and the rightful ruler of Egypt.

Siwa relies on farming. It is an amazing feat in the middle of the desert. The oasis has produced, some argue, the finest dates and olives in the world. Farmers tend to their crops with great care. They ensure that the water flows in and out of their fields in just the right way. They even pollinate the date palm trees by hand.

1. **The author discusses the oracle in paragraph 2 in order to**

   (A) contrast Alexander with the oracle

   (B) persuade us to visit the oracle in Siwa

   (C) show the cultural importance of Siwa

   (D) define the meaning of the word "oracle"

2. **The author discusses Alexander the Great in paragraph 3 in order to**

   (A) show the historical importance of Siwa

   (B) contrast Alexander with the gods

   (C) explain how he won the war with Egypt

   (D) define the meaning of "rightful ruler"

3. **Why does the author mention that they even pollinate the date palm trees by hand?**

   (A) To show what must be done to grow dates and olives

   (B) To illustrate how involved Siwan farmers are with farming

   (C) To prove that pollination is the best way to grow dates

   (D) To explain why Siwan farmers need fresh water supplies

oracle (n)
a priest for the gods of Greece, Egypt, and Rome

run out of (phr)
no longer to have something

divine (a)
relating to a god

feat (n)
an accomplishment

tend (v)
to pay attention to

pollinate (v)
to put pollen on a plant to make it grow fruit

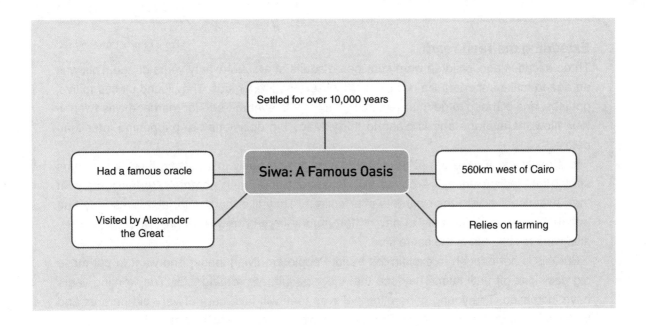

Read the following passage, and answer the questions.

Extending the Teen Years

Time Limit: 1 min. 50 sec.

Three decades ago, children were considered adults at around twenty years of age. This was an age to make important life decisions. Kids were no longer kids. They found places to live, got jobs, and planned to get married. In the 1970s, the average age for marriage was twenty-four. Now the average age is close to thirty. Many big decisions are happening later than before.

Is it really just a case of not growing up? Are people really just making their "teen" years stretch into their twenties? Are they still dependent upon their parents? Certainly many in their twenties live with their parents after college. They like the comfortable lives they had before. They want to be able to pay off the money they borrowed to pay for college. They also want to have fun at the same time.

But this is not enough to explain the trend. People are living longer and want to put these big decisions off until later. They see that older people are retiring later. The working years have increased. The young generation believes they will take care of very old parents and their own children for many years. They do not wish to hurry into this stage of life.

1. **Why does the author mention that kids were no longer kids?**

   Ⓐ To make the passage interesting to read
   Ⓑ To describe what kids do while young
   Ⓒ To emphasize the concept of adulthood
   Ⓓ To state the age of important life decisions

2. **The author uses the money they borrowed to pay for college as an example of which of the following?**

   Ⓐ Why children stay at home in their twenties
   Ⓑ How children should behave in their twenties
   Ⓒ What parents suggest that their children do
   Ⓓ Why college costs so much in the United States

3. **Why does the author mention that older people are retiring later?**

   Ⓐ To state that older people will retire
   Ⓑ To prove that this is the only cause
   Ⓒ To justify why we should not care for our parents
   Ⓓ To explain the trend of young people leaving home later

○ **decade (n)**
ten years

○ **stretch into (phr)**
to continue for a particular period of time

○ **trend (n)**
a general direction of change

○ **put off (phr)**
to postpone; to delay

○ **retire (v)**
to stop working

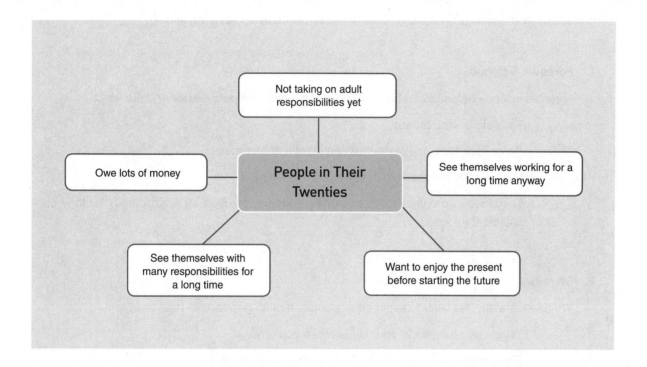

Building Summary Skills

A Put the following sentences in order to make appropriate summaries based on the long passages you worked on earlier. The first sentence is already provided.

1. Forensic Science

Forensic science helps collect information that is useful for police work and the law.

_____ The field is very broad.

_____ Police look for small clues that can identify the criminal.

_____ Many things are studied for forensic purposes.

_____ The clues can come from someone's body (blood, skin, or fingerprints), or they can be chemical (drugs).

2. Shyness

When we are shy, we wish to avoid other people. It often happens in new situations.

_____ Things can happen in your life to make you shy.

_____ Sometimes men and women feel shy around each other.

_____ Sometimes you are born that way.

_____ In some cultures, shyness is not valued, and in other cultures, it is a good quality to have.

3. A Famous Oasis

Siwa is a famous oasis, and it has sheltered people who cross the desert.

_____ Alexander the Great stopped in Siwa to consult him while conquering Egypt.

_____ A powerful priest lived there in ancient times.

_____ Farmers must be very careful when managing the land and plants.

_____ Siwa has a water source, it depends on farming, and it has some of the best dates and olives in the world.

4. Extending the Teen Years

Children are taking on adult responsibilities later in life.

_____ Children realize they will have to take care of their aging parents for longer periods of time, so children are not in a hurry to begin this long phase of their lives.

_____ It is true that they owe a lot of money for college, but they want to enjoy their lives as well.

_____ People are also working for many more years, and they are living longer, too.

_____ But are they just trying to keep living their teenage lives?

B Fill in the blanks with suitable words or phrases to complete the following summaries. Do not look at the previous page until you are finished.

1. Forensic Science

Forensic science helps collect (1)_____ that is useful for (2)_____ and the law. Police look for (3)_____ that can identify the (4)_____. The clues can come from someone's body (blood, skin, or (5)_____, or they can be (6)_____ (drugs). The field is very (7)_____. Many things are studied for (8)_____ purposes.

2. Shyness

When we are (1)_____, we wish to (2)_____ other people. It often happens in (3)_____ situations. Sometimes, (4)_____ feel shy around each other. Things can happen in your life to make you (5)_____. Sometimes you are (6)_____ that way. In some cultures, shyness is not (7)_____, and in other cultures, it is a (8)_____ to have.

3. A Famous Oasis

(1)_____ is a famous oasis, and it has sheltered people who cross the (2)_____. A powerful (3)_____ lived there in ancient times. (4)_____ stopped in Siwa to consult him while conquering (5)_____. Siwa has a (6)_____, it depends on (7)_____, and it has some of the best (8)_____ in the world. Farmers must be very careful when managing the land and plants.

4. Extending the Teen Years

Children are taking on adult (1)_____ later in life. But are they just trying to keep living their (2)_____? It is true that they owe a lot of money for (3)_____, but they want to (4)_____ their lives as well. People are also (5)_____ for many more years, and they are living longer, too. Children realize they will have to (6)_____ their aging (7)_____ for longer periods of time, so children are not (8)_____ to begin this long phase of their lives.

1. **The word it in the passage refers to**

   - (A) Tierra del Fuego
   - (B) name
   - (C) South America
   - (D) explorer

2. **The word notable in the passage is closest in meaning to**

   - (A) notorious
   - (B) remarkable
   - (C) challenging
   - (D) supporting

3. **The word altitude in the passage is closest in meaning to**

   - (A) height
   - (B) distance
   - (C) length
   - (D) shape

4. **According to the passage, all of the following are true EXCEPT:**

   - (A) The land is an island.
   - (B) The ocean is nearby.
   - (C) The place is home to wildlife.
   - (D) The land was set on fire.

5. **According to paragraph 3, why are the waters unique?**

   - (A) The people catch fish with shopping bags in winter.
   - (B) Many types of sea life and birds come there.
   - (C) The water is great for drinking.
   - (D) The ice has good nutritional properties.

6. **The author uses huge schools of sardines as an example of which of the following?**

   - (A) What the inhabitants like to catch
   - (B) How people catch fish
   - (C) Fish that come to the island
   - (D) Birds that come to the island

The End of the World

Tierra del Fuego is the end of the world. In geographical terms, it might just be. It is a small triangle of land that sits at the bottom of South America. The name means "Land of Fire." It was given the name by a famous explorer who saw the natives' fires on the shore. The island is shared by Argentina and Chile. Tierra del Fuego is notable for its unique geography.

However, the land is anything but fire. It rests at the southernmost tip of South America. The average temperature for the year is 5°C. In winter, it gets much colder. Much of the temperature differences are due to altitude. Rivers of ice form on the Andes Mountains to the west. Cold rain and winds chill the flat lands to the north and east.

It is easy to talk about the land of Tierra del Fuego. The waters that surround it also are unique. They are perhaps the most important in the world. They are home to all kinds of birds. The albatross is the most well-known. There are also whales, squid, and many fish. For a few days in summer, huge schools of sardines move into this part of the world. The local people can simply walk into the water and catch them with shopping bags. Schools of fish are everywhere. They can be caught without bait. These fish are of huge economic value to the locals and to the world.

Tierra del Fuego is a rare place. In such a small space, it contains varied land features: mountains, forests, and prairies. Two great oceans meet on either side. This group of features makes it home to a huge range of wildlife. The land has very long days in summer and short days in winter. It is a unique place on earth.

7. The phrase **keep a roof over their heads** in the passage is closest in meaning to

    (A) give them a home
    (B) hold an umbrella
    (C) put them in school
    (D) buy them a roof

8. According to paragraph 3, which of the following is NOT true?

    (A) The cost of living is increasing.
    (B) Two salaries are needed to pay bills.
    (C) Doctors are raising their fees.
    (D) Property prices are increasing.

9. The word **ensuring** in the passage is closest in meaning to

    (A) guaranteeing
    (B) making
    (C) benefiting
    (D) timing

10. The word **that** in the passage refers to

    (A) child
    (B) day care
    (C) benefit
    (D) time

11. The author mentions **latchkey kids** in order to

    (A) show the consequences of rising costs
    (B) describe what latchkey kids do
    (C) explain why latchkey kids are important
    (D) demonstrate the need for health care

12. According to the passage, which of the following is true of the cost of living 30 years ago?

    (A) One salary was enough to cover expenses.
    (B) Mothers needed to work long hours.
    (C) Fathers were paid in cash, not in checks.
    (D) The cost of living was the same as now.

Family and Money

The modern world is changing family relationships. The cost of living has had an influence on how the American family behaves. It may not be the best thing.

Several decades ago, the father went to work. His paycheck paid the bills. The mother stayed home. She might have volunteered at a local church or a community program. Children went to school. Sometimes they had a small job on weekends when they were teenagers.

In many parts of the United States, things are different. The cost of living is on the rise. The greatest increases in the cost of living are seen in property prices and in health care. Basically, one salary is not enough to buy or rent a house and pay the bills. As a result, both parents must work. This helps the family keep a roof over their heads, and they can go to the doctor when they need to.

When both parents work, it changes the amount of time that the child spends with them. Many parents put their children in day care. This has a benefit of ensuring the children's care. But it also reduces the amount of time that parents spend with their children in their early years. What is more, day care is an extra expense. Both parents must work more.

During the school years, it is often the case that children come home before their parents do. They are called latchkey kids because they let themselves in the door. Mother is not waiting at home to open the door for the child. This time alone puts him at risk to things like drugs or crime. The child may get in trouble more often because he is not supervised.

Rising expenses are changing how families live. While working hard for better lives, they open themselves up to different risks.

Vocabulary Review

Choose the word with the closest meaning to each underlined word or phrase.

1. The young tend not to offer their seats to the old on buses or subways.
   - (A) are inclined
   - (B) look after
   - (C) are prepared
   - (D) are willing

2. The company is threatened with bankruptcy.
   - (A) prevented
   - (B) confused
   - (C) faced
   - (D) chased

3. Modern civilization has resulted in a lot of benefits for people.
   - (A) formats
   - (B) advantages
   - (C) defects
   - (D) contracts

4. Some students go to study abroad at government expense.
   - (A) materials
   - (B) judgments
   - (C) requirements
   - (D) payment

5. A lot of students rely on their parents for advice and guidance on the social aspects of college life.
   - (A) depend on
   - (B) reply to
   - (C) mean to
   - (D) pass by

6. The scientist explored the bottom of the ocean with a lot of technological aids.
   - (A) surface
   - (B) ground
   - (C) opposite
   - (D) point

7. The man had to put off paying his debts.
   - (A) promise
   - (B) gather
   - (C) serve
   - (D) postpone

8. Most tree frogs change color to harmonize with their background.
   - (A) environment
   - (B) creation
   - (C) society
   - (D) pressure

9. Finally, the rumor about the actress was exposed.
   - (A) disappeared
   - (B) disclosed
   - (C) hidden
   - (D) discussed

10. No one should be discriminated against according to nationality, gender, or occupation.
    - (A) religion
    - (B) personality
    - (C) faith
    - (D) sex

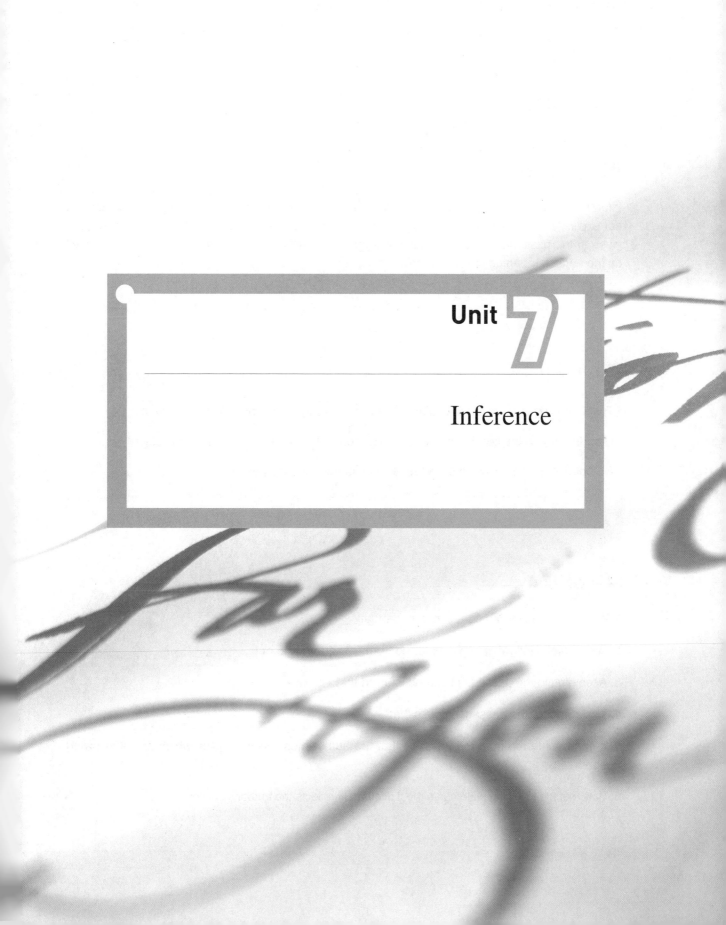

Unit 7

Inference

7 Inference

Overview

■Introduction

Inference questions ask you to understand an argument or an idea that is strongly suggested but not explicitly mentioned in the passage. Because the answers to these questions are not directly given in the passage, you should figure out the logical implications of the author's words as well as the surface meaning of those words.

■Useful Tips

• Think logically to draw a reasonable conclusion from what is implied in the passage.

• Remember that the correct answer does not contradict the main idea of the passage.

• Do not choose an answer just because it is mentioned in the passage.

■Question Types

1. Which of the following can be inferred about _____?

2. Which of the following can be inferred from paragraph X about _____ ?

3. According to the passage, it can be inferred that ~

4. The author of the passage implies that ~

5. It can be inferred from the passage that the author most likely believes which of the following about _____?

6. Which of the following statements most accurately reflects the author's opinion about _____?

Sample iBT Question

Which of the following can be inferred about secondhand smoke?

(A) It should be used between employees.

(B) It should be accepted in the airport.

(C) It should be considered very seriously at work.

(D) It should be recommended to servers in a restaurant.

Secondhand smoke is a serious issue in the U.S. It causes major health problems. Many people like to smoke in restaurants and bars. Nonsmoking customers can choose to go elsewhere. But what about employees? They cannot choose so easily. Servers are exposed to high levels of smoke. Their health is at risk.

 At first, the passage says secondhand smoke is a big problem in America. Then, it claims that people working in restaurants and bars may lose their health due to secondhand smoke. So you can infer that secondhand smoke in workplaces is not a good thing. So, the correct answer is (C).

Inference questions ask you to identify an idea that is not explicitly stated in the passage. The idea is strongly suggested or implied but never said. In order to make an inference based on some information in the passage, you need to use logical thinking. Your conclusion should not contradict the main idea of the passage.

Example

The body mass index (BMI) tells you if your weight is healthy. It is a ratio of height to weight. A person with a BMI of less than 20 is not heavy enough. A person with one of 25 is healthy. A person with a BMI of 30 is overweight. The index is not absolute. It serves only as a rough estimate of your healthy weight.

Which of the following can be inferred about the BMI?

- (A) It should be used as an absolute measure.
- **(B) It should be used as a general guideline.**
- (C) It should not be used to advise heavy people.
- (D) It should be used by the government for statistics.

In the summer, people need to take care. The heat can make them sick. The most serious sickness is heatstroke. There are a number of signs. One is a very high temperature. A second sign is a change in behavior. Dry skin is another sign. In many cases, the body cannot sweat to cool itself. It is possible to lose consciousness.

1. Which of the following can be inferred about heatstroke?

- (A) It can be avoided by staying in a cool place.
- (B) It is impossible to avoid in summer.
- (C) It only lasts for a short amount of time.
- (D) It is a chronic illness.

There is a difference between hard news and soft news. Hard news refers to topics that are serious and timely. These might include politics, crime, and war. Soft news refers to topics that are not so serious. Time is not an important factor in telling the news. Topics include sports and news about famous people.

2. The author of the passage implies that

- (A) hard news is more interesting than soft news
- (B) soft news is more interesting than hard news
- (C) hard news and soft news serve different purposes
- (D) hard news is the most valuable type of news there is

States' rights concern how a state has a separate government from the nation. Each state can decide on important matters for itself. One state may not allow the death penalty while another will. As long as it does not go against the laws of the national government, the state can do what it wants. For now, the nation has not decided on the death penalty. Each state can decide as it wishes.

3. **Which of the following can be inferred about states' rights?**
   - Ⓐ States make the death penalty a good punishment.
   - Ⓑ It is no longer necessary as an element of government.
   - Ⓒ States' rights cause debate over many issues.
   - Ⓓ Each state can decide on important issues.

Arthritis makes your joints swell painfully. As one grows older, the bones get less protected from the soft tissue around them. Joints can grow in size and become sore. It happens in many older people and more often in women than men. Nearly one third of Americans develop some form of the disease. In some cases, the joint is so painful that doctors must replace it.

4. **Which of the following can be inferred about doctors who treat arthritis?**
   - Ⓐ They are not sure what causes the disease.
   - Ⓑ They often have to replace joints.
   - Ⓒ They only treat women, not men.
   - Ⓓ They cannot easily treat the disease.

Reality TV has been very popular for a few years. Viewers like to watch normal people in normal situations. They think that something unusual can be made from daily life. But is it always reality? Sometimes a show will put normal people in unusual situations. They will go to strange places. And not all of the event is shown. Editors can pick which scenes to show. This changes how we see the event.

5. **The author of the passage implies that**
   - Ⓐ reality TV is somewhat artificial
   - Ⓑ reality TV is great programming
   - Ⓒ reality TV is unusual at times
   - Ⓓ reality TV is going to end soon

Practice with Short Passages

Read the following passage, and answer the questions.

Becoming a Reporter

Time Limit: 40 sec.

To be a reporter you need to do a few things. First, get a good education. World knowledge is very important. But going to a good university has another advantage. It can help you find your first good job because it has connections to news companies. Sometimes, your salary will be better with more education. Next, you have to specialize. There are many things to write about, and each has a different style. Third, you need work experience. Find companies that will help you learn the skills you need. This may be unpaid work. Fourth, understand what good reporters do. They know how to find good news stories. They know the difference between fact and opinion. They know how to protect their sources from harm. With the right background, skills, and hard work, journalism can be a great career.

General Comprehension

1. **What does work experience provide?**

   (A) It teaches you different styles.
   (B) It helps you find good stories.
   (C) It provides unpaid work.
   (D) It helps you get necessary skills.

2. **What are good reporters able to do?**

   (A) Find good stories and report responsibly
   (B) Find new stories and report what is said
   (C) Protect sources from hard work
   (D) Write opinions when they are needed

On the TOEFL Test

3. **Which of the following can be inferred about a first job?**

   (A) It provides enough world knowledge to build skills.
   (B) It is difficult to get even with the right background.
   (C) It pays enough for students to repay their college tuition.
   (D) It gives you connections to news companies.

4. **The author of the passage implies that**

   (A) reporting is not an easy thing to start doing
   (B) reporting is very easy to start doing
   (C) reporting is a job that everyone must try
   (D) reporting is becoming less important

advantage (n)
a positive aspect

connection (n)
a relationship

specialize (v)
to be an expert in a particular part of a subject or profession

style (n)
a particular way of writing

source (n)
people who give information

B Read the following passage, and answer the questions.

Cataracts

Time Limit: 30 sec.

Cataracts are very common. This is when the lens of your eye becomes cloudy. Half of all people over the age of sixty develop cataracts. Eye injury is a possible cause. The most common cause is the sun's UV rays. A study showed that airplane pilots were at high risk for cataracts. It is possible that sunlight is not safe when you are high in the sky. Some diseases can also cause cataracts. Of course, old age can cause it. Parts of the eye become weak over time. Doctors used to use needles to remove the cloudy parts. Now they usually replace the entire eye lens with a plastic lens. In most cases, patients can go home the same day as the surgery.

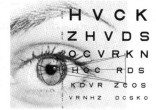

General Comprehension

1. What is the result of cataracts?

- (A) Your sight becomes very cloudy.
- (B) You get them over the age of sixty.
- (C) You get needles in your eye.
- (D) Your eye feels painful at times.

2. How do doctors treat cataracts?

- (A) They tell patients to go home.
- (B) They use needles to treat them.
- (C) They wait until you are old.
- (D) They usually replace the lens.

injury (n)
hurt

UV (a)
ultraviolet; the light beyond the normal range of colors humans can see

at risk (phr)
in danger

remove (v)
to take out; to get rid of

replace (v)
to get rid of something and put a new thing in its place; to substitute

patient (n)
someone who is receiving medical treatment

On the TOEFL Test

3. The author of the passage implies that

- (A) sunlight is dangerous to eyes at all times
- (B) sunlight is only dangerous at high altitudes
- (C) sunlight helps cloudiness in the eyes
- (D) sunlight makes the effects of diseases worse

4. Which of the following can be inferred from the passage about cataracts?

- (A) They are so common that they can be ignored.
- (B) They take a lot of money and time to treat.
- (C) They can develop from various causes.
- (D) They occur only in old people.

Read the following passage, and answer the questions.

McCarthy

Time Limit: 30 sec.

The 1950s were a scary time in America. A man named Joseph McCarthy wanted to gain power in government. He decided to use fear as his weapon. It was a time when the U.S. was afraid of a war with Russia. The country was afraid they would take over the U.S. Of course, the Russians were communists. McCarthy used this fear of communism. He would call people communist even if he had no evidence. This led to investigations, trials, and prison. Many public figures had their lives ruined by McCarthy. They could see that he was trying to become more powerful. They said he was being unfair. But he used fear to ruin their reputations.

General Comprehension

1. Why were the 1950s a scary time in America?

- (A) A man used fear as a way to get power in the government.
- (B) A man used to fear to help a powerful government.
- (C) A man no longer feared his government and was powerful.
- (D) A man put communists in power in government.

2. How did McCarthy ruin people's lives?

- (A) He would look for evidence of people being communists.
- (B) He would call communists to investigate people.
- (C) He would call them communists and put them on trial.
- (D) He would find how powerful they were and scare them.

On the TOEFL Test

3. What can be inferred about McCarthy?

- (A) He had very few friends.
- (B) He was not very honest.
- (C) He liked to chase communists.
- (D) He was a favored politician.

4. It can be inferred from the passage that the author most likely believes which of the following?

- (A) People should not abuse power.
- (B) People have to gain power.
- (C) People should not be afraid of power.
- (D) People have to share power.

gain (v)
to acquire; to get

weapon (n)
a tool for hurting or killing

evidence (n)
facts or physical signs that help to prove something

investigation (n)
an inspection; an examination

ruin (v)
to destroy

reputation (n)
people's opinion of you

144

D Read the following passage, and answer the questions.

Horses in the Bullfight

Time Limit: 50 sec.

Many horses are hurt each year in bullfights. The bull and the bullfighter are usually the center of attention. The crowd admires the bravery and skill of each. Sometimes, the bullfighter is on horseback. The horse also has skills. It is a highly-trained animal that works with the bullfighter. The horse and rider can move quickly in four directions at the slightest command. This is necessary to avoid the angry bull. The bull does not understand that a man is causing it pain. It only sees the horse. People do not know that the horse is blindfolded and has cotton stuffed in its ears. This prevents it from seeing and hearing the bull. If this were the case, the horse would be terrified. The horse depends on the bullfighter for its life in the ring. Sometimes, the bullfighter is not quick enough, and the bull kills the horse.

General Comprehension

1. **What is special about the horses in bullfights?**

   (A) They are able to move when they want to.
   (B) They are highly trained and help the bullfighter.
   (C) They do not need commands to avoid the bull.
   (D) They have cotton in their ears to protect them.

2. **The word this in the passage refers to**

   (A) the horse
   (B) the cotton stuffed in the horse's ears
   (C) seeing and hearing the bull
   (D) the bullfighter

Vocabulary

- **admire (v)**
  to like very much
- **bravery (n)**
  brave behavior; the quality of being brave
- **slight (a)**
  very small in degree or quantity
- **command (n)**
  an order; instructions
- **blindfolded (a)**
  with eyes covered
- **terrified (a)**
  very scared

On the TOEFL Test

3. **According to the passage, what can be inferred about how a horse is hurt?**

   (A) The horse sometimes slips on the ground when the bull charges.
   (B) The bullfighter does not give it the command to move in time.
   (C) The bullfighter charges the bull with the horse when he wants to.
   (D) The bull cannot see where it is going and accidentally hurts the horse.

4. **What can be inferred about what the bull thinks?**

   (A) It thinks the horse is causing it pain.
   (B) It does not want to fight the man.
   (C) It wants to run away.
   (D) It wants to please the crowd.

Practice with Long Passages

A Read the following passage, and answer the questions.

Time Limit: 1 min. 50 sec.

Standards in Reporting

The press is news sources like TV news and newspapers. It keeps people free to choose, to vote, and to think. The press keeps information flowing. For this system to work, there have to be standards. Good reporting can be explained through four ideas: harm, truth, privacy, and balance.

A reporter for a newspaper must think about harm. A writer should be careful about how he might hurt a person's feelings by asking questions. Children, for example, must be treated with care because they are sensitive. When gathering facts, a reporter must think about how he will affect the child.

Truth is another concern. A reporter must try to make as few errors as possible in reporting the facts. Facts should be said in a different way from opinions. This helps readers make better decisions.

Privacy is a worry. A reporter must balance the public's right to know with a person's right to a private life. Public figures like politicians do not have the same rights as normal people.

Balance is also necessary. If possible, both sides of a story should be told. When only one side of a story is told, the reporter may seem to favor that person.

1. **Which of the following can be inferred about harming sources?**

   (A) It is an easy thing to do in difficult situations.
   (B) Everybody does it at some point in their lives.
   (C) No one has ever done it in the reporting profession.
   (D) Reporters prefer to harm their sources if they can.

2. **Which of the following can be inferred from paragraph 3 about reporting the facts?**

   (A) It is simple to separate fact from opinion.
   (B) It is a challenge to separate fact from opinion.
   (C) Reporting the facts help readers make decisions.
   (D) Some newspapers do not always report facts.

3. **The author of the passage implies that**

   (A) reporting keeps people free
   (B) reporting is the best job to have
   (C) reporting requires responsibility
   (D) reporting is a tiring job

---

source (n)
a person or thing that provides information

harm (n)
hurt; damage

sensitive (a)
easily hurt

affect (v)
to influence

normal (a)
usual and ordinary

favor (v)
to treat better; to prefer

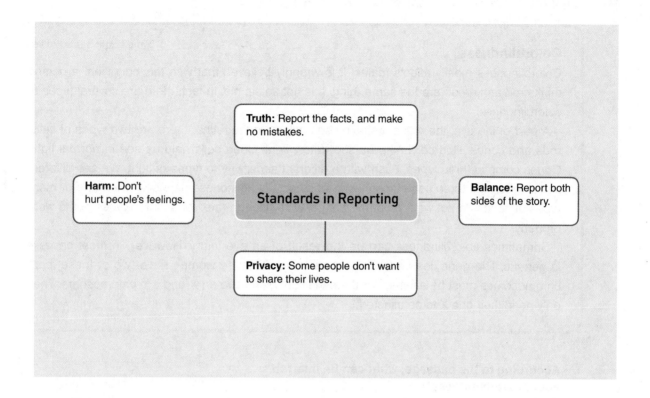

Read the following passage, and answer the questions.

Colorblindness

Time Limit: 1 min. 20 sec.

Colorblindness mostly affects males. It is wrongly believed that with this condition, a person thinks red and green are the same thing. It is not so simple. In fact, there are several types of colorblindness.

A part of the eye, the retina, helps us see colors. In the retina, there are two types of cells: rods and cones. Rod cells help us see in low light. Cone cells help us see in normal light. Cones come in three types, each with a different sensitivity to types of light. We see different colors when the three cone types work together. Colorblindness happens when one or more types of cones do not work properly. It is possible, though rare, for all three types not to work properly.

Sometimes colorblindness can be the result of an eye injury. However, in most cases it is genetic. The gene lies on the X chromosome. Because women have two of these, both chromosomes must be affected for the condition. Men have an X and a Y chromosome. They only need their one X to be affected.

1. **According to the passage, what can be inferred about colorblindness?**
   - (A) Relatively few women have this condition.
   - (B) It happens to men and women equally.
   - (C) No one has had it except men.
   - (D) It is a rare type of condition.

2. **Which of the following can be inferred about types of colorblindness?**
   - (A) Some types of colorblindness only affect women and not men.
   - (B) Some types of colorblindness stop you from seeing anything at all.
   - (C) It is possible that some people can only see in two shades: light and dark.
   - (D) Some types of colorblindness only affect men and not women.

3. **The author of the passage implies that**
   - (A) colorblindness is a great challenge for all people
   - (B) colorblindness is a great challenge for women
   - (C) colorblindness challenges the rods and cones
   - (D) colorblindness is usually passed on from parents

affect (v)
to influence

retina (n)
the area at the back of your eye

sensitivity (n)
the quality or state of reacting easily

properly (ad)
correctly; appropriately

rare (a)
not common

chromosome (n)
the part of the cell that carries genetic information

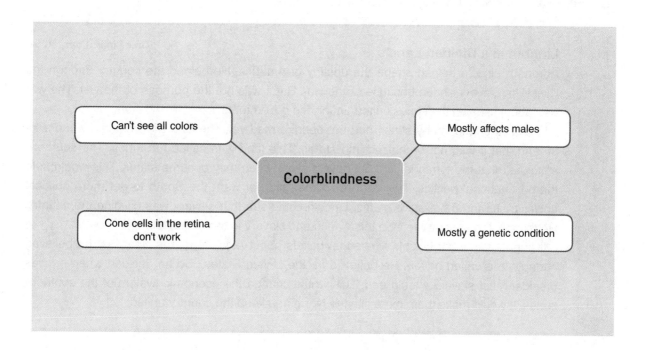

Read the following passage, and answer the questions.

Lincoln in a Divided Land

Time Limit: 1 min. 40 sec.

Abraham Lincoln helped shape the destiny of America. He helped the country through the Civil War. Slavery ended because of the war. But it was not the purpose of the war. The war was about keeping the states united under one government.

In Lincoln's time, many states had not been formed yet. The U.S. government owned a lot of land, but it was not organized into states. This land was called territories. The southern states felt that the territories should have slavery when they became states. This would help them in national politics. The northern states did not want the South to get more political power by having more slave states. Lincoln could see that slavery was dividing the country. He thought the best way to stop this was to end slavery in the entire country.

It is not clear what Lincoln's personal beliefs about race were. It is clear that he believed strongly in a united nation. He believed in "the United States." So he decided when he was president that slavery should end. This would change the economic system of the southern states. It would make them more like the North and keep the country united.

1. **According to paragraph 1, what can be inferred about Lincoln's role in America?**

   Ⓐ He made the United States what it is today.
   Ⓑ He was one of the most important presidents.
   Ⓒ He started the Civil War to stop slavery.
   Ⓓ He was the first president to start a Civil War.

2. **Which of the following can be inferred about the states' attitudes?**

   Ⓐ The southern states no longer wanted to have slavery.
   Ⓑ The southern states felt the northern states were going to get slaves.
   Ⓒ The northern states felt the southern states were getting too much political power.
   Ⓓ The northern states did not want to go to war.

3. **The author of the passage implies that**

   Ⓐ Lincoln was not a racist
   Ⓑ Lincoln was somewhat racist
   Ⓒ Lincoln believed that slavery was not a moral thing
   Ⓓ Lincoln favored the northern states

destiny (n)
the future

civil (a)
relating to the ordinary people of a country; not military or religious

purpose (n)
a goal or intention

political (a)
relating to politics

race (n)
an ethnic group having distinct physical differences

economic (a)
relating to the economy

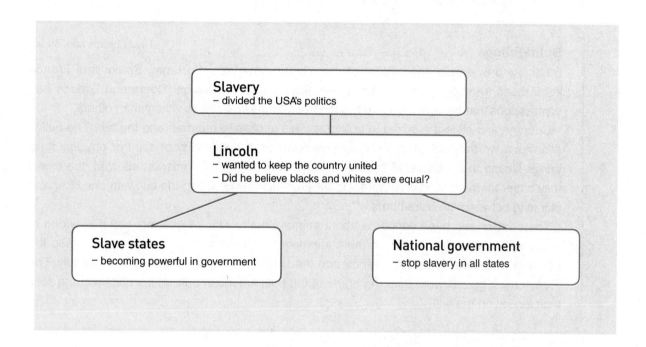

Read the following passage, and answer the questions.

Bullfighting

Time Limit: 1 min. 30 sec.

Bullfighting is part of the culture of many Latin countries. Portugal, Spain, and France keep these traditions. Countries in the Americas do, too. Ancient Rome and Greece had competitions that brought man and bull together. Some were more violent than others.

Courage and style are prized in bullfights. This applies to the man and the bull. The bull is seen as a worthy contestant who must be honored. A bull with poor spirit or physical form brings shame to the owner of the bull and the event. If the bullfighter is unskilled, the crowd may cheer for the bull. The bullfighter must show his skill by killing the bull with one blow and standing between the bull's horns.

There have long been concerns about animal cruelty. Many in society feel it is wrong to make an animal suffer. It is even more improper to kill them for entertainment. To keep the tradition, some countries like France and the U.S. have bullfights that are not deadly. The French must grab flowers from the horns of the bull. American bullfighters use Velcro to stick their lances on the bull.

1. The author of the passage implies that
   - (A) bullfighting should stop because it is an old tradition
   - (B) bullfighting is not important to some cultures
   - (C) each culture must balance tradition against animal cruelty
   - (D) each culture must make animal cruelty a crime

2. Which of the following can be inferred about bulls?
   - (A) They are selected to show strength and spirit.
   - (B) They are chosen to defeat the bullfighter.
   - (C) They do not have any skills against a bullfighter.
   - (D) They mean nothing to the people fighting them.

3. According to paragraph 3, what can be inferred about animal cruelty?
   - (A) It is not taken seriously in America.
   - (B) A lot of people do not care about it.
   - (C) Some cultures take it seriously.
   - (D) The French are cruel to animals.

tradition (n)
a custom or belief that has existed for a long time

competition (n)
a rivalry; a contest

apply to (phr)
to relate to

contestant (n)
a competitor

cruelty (n)
behavior that deliberately causes pain or suffering to people or animals

lance (n)
a long spear used by soldiers on horseback

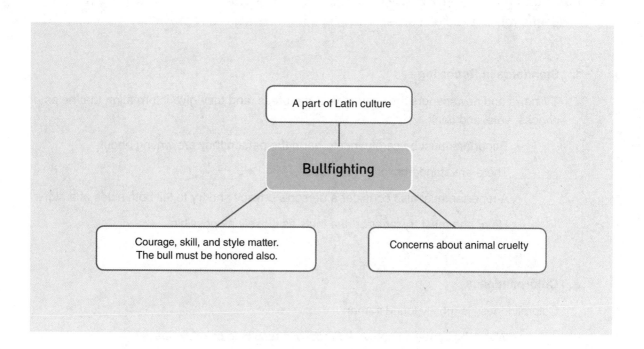

Building Summary Skills

A Put the following sentences in order to make appropriate summaries based on the long passages you worked on earlier. The first sentence is already provided.

1. **Standards in Reporting**

   TV news and newspapers are examples of the press, and they give information that helps people choose, vote, and think.

   _____ Reporters must be careful not to harm the person they are writing about.

   _____ There are standards for a good press.

   _____ A reporter must also consider a person's privacy and try to tell both sides of a story.

   _____ He or she must try to report the facts as closely as possible.

2. **Colorblindness**

   Colorblindness is mostly found in men.

   _____ When the cones do not work properly, it results in colorblindness.

   _____ The parts of the eye called cones help us see certain colors of light.

   _____ Most of the time, this condition is genetic, and it is passed on to children through the X chromosome.

   _____ Sometimes colorblindness happens because of an injury.

3. **Lincoln in a Divided Land**

   Lincoln came to power at a time when the United States was trying to decide on slavery.

   _____ This issue divided the North and South.

   _____ Many southern states wanted any new states to have slaves.

   _____ It would help increase their political power, but northern states did not want this.

   _____ Lincoln thought it was best to end slavery in the whole country because he believed that the country should be united.

4. **Bullfighting**

   Bullfighting is an old tradition in some countries.

   _____ Courage, form, and style are very important in this sport for both man and bull.

   _____ Some countries have bullfights that do not hurt the bull.

   _____ Some people think this sport is cruel because it is not fair to make animals suffer.

   _____ If the man has poor skills, the crowd will cheer for the bull, so the man must show his skill by killing the bull quickly.

B Fill in the blanks with suitable words or phrases to complete the following summaries. Do not look at the previous page until you are finished.

1. Standards in Reporting

TV news and (1)_____ are examples of the (2)_____, and they give information that helps people choose, (3)_____, and think. There are (4)_____ for a good press. (5)_____ must be careful not to harm the person they are writing about. He or she must try to report the (6)_____ as closely as possible. A reporter must also consider a person's (7)_____ and try to tell (8)_____ of a story.

2. Colorblindness

Colorblindness is mostly found in (1)_____. The parts of the eye called (2)_____ help us see certain (3)_____. When the cones do not (4)_____, it results in (5)_____. Sometimes colorblindness happens because of an (6)_____. Most of the time, this condition is (7)_____, and it is passed on to children through the (8)_____.

3. Lincoln in a Divided Land

Lincoln came to (1)_____ at a time when the United States was trying to decide on (2)_____. Many (3)_____ wanted any new states to have slaves. It would help increase their (4)_____, but (5)_____ did not want this. This issue (6)_____ the North and South. Lincoln thought it was best to (7)_____ slavery in the whole country because he believed that the country should be (8)_____.

4. Bullfighting

Bullfighting is an old (1)_____ in some countries. (2)_____, form, and style are very important in this sport for both (3)_____. If the man has (4)_____ skills, the crowd will cheer for the bull, so the man must show his skill by killing the bull (5)_____. Some people think this sport is (6)_____ because it is not (7)_____ to make animals suffer. Some countries have bullfights that do not (8)_____ the bull.

1. **The word regulates in the passage is closest in meaning to**

   Ⓐ controls
   Ⓑ adjusts
   Ⓒ forbids
   Ⓓ allows

2. **According to the passage, how many drugs make it to the market?**

   Ⓐ Nearly five thousand
   Ⓑ One of five thousand
   Ⓒ Five thousand only
   Ⓓ Over five thousand

3. **The author uses food supplements as an example of which of the following?**

   Ⓐ Things the FDA ignores
   Ⓑ Things the FDA controls
   Ⓒ Things the FDA buys
   Ⓓ Things the FDA rejects

4. **Which of the following can be inferred from paragraph 4 about labeling?**

   Ⓐ It is a necessary way to protect the public.
   Ⓑ It does not matter if people read the labels or not.
   Ⓒ It is only good if people can find the label.
   Ⓓ It has no use if doctors tell people what to do.

5. **The word achieves in the passage is closest in meaning to**

   Ⓐ develops
   Ⓑ increases
   Ⓒ controls
   Ⓓ accomplishes

6. **Which of the following is NOT discussed in the passage?**

   Ⓐ Requirements for labeling
   Ⓑ The approval of medical supplies
   Ⓒ Why pregnant women take drugs
   Ⓓ Controls for baby and medical food

The FDA

The FDA is the common name for the Food and Drug Administration. It is a government agency that makes consumer goods safe. It regulates food and the food supply. It also controls diet supplements. The FDA also makes sure that drugs and medical devices are safe and effective.

For drugs and medical machines to be approved, they must go through a lengthy process. There are many strict tests. First, anything that humans use must be tested on animals. This may take up to 6 years. Then, it must be tested with a few people. Testing on 15 to 20 people can last up to a year and a half. Third, a mid-sized group (100 to 500 people) is used. This often takes two years. Then a large group is tested over 3 years. Of 5,000 drugs discovered, only 5 enter trials. Of that, only one passes on to the market.

Food supplements like ginseng follow a different path. The FDA does not pre-test them as they do for drugs. The agency only controls these products if they are unsafe but are already being sold. Two exceptions are baby and medical food. Because those that use them are not strong, the FDA is more careful with these products.

Labeling is a major focus. A label must show what a product is for. For drugs, labels should say the name of the drug and what it is used for. It should also detail who should take it and list any side effects. It needs to detail directions for pregnant women, children, or old people. It also needs to detail safety information.

The FDA protects the public from harm. It achieves this through controls and labeling. It has standards for effectiveness in medical products. It also has standards for how information is shared.

7. **The word circumstances in the passage is closest in meaning to**

- (A) ability
- (B) environment
- (C) need
- (D) education

8. **The word issue in the passage is closest in meaning to**

- (A) accident
- (B) result
- (C) problem
- (D) copy

9. **The author uses banking and insurance practices as an example of**

- (A) fewer opportunities for some
- (B) better service at banks
- (C) the increase of opportunities
- (D) the greatest opportunity of all

10. **According to the passage, what do many people need to do to get ahead with their money?**

- (A) Borrow money
- (B) Buy a car
- (C) Own a house
- (D) Steal money

11. **Which of the following best expresses the essential information in the highlighted sentence?** *Incorrect* **answer choices change the meaning in important ways or leave out essential information.**

- (A) Insurance causes poor people to risk losing money.
- (B) Poor people risk losing money to insurance companies.
- (C) Money protects poor people from insurance risks.
- (D) Without insurance, poor people are more likely to suffer financial ruin.

12. **The author of the passage implies**

- (A) that everyone has the same opportunities in the USA
- (B) that we should do more to help immigrants in the USA
- (C) that people do not have the same opportunities as others
- (D) that the American dream is not what it seems

Less Opportunities

Opportunity can be expressed in terms of choice. People come to the U.S. for just this. They feel they have more choices. But choices are limited. Opportunity is not as easy to get as expected.

The circumstances are bad, as the statistics will tell. Wages are one point of concern. First, women earn 81 cents for every dollar a man earns. The gap is wider between educated women and men. Second, wages have increased 27% for the rich. They have only increased 1% for the poor. White men have gained the most. The number of poor minority men is growing.

Home ownership is seen as the key to a successful life. Fewer poor people have owned homes in the past twenty years. More middle and upper class people have owned them, but they are not at risk. With a home, it is possible to borrow money in times of trouble. This is a serious issue for poor people, who find themselves in trouble often.

Last, banking and insurance practices deny opportunity. It is difficult for the poor to get loans because of their background. If they do get a home loan, they must pay a higher rate because they are part of a high-risk group. These are the people who can least afford to pay extra fees. Also, 45 million people do not have insurance. Most of them are immigrants, minorities, and poor people. They cannot get health care. They are more at risk of losing everything they have without protection by insurance. Many poor people have no protection from high costs. When accidents happen, they must sell everything they have to pay their bills.

Vocabulary Review

Choose the word with the closest meaning to each underlined word or phrase.

1. Every soldier should obey commands in the military.
   - (A) problems
   - (B) rules
   - (C) orders
   - (D) methods

2. Seat belts decrease the risk of injuries in a car accident.
   - (A) wounds
   - (B) rewards
   - (C) stress
   - (D) help

3. Because of his low annual income, he cannot afford to have more children.
   - (A) separate
   - (B) manage
   - (C) hurry
   - (D) choose

4. Because of his improvement, many people admired him very much.
   - (A) defended
   - (B) expected
   - (C) respected
   - (D) understood

5. A lower price is impossible until production volumes increase.
   - (A) expand
   - (B) decline
   - (C) correct
   - (D) reduce

6. The biggest purpose in studying abroad is to see more of the world.
   - (A) result
   - (B) possibility
   - (C) production
   - (D) reason

7. In many western countries, women by tradition wear white dresses when they get married.
   - (A) consideration
   - (B) convention
   - (C) notification
   - (D) factor

8. If you look at the people around you, good listeners are very rare.
   - (A) typical
   - (B) often
   - (C) unusual
   - (D) consistent

9. It is important to season lamb properly with salt and pepper.
   - (A) correctly
   - (B) actually
   - (C) practically
   - (D) politely

10. There is a very strong connection between smoking and cancer.
    - (A) division
    - (B) split
    - (C) dispute
    - (D) relation

Unit 8

Insert Text

8 Insert Text

Overview

■Introduction

Insert Text questions ask you to determine where the best place for a given sentence would be in the passage. In this type of question, you will see four black squares appearing in one paragraph or spreading across the end of one paragraph and the beginning of the next. In either case, you need to understand the logical stream of the passage and focus on any grammatical connections between sentences such as conjunctions, pronouns, demonstratives, and repeated words or phrases.

■Useful Tips

• Put the sentence in each place next to the squares.

• Pay attention to the logical connection between sentences.

• Be familiar with connecting words, such as *on the other hand, for example, on the contrary, similarly, in contrast, furthermore, therefore, in other words, as a result, finally,* etc.

■Question Type

Look at the four squares [■] that indicate where the following sentence could be added to the passage.

[a sentence to be inserted into the passage]

Where would the sentence best fit?

Click on a square [■] to add the sentence to the passage.

Sample iBT Question

Look at the four squares [■] that indicate where the following sentence could be added to the passage.

In 1920, when American businessman Donald F. Duncan saw a Filipino play with a yo-yo, he entered into the yo-yo business.

Where would the sentence best fit?

> Click on a square [■] to add the sentence to the passage.

The yo-yo is a popular toy around the world. **A** Since the 16th century, Filipinos have used yo-yos to catch animals from trees. **B** Even now, Filipinos are considered the best yo-yoers. **C** Soon after, he succeeded in making the yo-yo the world's most famous toy. **D**

Correct Answer The new sentence is about American businessman Donald F. Duncan, and the pronoun *he* in the last sentence of the passage refers to the businessman. So **C** is the only place where the new sentence can fit.

Skill & Drill

Insert Text questions give you an example sentence and ask you where the best place for that sentence would be in the passage. You should understand the logical flow of the information in the passage. It is helpful to check out pronouns, linking words, demonstratives, and repeated words or phrases.

Example

Bono, a famous rock star, is well known for his other work. He is a humanitarian. He works to improve the lives of people in the poorest countries. **A** Bono feels that respect for rights is the first step to helping people. **B** Bono wants to help people help themselves. **C** That means that he wants to remove the structures that keep people poor. It may mean changing the economic rules for a country. It may mean helping people borrow money with a realistic way to pay it back. He wants to change unfair trade rules that hurt the poor.

Look at the three squares [■] that indicate where the following sentence could be added to the passage.

However, these countries must respect human rights.

Where would the sentence best fit? A

Bullying is a mean kind of behavior. It happens when a person scares or hurts someone who is weaker than the person is. **A** With children, this usually happens when there is no adult around. **B** A bully will call victims names and will make fun of how they do things. **C** He will say bad things about the victim to the victim's friends. A bully might even steal the victim's things. Bullying must be stopped at a young age so that children do not develop this behavior.

1. **Look at the three squares [■] that indicate where the following sentence could be added to the passage.**

   Bullies usually hurt people again and again.

   Where would the sentence best fit?

W.B. Yeats was an Irish poet. **A** He wrote about love, Irish myths, magic, and the spirit. **B** Yeats is one of the most important modern poets in English, but he liked to write poetry in traditional forms. **C** He liked to use rhymes and rhythms that older poets used. His poems had a commanding, timeless feeling about them. Yeats had a way of understanding the human experience. His ideas were so admired that he even had an influence in politics.

2. **Look at the three squares [■] that indicate where the following sentence could be added to the passage.**

   He was born in 1865.

   Where would the sentence best fit?

Human cloning raises some questions. First, we have to think about what it means to be unique. **A** Is it something that is important to our society? **B** In fact, it might be a necessary quality for all living things. **C** As unique people, our sense of self is at the center of everything. If we were cloned from someone else, our ideas of identity would change. That might not be for the better. Also, we have to think about relationships. When we clone someone, we are not affecting one person's life. We are affecting the lives of the people around them.

3. **Look at the three squares [■] that indicate where the following sentence could be added to the passage.**

   Being unique is a crucial human quality.

   Where would the sentence best fit?

Common law is an English legal system. It is used in many countries around the world. **A** Court decisions are based on the results of past cases. **B** One feature of common law is trial by jury. **C** A group of people decide guilt. Another feature is this: no one, not even the president, is above the law. He or she must follow the law as the common man does.

4. **Look at the three squares [■] that indicate where the following sentence could be added to the passage.**

   In other words, this law system takes history into account.

   Where would the sentence best fit?

There is some debate over the importance of Alexandria in Egypt. Was it more important as a center of knowledge or as a center of commerce? Some say that it was most important as a center of knowledge. It had a famous library, at one time the largest in the world. It attracted scholars from many countries. **A** Its contribution to present knowledge is no small feat. **B** Much of the grain from Egypt was sold in Alexandria. **C** It fed hungry nations and made the city rich. The city had great power because of this.

5. **Look at the three squares [■] that indicate where the following sentence could be added to the passage.**

   Others say that it was most important for trade.

   Where would the sentence best fit?

Practice with Short Passages

A   Read the following passage, and answer the questions.

Winston Churchill
Time Limit: 40 sec.

Winston Churchill was a great leader of Great Britain. He came from family of politicians and war heroes. As a young boy, he did poorly at school. But when he got older, he became fascinated by military studies. He finished eighth in his class at the Royal Military Academy. He next joined the British Army in India to learn the skills of a soldier. It was good experience for him. Then he quit the army and went to South Africa as a reporter. **A** He wanted to cover the war between the Dutch and the British. **B** Churchill insisted on fighting even though he was not a soldier. **C** He was captured by the Dutch. **D** He escaped after one month and crossed hundreds of miles to friendly lands. He returned to England a hero. Churchill ran for Parliament and won a seat. This was the beginning of his famous political career.

General Comprehension

1. **Which of the following is NOT true about Churchill?**

    (A) He was a poor student at school.
    (B) He graduated from a military school with honors.
    (C) He served the army in India.
    (D) He worked as a reporter in South Africa.

2. **What made Churchill a hero?**

    (A) He escaped from the Dutch enemy.
    (B) He helped England win the war.
    (C) He ran for Parliament.
    (D) He was famous in South Africa.

On the TOEFL Test

3. **Look at the four squares [■] that indicate where the following sentence could be added to the passage.**

    Prison was a difficult experience for him.

    Where would the sentence best fit?

become fascinated by (phr)
to be very interested in

military (a)
relating to soldiers or the armed forces

cover (v)
to report on

insist (v)
to demand

escape (v)
to get away; to run away

run for Parliament (phr)
to try to get elected to Parliament

B Read the following passage, and answer the questions.

Social Pressure on Women

Time Limit: 30 sec.

There is great social pressure for women to be pretty and successful. It causes a lot of stress. They learn from media that they are supposed to look beautiful like a movie star. They learn that beauty is something that other people will decide, not something they decide for themselves. **A** This movie star beauty conflicts with another message: women are supposed to be independent and successful at their careers. **B** Basically, they are supposed to be strong, smart, and very good at their work. **C** In many cases, they can become depressed. **D** These women say they do not want to care so much but feel it is impossible not to. By 30, the stress becomes less. Women learn not to care so much what other people think.

General Comprehension

1. **What creates pressure for women?**

   (A) They don't care about their appearance.

   (B) They feel conflicted about which career to choose.

   (C) They want to look like movie stars and become famous.

   (D) They are supposed to be good-looking and succeed in their careers.

2. **Why does the stress become less?**

   (A) Women learn not to worry about what people think.

   (B) Women get very good at their work and earn money.

   (C) Women decide to be pretty and successful.

   (D) Women just stop caring about how they look.

On the TOEFL Test

3. **Look at the four squares [■] that indicate where the following sentence could be added to the passage.**

   Most women between the ages of 16 to 25 feel that this causes a lot of pressure.

   Where would the sentence best fit?

○ **media (n)**
television, radio, newspapers, and news magazines

○ **be supposed to do (phr)**
to be expected or required to do

○ **conflict with (phr)**
to go against

○ **independent (a)**
taking care of oneself

○ **career (n)**
a life's work, esp. in business or in a profession

○ **depressed (a)**
very sad

C Read the following passage, and answer the questions.

Ezra Pound

Time Limit: 50 sec.

Ezra Pound was a famous American poet. He grew up in the U.S. but spent many years in Europe. He was influenced by visual artists and classical Chinese poetry. His poems were complex and delicate. Ezra lived in London for a few years. He met his hero, W.B. Yeats, there. They worked together on writing poetry. They influenced each other greatly. Ezra Pound also worked with James Joyce and T.S. Elliot. **A** After World War I, Pound moved to Italy. **B** He also thought that Italian society at the time was a good and moral society. **C** It was not destroyed by capitalism. **D** During World War II, he was arrested by the Americans. They said he was speaking out against America. He went to jail. During these twelve years, he was able to produce some incredible poems that showed his appreciation for life around him.

General Comprehension

1. **All of the following influenced Ezra Pound EXCEPT**

   Ⓐ Chinese poetry
   Ⓑ W.B. Yeats
   Ⓒ Italian capitalism
   Ⓓ visual artists

2. **How did imprisonment change the way Ezra wrote?**

   Ⓐ He was able to meet James Joyce.
   Ⓑ He learned that society was moral and fair.
   Ⓒ He was able to speak out against America.
   Ⓓ He developed an appreciation for life around him.

visual (a)
relating to being seen; seeable

complex (a)
not simple; complicated

delicate (a)
made in a fine, sensitive manner

speak out (phr)
to oppose; to protest

incredible (a)
amazing; unbelievable

appreciation (n)
understanding and liking

On the TOEFL Test

3. **Look at the four squares [■] that indicate where the following sentence could be added to the passage.**

   He always loved Italian art.

   Where would the sentence best fit?

D Read the following passage, and answer the questions.

Hooliganism

Time Limit: 50 sec.

Hooligans are people who cause trouble at sporting events. They are fans who like to cause fights. They often damage the area around a sports match. The term "hooligan" was first used in a London police report in 1898. This violence has a long history. In 532 AD, thousands of people died in fights that lasted a week. They were started by fans at a race. In modern times, soccer has had the most problems with fan violence. This has been going on since the 1950s in England. **A** Italy has had a similar problem. **B** This sport violence has spread to other countries. **C** It has made it difficult for non-violent fans to enjoy sports in a safe way. **D** The violence also makes it difficult for shops around soccer fields to open safely. They have strict laws to punish fans that cause trouble.

General Comprehension

1. What are hooligans?

   Ⓐ Soccer fans who live in England
   Ⓑ Sport fans who like to cause trouble at sports matches
   Ⓒ Sport fans who died in fights in 1898
   Ⓓ Soccer fans who come from England to Italy

2. How long has sports violence been going on?

   Ⓐ For a few years
   Ⓑ For a few decades
   Ⓒ For a hundred years
   Ⓓ For over a thousand years

On the TOEFL Test

3. Look at the four squares [■] that indicate where the following sentence could be added to the passage.

It has almost ruined national sports in some cases.

Where would the sentence best fit?

---

damage (v)
harm; injure; destruct

violence (n)
using physical force to hurt or break

last (v)
to continue

similar (a)
almost the same

spread (v)
to reach more and more people

strict (a)
requiring obedience; not flexible

A Read the following passage, and answer the questions.

Time Limit: 1 min. 50 sec.

Betty Friedan

Betty Friedan argued for women's rights in America. The experiences in her life and her education gave her a powerful voice. She was able to change how society views women.

   Friedan was born in 1921. She studied psychology at Smith College. She also worked at the college newspaper. Friedan passed up graduate studies at UC Berkley. **1A**

   Friedan married and had three children. **1B** She started writing for women's housekeeping magazines. **1C** She was bored and unhappy. **1D** Her home life did not challenge her abilities. In 1957, Friedan questioned Smith graduates to see if they were happy with their lives. She found that many of them were not. **2A** Their lives existed only for the success of their husbands and children. **2B** Friedan wrote about how society pushes women to live at home. **2C** They were meant to live for their families and not have interesting, challenging careers. **2D** The book *The Feminine Mystique* became very famous. Twelve years later, she and her husband divorced. Friedan went on to work for a new image for women. They should take part in society in many more ways than being wives. She said that women should be in equal partnerships with men.

---

1. **Look at the four squares [■] that indicate where the following sentence could be added to the passage.**

   She wanted to write about the rights of workers.

   Where would the sentence best fit?

2. **Look at the four squares [■] that indicate where the following sentence could be added to the passage.**

   These women had no feeling of importance.

   Where would the sentence best fit?

argue (v)
to give reasons to support your opinion; to discuss

psychology (n)
the scientific study of human mind

pass up (phr)
not to make use of an opportunity

push (v)
to force

challenging (a)
demanding

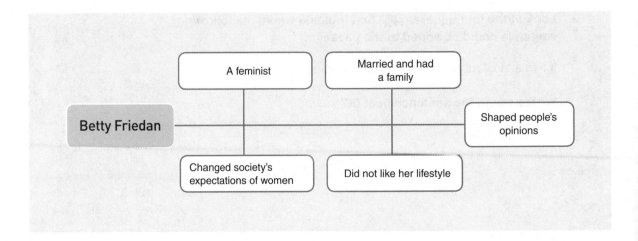

B Read the following passage, and answer the questions.

Child Obesity

Time Limit: 1 min. 50 sec.

Being fat is a normal part of many people's childhoods. However, obesity means having too much fat. Children with this problem may stay like this as adults. **1A** It causes health problems that last a long time.

1B This number has grown since the 1970s. **1C** Some children are more at risk than others. **1D** A family history of weight problems is one risk. Smoking or a lazy lifestyle is another risk.

Obesity is not just a personal problem. It is a social problem. An obese person suffers health problems, of course. But when there are too many obese people, society must start paying the costs. Health care costs more, schools have more problems, and people become less productive.

Some of the causes of obesity are social. **2A** Schools do not provide healthy living choices. **2B** Food companies are allowed to advertise or sell junk food in schools. **2C** Even worse, many schools must cut their physical education programs because of budgets. **2D** At home, there is too much TV and too many video games. Parents do not eat well either. They should show what good living habits are. They should not buy too much of the wrong kinds of food. It is important to teach healthy behavior at a young age.

1. **Look at the four squares [■] that indicate where the following sentence could be added to the passage.**

   In the U.S., about 15% of children are obese.

   Where would the sentence best fit?

2. **Look at the four squares [■] that indicate where the following sentence could be added to the passage.**

   Children do not get enough exercise.

   Where would the sentence best fit?

normal (a)
usual and ordinary

at risk (phr)
in danger; at stake

productive (a)
constructive; fruitful

advertise (v)
to promote a product or service

budget (n)
a plan for money

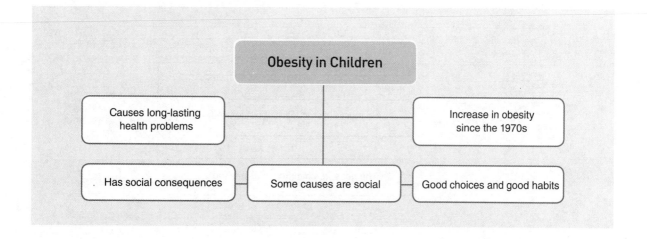

Read the following passage, and answer the questions.

The Literary Form of Tragedy

Time Limit: 1 min. 40 sec.

A tragedy is one of several kinds of plays. The form has been part of Western culture for thousands of years.

1A A tragedy is about a hero who has something bad happen to him. **1B** This bad event is connected to the hero's actions. **1C** This is because of a weakness in his personality, called a tragic flaw. **1D** In many cases, the gods are angered by the hero. They make the hero live through a bad event. It is especially cruel, and the hero must suffer. The audience must see this bad event in order to understand the hero's flaw. They must also see his suffering.

At some point, the hero realizes his wrongs. He goes through some kind of learning process. Then, the gods decide to stop his punishment. In the play, the god will come down from the sky to deliver his message. He then frees the hero from his suffering.

The audience goes through the changes of emotions from horror to relief. **2A** This is called catharsis. **2B** It means emotional healing. **2C** These simple ideas have lasted for thousands of years. **2D**

1. **Look at the four squares [■] that indicate where the following sentence could be added to the passage.**

   Tragedy has a few key elements.

   Where would the sentence best fit?

2. **Look at the four squares [■] that indicate where the following sentence could be added to the passage.**

   The Greek poets felt that this was a necessary part of a good tragedy.

   Where would the sentence best fit?

personality (n)
a person's whole character and nature

tragic (a)
extremely sad; miserable

flaw (n)
a weakness; a defect

anger (v)
to make angry

cruel (a)
very harsh; very painful

relief (n)
feeling better after a bad event; comfort; ease

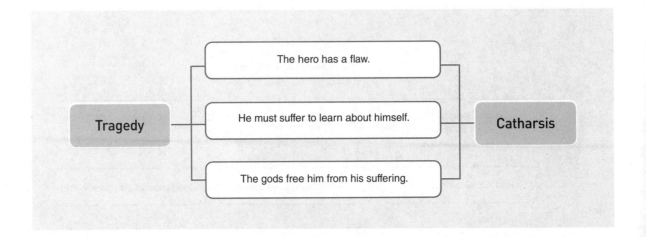

D Read the following passage, and answer the questions.

Paralympics

Time Limit: 1 min. 30 sec.

The Paralympic Games are held every Olympic year. **1A** The games give athletes the chance to show their skills. **1B** Their bodies are disabled in some way. **1C**

The Paralympics begin three weeks after the Olympic Games. **1D** Its athletes get to use the same fields and stadiums as the athletes in the regular Olympics. The prefix *para* means "beside" in Greek. These games are held in addition to the others.

To be in the games, athletes must have a disability. There are five types. Some do not have arms or legs. Some have brain damage. They have poor balance. Some athletes are in wheelchairs. Some others are blind. Some have birth defects. The great thing about these games is the attention to their skills. Their disability is not the focus.

The sports competition first started in England. It was for English soldiers who came back hurt from World War II. **2A** The first official Paralympic Games were held in 1960. **2B** There were four hundred athletes who came. **2C** The most recent games had nearly four thousand athletes from 136 countries. **2D**

1. **Look at the four squares [■] that indicate where the following sentence could be added to the passage.**

   But these athletes are different.

   Where would the sentence best fit?

2. **Look at the four squares [■] that indicate where the following sentence could be added to the passage.**

   Soon, other countries started sending their people.

   Where would the sentence best fit?

○ **athlete (n)**
a person who does a sport; a sportsperson

○ **disabled (a)**
not having normal ability; handicapped

○ **defect (n)**
a physical problem; an imperfection

○ **competition (n)**
a rivalry, contest, or race

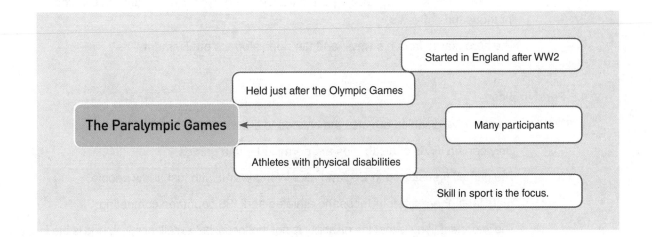

Started in England after WW2

Held just after the Olympic Games

The Paralympic Games

Many participants

Athletes with physical disabilities

Skill in sport is the focus.

Building Summary Skills

A Put the following sentences in order to make appropriate summaries based on the long passages you worked on earlier. The first sentence is already provided.

1. **Betty Friedan**

   Betty Friedan was a feminist, and she argued for women to be treated fairly in society and in marriage.

   _____ She asked other female college graduates how they felt.

   _____ Friedan had a family, but she was not happy with her life as a housewife.

   _____ She said women should take part in society more actively and be seen as equal to men.

   _____ Friedan discovered that they felt the same way, so she wrote a book about it.

2. **Child Obesity**

   Children with obesity might have long lasting health risks.

   _____ Obesity also affects society because it affects the cost of health care and creates social problems.

   _____ There are more children today with this problem than in the 1970s.

   _____ We can change how schools and companies operate to decrease the risk of obesity, and we should allow better food choices and promote good behavior.

   _____ Some children are more likely to be obese than others.

3. **The Literary Form of Tragedy**

   A tragedy is a traditional form of theater.

   _____ The audience experiences a range of emotions while watching the play.

   _____ It has a hero who, because of his personality, gets put into a bad situation where he must suffer.

   _____ This emotional change is a key part of tragedy, and this form of drama has lasted for thousands of years.

   _____ The hero learns from his ways, and the gods stop his punishment.

4. **Paralympics**

   The Paralympics give disabled athletes the chance to show their skills.

   _____ Only certain kinds of disabilities are permitted in the games.

   _____ The games first started in England after World War II with just a few people.

   _____ Years later, there are four thousand athletes and 136 countries competing.

   _____ The important thing is that the disability is not the focus, but excellence in sports is the focus.

Unit **8** | Insert Text

B Fill in the blanks with suitable words or phrases to complete the following summaries. Do not look at the previous page until you are finished.

1. Betty Friedan

Betty Friedan was a (1)_____, and she argued for women to be treated (2)_____ in society and in marriage. Friedan had a family, but she was not (3)_____ with her life as a (4)_____. She asked other female (5)_____ how they felt. Friedan discovered that they felt the same way, so she wrote (6)_____ about it. She said women should take part in society more (7)_____ and be seen as (8)_____ to men.

2. Child Obesity

Children with (1)_____ might have long lasting health risks. There are more children today with this problem than in the (2)_____. Some children are more likely to be (3)_____ than others. Obesity also affects (4)_____ because it affects the cost of (5)_____ and creates social problems. We can change how (6)_____ operate to decrease the risk of obesity, and we should allow better (7)_____ and promote good (8)_____.

3. The Literary Form of Tragedy

A (1)_____ is a traditional form of (2)_____. It has a hero who, because of his (3)_____, gets put into a (4)_____ situation where he must (5)_____. The hero learns from his ways, and the gods stop his (6)_____. The audience experiences a range of (7)_____ while watching the play. This emotional change is a (8)_____ part of tragedy, and this form of drama has lasted for thousands of years.

4. Paralympics

The Paralympics give (1)_____ athletes the chance to show their (2)_____. Only certain kinds of (3)_____ are permitted in the games. The important thing is that the disability is not the focus, but (4)_____ in sports is the focus. The games first started in (5)_____ after (6)_____ with just a few people. Years later, there are (7)_____ athletes and (8)_____ countries competing.

1. **According to the passage, what was Smith's goal?**

   (A) To put the geology of his country on paper
   (B) To become a famous scientist
   (C) To help coal companies grow
   (D) To study the way farmers work

2. **Look at the four squares [■] that indicate where the following sentence could be added to the passage.**

   This work led him to a discovery.

   Where would the sentence best fit?

   Click on a square [■] to add the sentence to the passage.

3. **The word those in the passage refers to**

   (A) fossils
   (B) features
   (C) layers
   (D) miles

4. **The word ancient in the passage is closest in meaning to**

   (A) local
   (B) old
   (C) early
   (D) recent

5. **The author discusses Smith's travels in paragraph 4 in order to**

   (A) complain about Smith's methods
   (B) show how much Smith cared about his work
   (C) explain how traveling was necessary
   (D) show what traveling was like back then

6. **The word precise in the passage is closest in meaning to**

   (A) strict
   (B) careful
   (C) complex
   (D) accurate

William Smith

William Smith lived in the late 1700s. He was an engineer. He had a simple discovery that led him to a life's work. He wanted to map the geology of England.

Smith came from a farming family in the west of England. His father died when he was young. Smith was raised by his uncle. He had a basic education but taught himself about geography from books. He showed an early interest in fossils that he found near where he lived.

A When Smith grew older, he became an engineer. **B** He worked for coal companies checking the quality of the land. **C** He had to drain water from places and see how easy it was to dig. **D**

Smith had to build a canal for a coal company. He saw as he dug that the earth had different layers. He noticed that each layer had certain kinds of fossils. As he traveled across England, he noticed these same features. Smith believed that the layers of earth in the north of England were connected to those in the south. He understood that these layers told an ancient history of the land. Soon, Smith had traveled all over England. Sometimes he traveled thousands of miles each year by horse and coach to observe the layers of the land.

Smith did his best to share his knowledge with everyone. He made maps that told what kinds of rock, earth, and plants grew in the different parts of England. He talked at farmers' meetings and at dinner parties. Smith also wrote several books.

Smith was very skilled. Many methods for observing land features are still used today. His maps were very precise and can still be used today. Many geological terms that he created are also used.

7. **According to the passage, what was the purpose of sports?**

  Ⓐ To stop people from being angry at the king
  Ⓑ To stop people from working too much
  Ⓒ To keep people busy so they would not fight
  Ⓓ To keep people happy and in good shape

8. **The word regular in the passage is closest in meaning to**

  Ⓐ systematic
  Ⓑ hopeful
  Ⓒ even
  Ⓓ common

9. **The author discusses tug-of-war in paragraph 3 in order to**

  Ⓐ explain how tug of war is not fashionable
  Ⓑ provide another example of an old game played today
  Ⓒ state his opinion on ancient Egyptian games
  Ⓓ contrast its simplicity with the complexity of other games

10. **The word these in the passage refers to**

  Ⓐ sports
  Ⓑ people
  Ⓒ the army and the temple
  Ⓓ skills

11. **Look at the four squares [■] that indicate where the following sentence could be added to the passage.**

  The king would run to show he had the mental strength to guide his country.

  Where would the sentence best fit?

  Click on a square [■] to add the sentence to the passage.

12. **The word entombed in the passage is closest in meaning to**

  Ⓐ hidden
  Ⓑ buried
  Ⓒ portrayed
  Ⓓ killed

Ancient Egyptian Sports

Many of the sports in ancient Egypt are still practiced today. In fact, many of the basic elements of sports, like rules and uniforms, were first used by Egyptians. The sports had important functions in society. Some were played for fun and fitness. Others were played to make stronger warriors and leaders.

The first group of sports, mostly for fun, was those like rowing, hunting, and the high jump. Hunting and fishing could be enjoyed by the kings and regular people. The same was for rowing. Rowing needs a lot of strength. Teams of people got into boats and followed the commands of a leader. He would give regular, sharp calls to tell them when to row. This technique is still used for rowing teams today.

Another popular game was tug-of-war. This was a game where two teams had to pull each other over a line. If a team fell forward, they lost. This game is still played today in the country.

The second group of sports prepared people for the army and the temple. These included boxing, horse riding, running, and archery. **A** They were ways to work on skills for fighting. **B** They were also ways to work on mental and spiritual power. **C** Running a marathon was a good example of this. **D**

Hockey was another Egyptian game. There are pictures where people are entombed that show the game. Players held tree branches with a bent end, just like modern hockey sticks. They had to hit a ball made of leather that was brightly colored.

These sports were a part of Egyptian culture. They kept the people happy and fit. The basic rules were created thousands of years ago. They are still seen in some form today.

Vocabulary Review

Choose the word with the closest meaning to each underlined word or phrase.

1. Drunk driving can lead to some tragic results.
   (A) compacted   (B) miserable   (C) peaceful   (D) delighted

2. The bank insists on the store making its payment in full.
   (A) persists in   (B) approves of   (C) objects to   (D) watches

3. There are a lot of defects in the machine.
   (A) interest   (B) acquisitions   (C) treatments   (D) imperfections

4. Chocolate is made by a complex process.
   (A) strange   (B) careless   (C) complicated   (D) simple

5. The company is pushing the sale of its new products on the market.
   (A) spreading   (B) forcing   (C) staying   (D) serving

6. Competition is not evil in itself.
   (A) Rivalry   (B) Combination   (C) Harmony   (D) Settlement

7. When women have no one to love, they feel lonely and depressed.
   (A) joyful   (B) sufficient   (C) sad   (D) excited

8. The bridge connects the land between two small towns.
   (A) delivers   (B) links   (C) secedes   (D) divides

9. The school has very strict rules about the dress code.
   (A) delicate   (B) firm   (C) vulnerable   (D) soft

10. The view of the sunset was incredible.
    (A) proper   (B) restless   (C) flat   (D) unbelievable

PART 3

Reading to Learn

In this part, the reading comprehension questions include: prose summary and fill in a table. The learning objectives of these reading comprehension questions are to recognize the major ideas and the relative importance of information in a passage and to organize the main ideas and other important information in the appropriate categories.

Prose Summary

Prose Summary

Overview

■Introduction

Prose Summary questions are a new type of question on the TOEFL® iBT. In this type of question, you will be asked to complete a summary chart by choosing three most important ideas from six choices. In order to solve Prose Summary questions, you should understand the overall theme of the passage and distinguish important ideas from minor ones in the passage.

■Useful Tips

- Try to understand the overall structure of the passage.

- Write down the main idea of each paragraph on your scratch paper.

- Distinguish major points from minor details in the passage.

- Incorrect answer choices usually deal with the minor points of the passage or are not mentioned in the passage.

■Question Type

Directions: An introductory sentence for a brief summary of the passage is provided below. Complete the summary by selecting the THREE answer choices that express the most important ideas in the passage. Some sentences do not belong in the summary because they express ideas that are not presented in the passage or are minor ideas in the passage. **This question is worth 2 points.**

[An introductory sentence]

-
-
-

Answer Choices

1. XXXXXXXXXXXXXXXXXXXXXXXXXXXX
2. XXXXXXXXXXXXXXXXXXXXXXXXXXXX
3. XXXXXXXXXXXXXXXXXXXXXXXXXXXX

4. XXXXXXXXXXXXXXXXXXXXXXXXXXXX
5. XXXXXXXXXXXXXXXXXXXXXXXXXXXX
6. XXXXXXXXXXXXXXXXXXXXXXXXXXXX

Sample iBT Question

The New Deal

The New Deal was designed by President Roosevelt in the 1930s. He wanted to help people who suffered in the Great Depression. Millions of people were poor. The banking system was not reliable. Roosevelt wanted to help the poor. He also wanted to improve the economy. Most of all, he wanted to prevent future problems.

The New Deal included work programs. It gave people jobs in cities and in the country. It also included social security. This insurance gave poor people money when they were too old to work. If a worker lost his job, he got unemployment insurance. To make banks safe, the New Deal provided deposit insurance. People received money from the government if a bank lost their money. These steps put people on their feet again.

Directions: An introductory sentence for a brief summary of the passage is provided below. Complete the summary by selecting the THREE answer choices that express the most important ideas in the passage. Some sentences do not belong in the summary because they express ideas that are not presented in the passage or are minor ideas in the passage. *This question is worth 2 points.*

President Roosevelt implemented the New Deal policy during the Great Depression.
-
-
-

Answer Choices

1. The New Deal was intended to boost the economy by providing people with jobs.

2. The Great Depression was an economic crisis in the 1930s.

3. The policy attempted to make the banking system more trustworthy.

4. Social security was strengthened by the New Deal.

5. The government encouraged people to deposit their money in banks.

6. The New Deal made people more dependent on the government.

 Choices 1, 3, and 4 are correct because they represent major ideas in the passage. Choice 2 is incorrect since it is just a minor idea. Choices 5 and 6 are also incorrect; they are irrelevant to the passage.

Skill & Drill

Prose Summary questions ask you to complete a summary chart with the most important ideas from the passage. The topic sentence will be given for the summary. It is important that minor ideas or ideas that are not mentioned in the passage be avoided.

Example

If there is not enough rain, farmers must bring water to their plants in other ways. In the short term, this is a good thing, but in the long term, it could be dangerous for the land. In most cases, this water contains small amounts of salt. Normally, this is not a bad thing, but over time, the salt starts to build up in the soil. Eventually, there is so much salt that the soil is no good for farming. Farmers need to be careful about how water flows through the earth to control the salt level.

Directions: An introductory sentence for a brief summary of the passage is provided. Complete the summary by selecting the TWO answer choices that express the most important ideas in the passage.

Watering crops has some considerations.
- It is good for plants.
- It can cause a buildup of salt.

- Ⓐ It is good for plants.
- Ⓑ It can cause a buildup of salt.
- Ⓒ It is good for the land in the long term.

Scarcity means not to have enough. If you need something that is scarce, you have to decide what to do. For example, when gasoline is scarce, the price goes up. You have to decide if you are going to pay that price. But what do you do if you do not want to pay? You could look in another place, but you may have to travel far. Or you could just learn to live without it. In the case of gasoline, you may not drive so often. You may ride your bike or share a ride with someone else.

1. **Directions:** Complete the summary by selecting the TWO answer choices that express the most important ideas in the passage.

   When necessary things are scarce, people have to make decisions.
   -
   -

   Ⓐ The price of gasoline goes up.
   Ⓑ You have to make decisions about rising prices.
   Ⓒ You may pay more or go elsewhere.

The philosophy of law is called jurisprudence. This means "knowledge of law." People who study this try to understand the reasons for certain laws, how they are organized, and how they are used. It is important to know how laws affect our society. Students of law can look at laws that are currently in use. In addition to the benefits, there may be some results that were not expected. Students can also study the ideas of new laws. As crimes change, there is always a need for new laws.

2. **Directions:** Complete the summary by selecting the TWO answer choices that express the most important ideas in the passage.

    Jurisprudence means the philosophy of law.
    -
    -

    A The study of jurisprudence is used in developing new laws.
    B Certain laws have benefits and disadvantages in our society.
    C People study current laws to see how they affect society.

The number of dollar bills in use must be controlled. If the government prints too much money, prices will rise. At first it does not seem logical. But more money means that people have more to spend. In this situation, it is easy to raise prices because people can afford it. But there is another effect. If the economy doubles the amount of bills, then it cuts the actual value of all the bills in half. Then you have to pay workers twice as much for them to get the same value. These new costs force prices to rise.

3. **Directions:** Complete the summary by selecting the TWO answer choices that express the most important ideas in the passage.

    The amount of money in use in a country affects the economy.
    -
    -

    A Too much money results in decreasing the money's value.
    B Prices rise because people have more money.
    C Printing too much money has other effects.

Practice with Short Passages

A Read the following passage, and answer the questions.

The Liability of Drunk Driving

Time Limit: 30 sec.

Drunk driving is a major factor in traffic accidents. When a drunk driver has an accident, a number of things happen. If the driver hurts someone or property gets damaged, the victims can sue the driver. This is because the driver must be responsible for his acts. In law terms, "liable" means responsible. But liability does not stop at the driver. In the United States, victims of an accident can also sue the bar where the driver got his alcohol. They can even sue the bartender. It is believed that because the bar "helped" the driver get drunk, the bar is also at fault for the accident. This means that these places must be very careful. They should not allow people to get drunk.

General Comprehension

1. **The word liability in the passage is closest in meaning to**

   (A) caution
   (B) credibility
   (C) responsibility
   (D) recklessness

2. **Why can the bartender be sued in a drunk driving accident?**

   (A) He is responsible for the person drinking.
   (B) He wanted to get the person drunk.
   (C) He had no control over the drinker.
   (D) He knows how to make drinks.

---

property (n)
possessions; belongings; assets

victim (n)
a person who is hurt

sue (v)
to start a legal case against someone; to take someone to court

bartender (n)
the person who serves alcohol at a bar

be at fault (phr)
be responsible for; be to blame

On the TOEFL Test

3. **Directions:** An introductory sentence for a brief summary of the passage is provided below. Complete the summary by selecting the TWO answer choices that express the most important ideas in the passage.

   Drunk driving carries a lot of consequences, especially if there is an accident.

   -
   -

   (A) The bar and bartender can be named in the lawsuit and must be careful.
   (B) The driver can be sued by the victims of the accident.
   (C) The victim of the accident becomes very upset.
   (D) The family of the victim can sue the drunk driver.

B Read the following passage, and answer the questions.

The Advantages of Crop Rotation

Time Limit: 50 sec.

Crop rotation was a great advance for society during the Middle Ages. Special farming techniques made it easier than before to grow food. This allowed populations to grow. The idea was simple. Each kind of plant takes different nutrients from the earth. It also attracts specific kinds of insects. So if you grow the same plant in the same place all the time, eventually the earth will not have what it needs to grow. What does grow will be eaten by insects.

People in the Middle Ages learned that if you grow different plants in the same spot every season, the second plant would replace what the first plant took from the earth. If you grow a plant that cows like to eat, then their manure will add more nutrients back into the earth. This was a new discovery. So every season, people grew a different crop. The earth became better for growing, and there was more food.

General Comprehension

1. **What is crop rotation?**

    Ⓐ A method for farming plants
    Ⓑ A way of moving animals around
    Ⓒ A means to keep animals
    Ⓓ A way to grow corn

2. **What effect does growing the same plant repeatedly have?**

    Ⓐ It takes different nutrients from the earth.
    Ⓑ It attracts insects which eat the plants.
    Ⓒ It attracts insects and ruins the soil.
    Ⓓ It makes the soil better for growing.

On the TOEFL Test

3. **Directions:** An introductory sentence for a brief summary of the passage is provided below. Complete the summary by selecting the TWO answer choices that express the most important ideas in the passage.

    Crop rotation was a great farming method.

    -
    -

    Ⓐ Old methods made it difficult to grow strong plants.
    Ⓑ Old methods ruined the soil in the Middle Ages.
    Ⓒ New methods replaced nutrients in the soil.
    Ⓓ New methods allowed animals to eat.

---

rotation (n)
taking turns to do a particular job

advance (n)
progress; development

nutrient (n)
a substance that helps plants and animals grow

specific (a)
particular

replace (v)
to put back what you took out

manure (n)
animal waste that is spread over the soil to help plants grow

Read the following passage, and answer the questions.

Sleep Disorders

Time Limit: 50 sec.

There are three major kinds of sleep disorders: you cannot sleep, you must always sleep, or your breathing affects sleep. The first kind, insomnia, means that you cannot sleep well. You may have a hard time falling asleep, or you keep waking up. During the day, you may feel sleepy or stressed. You may have a hard time concentrating. The second kind, narcolepsy, is called the sleeping sickness. You cannot control when you fall asleep, even during the day. In fact, if you get excited, your body tries to fall asleep. When you wake up, you cannot move or talk. The third kind is called sleep apnea. It is a breathing problem while sleeping. Usually, your throat starts to close. This may be because of drinking alcohol or being too heavy. The muscles do not have enough control. Other times, the brain does not send the signal to breathe. Then you wake up.

General Comprehension

1. **What is insomnia?**

   (A) When you cannot sleep well if at all
   (B) When you have to sleep all the time
   (C) When you keep sleeping in the day
   (D) When you wake up in the afternoon

2. **What is the difference between narcolepsy and sleep apnea?**

   (A) Alcohol is used to treat apnea but not narcolepsy.
   (B) Apnea is like narcolepsy but more severe.
   (C) Apnea involves breathing, but narcolepsy does not.
   (D) Apnea and narcolepsy only happen during the daytime.

disorder (n)
a problem or disease that affects a person's mind or body

have a hard time V-ing (phr)
have difficulty V-ing

concentrate (v)
to focus on

muscle (n)
body tissues on the bones which are used to make movements

On the TOEFL Test

3. **Directions:** An introductory sentence for a brief summary of the passage is provided below. Complete the summary by selecting the TWO answer choices that express the most important ideas in the passage.

   There are three types of sleeping disorders.
   -
   -

   (A) Sleep apnea relates breathing to waking up.
   (B) Sleep apnea relates alcohol to waking up.
   (C) Insomnia and narcolepsy describe the ability to control falling asleep.
   (D) Insomnia and narcolepsy do not involve the use of medication.

D Read the following passage, and answer the questions.

Game Theory

Time Limit: 50 sec.

Economists study the use of choice. They call it Game Theory. The result depends on the choices of all the people involved. Sometimes we have to make decisions that are selfish. The decision will make our lives better but will not help the people around us. It may even hurt them. Other times, we make decisions that are best for everyone but are not the best for ourselves. For example, imagine that there is garbage all over a town. The town does not look pretty at all. Tourists do not want to visit. The shop owners agree that the best thing for the town is to go out and clean it up. If one shop owner cleans it up, everyone benefits. However, that owner is using his own time. He is not getting paid for his work, and no one is helping him.

General Comprehension

1. **What does Game Theory describe?**

   (A) What selfish decisions are
   (B) How people use choices
   (C) Why tourists visit places
   (D) How to pay people for doing work

2. **The word selfish is closest in meaning to**

   (A) greedy
   (B) alone
   (C) bold
   (D) aggressive

○ **depend on** (phr)
 to rely on
○ **involve** (v)
 to include
○ **selfish** (a)
 not thinking about others, just oneself
○ **hurt** (v)
 to cause pain
○ **benefit** (v)
 to gain advantage

On the TOEFL Test

3. **Directions:** An introductory sentence for a brief summary of the passage is provided below. Complete the summary by selecting the TWO answer choices that express the most important ideas in the passage.

   This passage describes Game Theory.

   -
   -

   (A) Game Theory is important due to its usefulness.
   (B) Game Theory is based on the use of choice.
   (C) People tend to make selfish decisions.
   (D) People make decisions for their benefit or for others' benefit.

Practice with Long Passages

A Read the following passage, and answer the question.

Time Limit: 1 min. 50 sec.

Miranda Rights

According to US law, a person has the right to silence if police ask him about a crime. He also has the right to a lawyer if he goes to jail for a crime. The reason for these rights is simple: police cannot force a person to say anything that will make him guilty. An arrested person must know this.

The Miranda Rights are something that police say when you are arrested. They say, "You have the right to remain silent. If you give up that right, anything you say can and will be used against you in a court of law. You have the right to a lawyer during questioning. If you cannot afford a lawyer, one will be given at no cost. During questioning, you may decide not to answer if you choose." The police make sure the person understands this. They may have to say the Miranda Rights in the person's own language.

Criminals have been set free because the police did not do a good job of reading them their rights. It is important in any society for criminals to know the law but also to know their rights. This is a way to make sure that a society is fair for everyone.

Directions: An introductory sentence for a brief summary of the passage is provided below. Complete the summary by selecting the THREE answer choices that express the most important ideas in the passage. Some answer choices do not belong in the summary because they express ideas that are not in the passage or are minor ideas in the passage.

according to (phr)
in the words of

crime (n)
a serious, illegal act

force (v)
to require

guilty (a)
having broken a law;
at fault

afford (v)
to have enough money

fair (a)
having justice

The right to silence is an important right.
-
-
-

Answer Choices

(A) Police cannot force you to say something against your will.

(B) You can be set free if your rights have been abused.

(C) Anything you say can be used against you in a court of law.

(D) Criminals have to be set free if the police do not do their job.

(E) Police read you your Miranda Rights when you are arrested.

(F) Criminals are set free if they do not know the law.

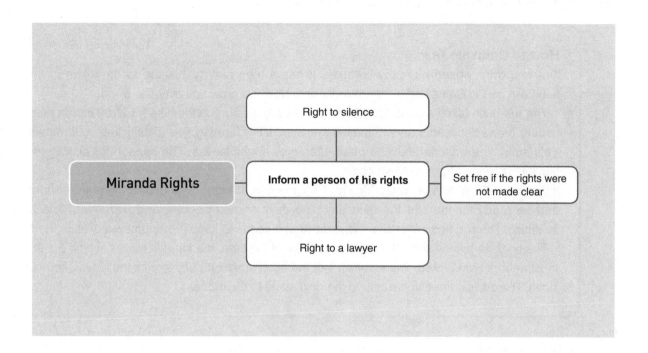

Read the following passage, and answer the question.

How to Cultivate Tea

Time Limit: 1 min. 50 sec.

Tea is a drink prized by many cultures. It has a long history. It used to be grown in the southern part of China and northern India only. Now it is grown all over the world.

The tea bush takes around four years to start producing good leaves for tea. The tea plant usually grows between 5 and 15 meters in the wild. For farming, it is usually kept to 2 meters. This small size ensures that the plant often grows new leaves. The season for picking tea leaves lasts from March to November.

Tea bushes like lots of water. Ideally, it should rain at night. This allows the plant to drink and be ready for the sun the next day. The days should be long and warm with lots of sunshine. The sun and water give the plant what it needs to keep growing new leaves.

The best tea leaves are picked by hand. Most of the time, the top two leaves, which are the most delicate, are picked. The small size of the bush makes it easy to pick the leaves from all sides. The tea is carried in baskets to the next stage in the process.

Directions: An introductory sentence for a brief summary of the passage is provided below. Complete the summary by selecting the THREE answer choices that express the most important ideas in the passage. Some answer choices do not belong in the summary because they express ideas that are not in the passage or are minor ideas in the passage.

prize (v)
to value; to esteem

in the wild (phr)
not farmed

ensure (v)
to make sure

ideally (ad)
in the best situation

delicate (a)
fragile

There are a few considerations to growing tea.

-
-
-

Answer Choices

(A) Four-year-old tea plants are kept small to produce lots of hand-picked leaves.

(B) Rain should fall at night instead of the day to feed the plant.

(C) The tea is carried in baskets to the next stage of the process.

(D) The tea plant produces the most leaves from March to November in warm, wet climates.

(E) Tea bushes like a lot of water and sunshine.

(F) The two top leaves are very delicate and must be picked by hand.

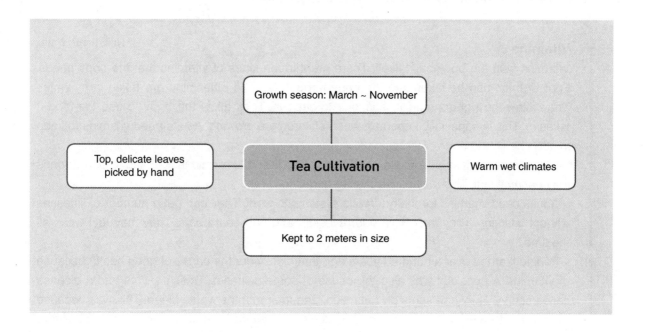

Read the following passage, and answer the question.

Vitamins

Time Limit: 2 min.

Vitamins help the body build itself. There are thirteen kinds of vitamins that the body needs. Four of them can be taken into the body through fat. The other nine are taken in by water. They allow the right chemical reactions to happen. They allow the body to use the food it takes in. This is especially important when children are growing. Adults need vitamins to keep in good health.

Children need vitamins to build good bones and tissue. If a child lacks Vitamin D, his bones may become soft. This may cause the leg bones to curve.

Adults need vitamins for their nervous systems to work. They can get a number of illnesses without vitamins. They may have poor eyesight and bad heartbeats. They may feel weak all the time.

People learned over a hundred years ago that diets were the cause of good health because of vitamins. A poor diet was also the cause of some diseases. British sailors had a disease called scurvy. They had spots on their skin, and their mouths would bleed. This was because they did not have enough Vitamin C. A doctor discovered this cause and made sure that lemons and limes were put on all the ships.

Directions: An introductory sentence for a brief summary of the passage is provided below. Complete the summary by selecting the THREE answer choices that express the most important ideas in the passage. Some answer choices do not belong in the summary because they express ideas that are not in the passage or are minor ideas in the passage.

Vitamins are necessary for the body.

-
-
-

Answer Choices

(A) Adults and children need vitamins for strong bones, eyes, their heart, and nervous system.

(B) Spots on the skin and sore mouths are indications of a lack of vitamins.

(C) Scurvy used to affect British sailors until doctors put lemons and limes on ships.

(D) The quality of diet, it has been discovered, has been linked to vitamin intake and health.

(E) The right chemical reactions happen when the body is treated well.

(F) There are thirteen different kinds of vitamins in the body.

reaction (n)
a response; an answer

tissue (n)
a group of cells that form different parts of animals and plants

lack (v)
to be without (something needed)

curve (v)
to bend

spot (n)
a mark that looks different from its background

bleed (v)
to lose blood

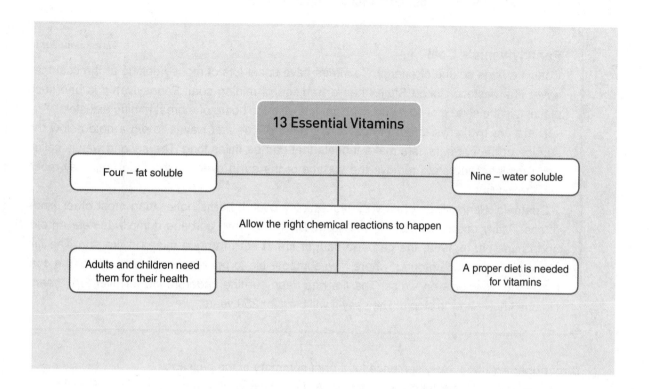

Read the following passage, and answer the question.

Pennsylvania's Coal

Time Limit: 2 min.

Coal is a huge source of energy. Countries have spent lots of money getting at the coal they have. The eastern United States has a tradition of mining coal. Pennsylvania is one such place. It is the source of so much coal, but it is also the home of a great mining disaster.

There are two ways to get at coal in the ground. The first way is to dig a hole below the surface of the earth. Miners make tunnels that can be miles long. The second way is called open mining. Miners will remove the surface of the earth over a huge area until they reach what they want.

Centralia, Pennsylvania has very high-quality coal. It burns hotter than most other kinds of coal. Many open mines are in that town. Sadly, the town garbage dump was near an old, open mine pit. In 1962, the garbage caught fire. It set the open mine on fire, too. The fire started burning underground, where it was impossible to put out. The fine quality of the coal made the disaster even worse. The fire has been burning underground for over forty years. No one knows how to stop it. They say it will burn for 250 years.

Directions: An introductory sentence for a brief summary of the passage is provided below. Complete the summary by selecting the THREE answer choices that express the most important ideas in the passage. Some answer choices do not belong in the summary because they express ideas that are not in the passage or are minor ideas in the passage.

Pennsylvania has a great mining tradition and a sad history.

-
-
-

source (n)
a supply

get at (phr)
to reach

mine (v)
to take minerals from under the earth's surface

surface (n)
the top part

remove (v)
to take away; to get rid of

put out (phr)
to extinguish a fire

Answer Choices

(A) The town garbage dump was near an old, open mine.

(B) The coal near a town caught fire and has been burning for decades.

(C) The town of Centralia has many open mines.

(D) Pennsylvania uses open mining to get coal from the ground.

(E) No one knows how to make the fire burn for 250 years.

(F) There is good, quality coal in Pennsylvania.

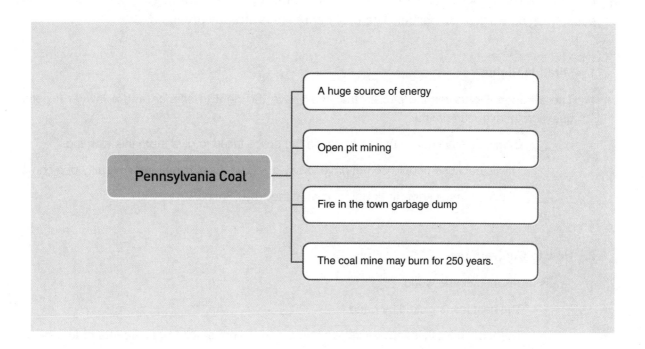

Building Summary Skills

A Put the following sentences in order to make appropriate summaries based on the long passages you worked on earlier. The first sentence is already provided.

1. **Miranda Rights**

   The Miranda Rights remind people that they have the right to silence and a lawyer if police question them about a crime.

   _____ Criminals have been set free because the police failed to give them this warning.

   _____ This is because people do not have to say anything that will make them guilty of a crime.

   _____ All people must know their rights, even if they are criminals.

2. **How to Cultivate Tea**

   Tea is drunk all over the world.

   _____ The best tea is picked by hand.

   _____ The tea plant takes four years to mature and is kept small to ensure lots of leaves and easy picking.

   _____ It grows well in climates that are warm and wet.

   _____ The delicate, top leaves are picked and carried in baskets to the next stage of processing.

3. **Vitamins**

   Vitamins are necessary for the body to build itself and stay healthy.

   _____ Some diseases occur if you do not eat well.

   _____ Some are taken in through fat and others through water.

   _____ People have learned that their diets are the key to getting enough vitamins.

   _____ Children need vitamins to grow strong bones and organs, and adults need them for strong nervous systems.

4. **Pennsylvania's Coal**

   Pennsylvania has provided a lot of coal, which is an important fuel.

   _____ There are many coal mines there.

   _____ One of the coal mines caught fire and started burning underground.

   _____ Open mining was used in a town called Centralia, where there is high-quality coal.

   _____ It is impossible to put out the fire, and it may burn for 250 years.

B Fill in the blanks with suitable words or phrases to complete the following summaries. Do not look at the previous page until you are finished.

1. Miranda Rights

The (1)_____ remind people that they have the right to (2)_____ and a (3)_____ if police question them about a crime. This is because people do not have to (4)_____ anything that will make them (5)_____ of a crime. Criminals have been (6)_____ because police failed to give them this (7)_____. All people must know their rights, even if they are (8)_____.

2. How to Cultivate Tea

(1)_____ is drunk all over the world. The tea plant takes (2)_____ years to mature and is kept (3)_____ to ensure lots of leaves and easy (4)_____. It grows well in climates that are (5)_____ and (6)_____. The best tea is picked (7)_____. The delicate (8)_____ are picked and carried in baskets to the next stage of processing.

3. Vitamins

Vitamins are (1)_____ for the body to build itself and stay (2)_____. Some are taken in through (3)_____ and others through (4)_____. Children need vitamins to grow strong (5)_____ and organs, and adults need them for strong (6)_____. People have learned that their (7)_____ are the key to getting enough vitamins. Some (8)_____ occur if you do not eat well.

4. Pennsylvania's Coal

Pennsylvania has provided a lot of (1)_____, which is an important (2)_____. There are many (3)_____ there. Open mining was used in a town called (4)_____, where there is high-quality coal. One of the coal mines caught (5)_____ and started burning (6)_____. It is impossible to (7)_____ the fire, and it may burn for (8)_____ years.

1. **The word rotate in the passage is closest in meaning to**

   (A) spin   (B) stir   (C) clean   (D) change

2. **The author mentions plant compost in the passage as an example of which of the following?**

   (A) A way to add nutrients back to the soil
   (B) A type of pesticide
   (C) A kind of fertilizer
   (D) A way to avoid labor

3. **The word they in the passage refers to**

   (A) pesticides   (B) bad insects   (C) farmers   (D) weeds

4. **According to the passage, what replaces the chemical treatment of crops?**

   (A) topsoil
   (B) weed killer
   (C) animal feed
   (D) human labor

5. **Directions:** An introductory sentence for a brief summary of the passage is provided below. Complete the summary by selecting the THREE answer choices that express the most important ideas in the passage. Some answer choices do not belong in the summary because they express ideas that are not in the passage or are minor ideas in the passage. **This question is worth 2 points.**

   Organic farming tries to use natural means to grow plants.

   -
   -
   -

   Answer Choices

   (A) It relies on crop rotation, manure, and plant compost to keep the soil rich.

   (B) Organic food costs more, but it is worth the expense.

   (C) This natural means keeps plants and people healthy.

   (D) It avoids the use of pesticides, which kill good animals as well as bad ones.

   (E) It has been used for thousands of years and has been very successful.

   (F) It is the only farming technique that works all over the world.

Organic Farming

The idea behind organic farming is to use no chemicals. Farmers must use natural means to make plants grow strong and protect them from insects. It is believed that without chemicals, these plants will make better food for humans. But the idea is bigger than that. Organic farming respects all plants and animals in the environment. This kind of farming should improve nature's health.

Fertilizers are chemicals that give plants strength. If a farmer grows the same plant over and over in the same place, the soil will lose its ability to feed the plant. The farmer must add fertilizer to help the soil. Organic farmers do not add fertilizer. They will rotate crops or use animal manure and plant compost to make the soil rich again. Compost is made from plant material that has broken down into soil. It has all the food a plant needs to grow.

Pesticides are also avoided. These are chemicals that kill pests like bad insects or animals. Organic farmers have other ways to deal with pests because pesticides kill good animals and insects that protect the plants. Foxes and snakes eat the mice. Some insects like ladybugs eat the bad insects. And of course there are weeds. These are the plants that farmers do not want because they steal growing space from the good plants. To stop weeds, organic farmers can scrape the soil several times. Eventually, the weeds will die.

Organic farming usually needs a lot of human labor to do the job of chemicals. This is one reason that organic food costs more. But when we think about the health of the earth, its plants, and its animals, perhaps it is worth it. In the end, a healthy planet means that we will be healthy, too.

6. **The word barriers in the passage is closest in meaning to**

   (A) bans   (B) disputes   (C) obstacles   (D) documents

7. **In paragraph 2, why does the author give details about how the WTO helps trade?**

   (A) To illustrate how the WTO improves international trade
   (B) To complain about the actions of the WTO
   (C) To distinguish between the WTO and banks
   (D) To promote discussion about the WTO

8. **According to the passage, all of the following are true EXCEPT:**

   (A) The WTO wants to improve trade by lowering taxes.
   (B) The WTO wants to make trade better.
   (C) Poor countries are not given priority.
   (D) Trade means the buying and selling of goods.

9. **In stating that the WTO helps poor countries get ahead, the author means that it helps them**

   (A) make more decisions   (B) improve their situations
   (C) feed the poor   (D) elect a leader

10. **Directions:** An introductory sentence for a brief summary of the passage is provided below. Complete the summary by selecting the THREE answer choices that express the most important ideas in the passage. Some answer choices do not belong in the summary because they express ideas that are not in the passage or are minor ideas in the passage. *This question is worth 2 points.*

    The WTO provides a way for countries to improve trade.

    •
    •
    •

    Answer Choices

    (A) Countries should try to come up to the level of the richest country.

    (B) Countries should allow goods and services to cross borders easily.

    (C) Countries should lower tariffs and make investors feel secure.

    (D) Countries should allow time to organize political protests.

    (E) Countries should be fair to one another and help poor members.

    (F) Countries should never stop themselves from raising taxes.

WTO

The World Trade Organization (WTO) has 149 member countries. They are looking to improve trade. Trade means the buying and selling of goods. The WTO provides a place where these countries can talk about what they need. The goal of the WTO is to make trade grow by removing legal barriers between countries.

The WTO helps trade in several ways. First, it asks countries to treat each other equally. They should not give special trade deals to one country and not to another. Also, these countries should not try to stop foreign products from any one country. The idea is that goods and services should be able to cross borders easily. A second way to improve trade is to lower tariffs. These are special taxes for things bought and sold. A third way to strengthen trade is to make sure that the rules will stay the same. In order for people to invest their money, they need to feel secure for the future. A fourth way is to allow greater competition between countries. The central belief is that competition makes for a stronger economy. The last way to improve trade is to help countries that are poor. They need help coming up to the level of modern countries. They can be helped by allowing them extra time to get their systems in order. They can be given priority in making deals with other countries.

Free and easy trade is the WTO's goal. It supports rich countries and helps poor countries get ahead. It is one way of improving the lives of more people in the world. It asks countries to make laws that help this process. Every year, more countries apply to be in the WTO. They see membership as a good thing.

Choose the word with the closest meaning to each underlined word or phrase.

1. Parents should be very careful with their baby's delicate skin.

    (A) sufficient   (B) pretty   (C) sweat   (D) fragile

2. The water source in this country is not infinite.

    (A) supply   (B) prevention   (C) negligence   (D) demand

3. The governments can manage to import specific items.

    (A) normal   (B) particular   (C) various   (D) common

4. Allergies are the body's natural reaction to any foreign substance.

    (A) introduction   (B) comparison   (C) opinion   (D) response

5. People should remove their bicycles from the hallway.

    (A) add   (B) depart   (C) take away   (D) file

6. The company can save money on insurance benefits from next year.

    (A) advantages   (B) alarms   (C) faults   (D) decisions

7. We must concentrate our efforts on improving our environment.

    (A) overcome   (B) focus   (C) express   (D) complete

8. Many people are likely to prize possessions such as expensive cars or big houses.

    (A) compare   (B) sorrow   (C) ignore   (D) value

9. Firefighters are good at putting out fires.

    (A) extinguishing   (B) observing   (C) recording   (D) firing

10. What is a major product in Canada?

    (A) insignificant   (B) boring   (C) primary   (D) inferior

Unit 10

Fill in a Table

10 Fill in a Table

Overview

■Introduction

Fill in a Table questions ask you to recognize and organize major ideas and important supporting information from across the passage. Then, you should classify them into the appropriate categories. Passages used for this type of question usually have particular types of organization such as compare/contrast, cause/effect, or problem/solution. A five-answer table is worth 3 points, and a seven-answer table is worth 4 points.

■Useful Tips

• Look at the categories of information in the table first.

• Using your scratch paper, make an outline of the passage according to these categories.

• Distinguish between major and minor information in the passage.

• Wrong answers usually include information that is not mentioned in the passage or that is not directly relevant to the categories in the table.

■Question Type

Directions: Complete the table below to summarize information about X discussed in the passage. Match the appropriate statements to the categories with which they are associated. TWO of the answer choices will NOT be used. *This question is worth 3 points.*

Answer Choices
1.
2.
3.
4.
5.
6.
7.

Category 1
•
•
•

Category 2
•
•

Sample iBT Question

The Effects of Weather

It was a brutal winter in eastern Canada this year. It comes as a surprise because last winter was so mild. The cold was bad for many people but good for some.

This year saw record low temperatures for long periods of time. There were nearly 25 days below −20℃. This was worsened by wind. It made temperatures feel even lower. Snow days, when schools close because of snow, actually became "cold days." A few schools had to close because the weather froze pipes, and disabled heating systems. The cold also impacted agriculture. Forty percent of the grapevines had to be replaced in a few areas.

The cold was good for some people, however. Energy suppliers increased sales to match the heating demand. Clothing suppliers were quick to see opportunities also. They were able to sell lots of winter clothing. The cold weather also created ideal conditions for winter sports. This helped tourism and helped people appreciate the cold. Despite its negative effects, people were able to find the upside.

Directions: Complete the table below to summarize information about the positive and negative effects of the cold weather in eastern Canada. Match the appropriate statements to the types of effects with which they are associated. TWO of the answer choices will NOT be ··sed. **This question is worth 3 points.**

Positive Effects	Negative Effects
• • •	• •

Answer Choices

1. Clothing suppliers made profits.

2. Some schools were shut down.

3. Winter sports attracted a lot of foreigners.

4. Energy suppliers benefited from the weather.

5. Agriculture was damaged.

6. All retailers enjoyed increases in sales.

7. The local tourism industry temporarily boomed.

 According to the passage, choices 1, 4, and 7 represent positive effects of the cold weather, and choices 2 and 5 belong to negative effects. Choice 3 includes information that is not mentioned in the passage—"a lot of foreigners." Choice 6 makes an incorrect overgeneralization.

Fill in a Table questions ask you to identify and organize the major ideas of the passage into table categories. They are similar to the Prose Summary questions in that they ask for important information.

Example

Our bodies have an internal clock. We have regular patterns of feeling hungry, sleeping, and waking. The cells in our bodies also repair themselves according to the clock. The clock is located in two places. First, cells in our liver affect when we eat. Second, a small group of cells in our brain controls the body clock. They respond to sunlight so our bodies are on a similar schedule as the sun. If we travel around the world by plane, our bodies adjust themselves to the local time. Of course, this takes a few days, so our bodies experience jet lag.

Directions: Complete the table below by matching TWO of the five answer choices with the functions of liver and brain.

Liver	Brain
• We experience hunger.	• The sun affects us.

Ⓐ We travel around the world.
🅑 The sun affects us.
Ⓒ Our bodies adjust to local time.
🄳 We experience hunger.
Ⓔ We experience jet lag.

An earthquake happens when the surface plates of our earth move. Sometimes the plates rub together. These are called interplate quakes. When there is a sudden slip between the plates, energy is released in the form of shock waves. Both plates shake like a guitar string when it is picked. Quakes can also happen when a crack in the middle of a plate forms. These are called intraplate quakes. They often surprise scientists because they happen in places that they do not ever expect earthquakes.

1. **Directions:** Complete the table below by matching TWO of the five answer choices with the kinds of earthquakes.

Interplate Quakes	Intraplate Quakes
•	•

Ⓐ Both shake like guitar strings.
Ⓑ Plates rub together and slip.
Ⓒ Plates crack in the middle.
Ⓓ Surface plates move.
Ⓔ Energy is released in waves.

The word *nebula* used to refer to anything that was not a planet or a comet. This meant that galaxies and clusters of stars were kinds of nebulas. Nebula should really refer to clouds of dust and gas in space. In fact, the word *nebula* means "cloud" in Latin. One kind of nebula is made of gas. When the hot gas cools, it lets out light. Usually these nebulas are red. Another kind is made of dust. They reflect the light of stars nearby. Another kind of dust nebula blocks the light of something shining behind it.

2. **Directions:** Complete the table below by matching THREE of the five answer choices describing the types of nebulas.

Gaseous Nebula	Dust Nebula
•	• •

  Ⓐ It is a group of planets.
  Ⓑ Starlight reflects off its particles.
  Ⓒ It is anything that is not a comet.
  Ⓓ Red light usually escapes as gases cool.
  Ⓔ It can block light.

The Erie Canal was a water highway that connected the Hudson River in New York to the Great Lakes. Before the canal, travel and trade were difficult. People and goods had to move across land in carts. They sometimes used rivers, but they depended too much on the weather. Travel and trade were expensive, slow, and dangerous. After the canal was built, things got better. First, it cut costs and time in moving goods. This increased trade. Crops that grew in the west could be sold in Europe. Second, people were able to move west and increase the size of the USA more easily.

3. **Directions:** Complete the table below by matching THREE of the five answer choices contrasting the times before and after the Erie Canal was built.

Before	After
•	• •

  Ⓐ The US was wealthy.
  Ⓑ Travel was slow, costly, and perilous.
  Ⓒ It became easier for the Indians to move westward.
  Ⓓ People were able to move west easily to explore.
  Ⓔ It was cheaper to move goods.

Practice with Short Passages

A Read the following passage, and answer the questions.

Black Holes

Time Limit: 50 sec.

Black holes are difficult to see. They neither give off nor reflect light because gravity pulls everything in. The only way physicists know a black hole exists is by seeing the things falling into it. As it enters, the object will be squeezed and give off heat and light. This radiation can be seen. Black holes are sometimes formed by a star that dies. Only large stars can become black holes. The star collapses into its center, where it becomes very small but still has gravity. This is the heart of a black hole. Sometimes a black hole is formed by a large cloud of gas. It shrinks because of the gravity that is created between the gas molecules. The Hubble Telescope took a picture of this kind of black hole. Scientists think that such a black hole is right at the center of our own galaxy.

General Comprehension

1. The word **radiation** in the passage is closest in meaning to

   Ⓐ gas
   Ⓑ energy
   Ⓒ liquid
   Ⓓ dust

2. According to the passage, what is the defining characteristic of a black hole?

   Ⓐ a galaxy
   Ⓑ gas
   Ⓒ a star
   Ⓓ gravity

> **give off (phr)**
> to produce something and send it out; to emit
>
> **reflect (v)**
> to throw back light, heat, sound, etc. from a surface
>
> **squeeze (v)**
> to compress
>
> **collapse (v)**
> to fall inwards and become smaller
>
> **gravity (n)**
> the force that attracts objects in space towards each other
>
> **shrink (v)**
> to get smaller

On the TOEFL Test

3. **Directions:** Complete the table below by matching THREE of the five answer choices with the ways black holes are formed.

First way of formation	Second way of formation
• •	•

   Ⓐ Only large stars can form black holes.
   Ⓑ The center of the hole becomes black.
   Ⓒ A large cloud of gas gets very small.
   Ⓓ The death of a star is a cause.
   Ⓔ The center of a galaxy collapses.

B Read the following passage, and answer the questions.

Sumerian Civilization

Time Limit: 50 sec.

The Sumerians made many advances. They first improved agriculture. They later established a military. The Sumerians are thought to have invented the wheel. It was first used for pottery, which was essential for storing crops. Then it was used for grinding grain. Last, it was then used for farm and military vehicles. Sumerians were the first to use writing and math, even before the Egyptians. This helped them organize their society. These systems were used to keep track of food storage and trade. The military used it to keep track of men, weapons, and supplies. They were the first to study the stars and sun in a serious way. It helped them tell time so they could decide when to plant crops. A way of reading the stars also helped them plan when to attack their enemies. They believed that the stars could speak of their success or failure.

General Comprehension

1. The word advances in the passage is closest in meaning to

- (A) merits
- (B) innovations
- (C) approaches
- (D) inventions

2. According to the passage, what did the Sumerians believe the stars could tell?

- (A) The stars could tell how to keep track of men.
- (B) The stars could tell how to grind grain.
- (C) The stars could tell how to store food for winter.
- (D) The stars could tell how to proceed with a battle.

pottery (n)
the skill of making pots and dishes out of clay

grind (v)
to smash

keep track of (phr)
to monitor

storage (n)
the keeping of food

On the TOEFL Test

3. Directions: Complete the table below by matching THREE of the five answer choices with the ways advances supported agriculture and the military.

Agriculture	Military
• •	•

- (A) They were the first to invent the wheel.
- (B) The Sumerians were the first to use writing.
- (C) The stars told when it was time to plant.
- (D) The wheel was used for carts in battle.
- (E) Writing kept track of food storage.

Read the following passage, and answer the questions.

Termite Colony

Time Limit: 50 sec.

Termites live in large groups called colonies. There can be millions of these insects living together. The colony survives by cooperation between the different kinds of termites. Each nest has at least one king and queen. Their role is to produce more termites, not to direct the life of the colony. A termite queen can lay thousands of eggs each day. Its body can grow up to ten centimeters with eggs. The eggs grow into young termites called nymphs. Worker termites are blind. They are in charge of looking for food, feeding soldiers and young termites, and taking care of the nest. Soldier termites must defend the nest. Their heads grow a protective covering. However, their jaws are so large they must be fed by worker termites. With this type of organization, the colony is able to achieve more than a single individual ever could.

General Comprehension

1. The word cooperation in the passage is closest in meaning to

   (A) corroboration
   (B) cohabitation
   (C) conflation
   (D) collaboration

2. The word their in the passage refers to

   (A) soldier termites
   (B) the king and queen
   (C) nymphs
   (D) worker termites

colony (n)
a group of plants or animals that live together or grow in the same place

cooperation (n)
working together

be in charge of (phr)
be responsible for

On the TOEFL Test

3. **Directions:** Complete the table below by matching FOUR of the five answer choices with the kinds of termites and their roles.

Queen	Soldier	Worker
•	•	• •

   (A) They have large jaws.
   (B) They lay eggs.
   (C) They cannot see.
   (D) They look for food.
   (E) They have large bodies.

D Read the following passage, and answer the questions.

The Theory of Continental Drift

Time Limit: 50 sec.

Continental drift is an old theory of geology. It is older than the theory of plate tectonics. Early scientists saw that the different land masses had shapes that fit together. They also noticed that their geologies were similar. Africa and South America had many similarities. The same types of fossils were found in both places. Even today there is a type of earthworm that is found in both places. Scientists learned that at one time all the land was stuck together. The great land mass was named "Pangaea." The land moved apart over time. The problem was to explain how the land masses moved apart. Scientists could not understand how whole continents could move through the rock on the sea floor. Eventually, they learned that even the sea floor spreads in certain places. This gave rise to the idea of floating plates and plate tectonics.

General Comprehension

1. **The phrase gave rise to in the passage is closest in meaning to**
    (A) began
    (B) lifted
    (C) spread
    (D) moved

2. **According to the passage, why did the idea of continental drift not work?**
    (A) Scientists found fossils of earthworms in South America.
    (B) Scientists did not know why continents stopped moving.
    (C) Scientists could not explain how continents could move through rock.
    (D) Scientists believed that the land was stuck together in places.

theory (n)
a formal idea or set of ideas that is intended to explain something

drift (n)
a slow, steady movement from one place to another

stuck (a)
fixed in one place

eventually (ad)
in the end

float (v)
to move slowly on the water or in the air

On the TOEFL Test

3. **Directions:** Complete the table below by matching FOUR of the five answer choices that contrast continental drift with plate tectonics.

Continental Drift	Plate Tectonics
• •	• •

(A) Continents do not move.
(B) Continents had some similar geology.
(C) The sea floor has spread zones.
(D) Plates float over the earth's core.
(E) Continents had shapes that seemed to fit together.

Practice with Long Passages

A Read the following passage, and answer the question.

Man's Perception of the Universe

Time Limit: 1 min. 40 sec.

Man has been watching the night sky for thousands of years. It has held his imagination and also has served in his search for knowledge.

Our ancestors first noticed that the stars moved across the sky but kept the same patterns. They grouped the stars into familiar shapes. These shapes guided man in his travels and told him when to plant his crops. These shapes also were the focus of stories and beliefs. For hundreds of years, people believed that the earth and man were the center of the universe. In 1543, Copernicus proved that this was wrong. In fact, the earth travels around the sun. It opened up the way for a deeper understanding of the universe. Galileo later used telescopes to learn more about the sun and the planets.

Finally, the idea of gravity made the universe come together. This was thanks to Isaac Newton. Gravity makes a small object move towards a large one. It explained how our solar system was formed. It explains how the planets move around the sun. It explains how comets move the way they do around our solar system. Our understanding of gravity helps us explore space.

Directions: Complete the table below by matching FIVE of the seven answer choices with the impact of Copernicus and Newton.

Copernicus
-
-

Newton
-
-
-

Ⓐ Gravity explains why small objects move towards larger ones.
Ⓑ The generation of our solar system can be explained.
Ⓒ The earth orbits the sun.
Ⓓ Telescopes were used to survey the objects in the sky.
Ⓔ Man is not at the center of the universe.
Ⓕ Man had many beliefs and stories about the universe.
Ⓖ Comets move around the solar system because of gravity.

perception (n)
understanding

search (n)
an attempt to find someone or something

gravity (n)
the force that pulls two objects together

comet (n)
a bright object with a long tail that travels around the sun

explore (v)
to travel around a place to learn about it

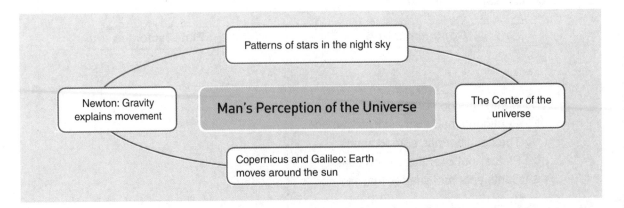

B Read the following passage, and answer the question.

Lewis and Clark and the Louisiana Purchase

Time Limit: 1 min. 50 sec.

President Jefferson bought the land west of the Mississippi from Napoleon, the ruler of France, in 1803. This created several challenges for the young country at the time, but the advantages were great.

Many people did not like the idea at the time. Some thought that "buying" from the French was not necessary. It could be taken because the French had no military power in North America. Some did not believe the president had the power to buy land. Others felt that buying this land would upset their Spanish neighbors. Yet others still worried that new states would take power away from the old states.

Despite the concerns, the purchase doubled the country's land in 1803. At first, however, President Jefferson and the rest of America knew almost nothing about this new land. They did not know what resources could be used. They were to learn that it had abundant resources. Vast amounts of land could be used for farming. There were minerals in the earth to be mined. Most importantly, there were great rivers that would help the economy grow. The president sent a team, headed by Lewis and Clark, to explore the land. They traveled over eight thousand miles in twenty-eight months. The team made many maps and took many notes. This information was used to plan the future of the United States.

Directions: Complete the table below by matching FIVE of the seven answer choices with the pros and cons of the Louisiana Purchase.

Pros
- •
- •

Cons
- •
- •
- •

- (A) Spain was a power to fear.
- (B) There was a supply of mineral resources.
- (C) The exploration team had many maps.
- (D) There was vast land to explore.
- (E) There was no need to buy from the French.
- (F) New states would shift the balance of power.
- (G) There were rivers to support the economy.

○ **challenge (n)**
a difficulty

○ **upset (v)**
to make someone unhappy

○ **purchase (n)**
a thing that was bought

○ **double (v)**
to make something twice the size

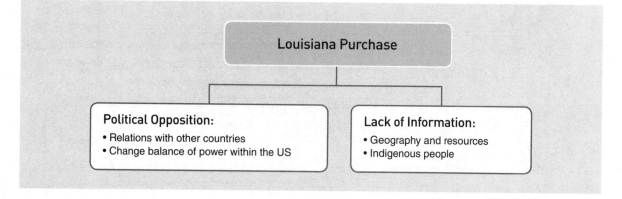

Read the following passage, and answer the question.

The Opossum

Time Limit: 1 min. 40 sec.

Marsupials are mammals that have a pouch. The female keeps its babies in the pouch until they are old enough to live outside the pouch. The only marsupial in North America is the opossum.

The opossum is about the size of a large cat. Its fur is grey, and it has a pink nose, feet, and tail. They have large, black eyes for seeing at night when they move around the most. Even though they have fifty very sharp teeth, they are very gentle animals. They try to avoid any kind of fight.

Opossums are very adaptable. They can live in many places, including trees and underground. They eat all kinds of food, both plants and animals. They eat insects, mice, small snakes, grass, leaves, and berries.

The opossum have a variety of defenses. They are mostly immune to snake poison. They usually do not get rabies, a nasty disease, because of the temperature of their blood. Their most famous defense is to play dead. Because most animals do not eat dead things, it is a good defense. The opossum will turn on its back and show its teeth. It will produce a bad smell near its tail. Usually the other animal will go away.

Directions: Complete the table below by matching FIVE of the seven answer choices with the adaptability and defenses of opossums.

Adaptability
-
-

Defenses
-
-
-

Ⓐ They have a variety of homes.
Ⓑ Snake poison does not usually affect them.
Ⓒ Their blood temperature prevents rabies.
Ⓓ Opossums are as large as cats.
Ⓔ They avoid fights.
Ⓕ Opossums can eat many different things.
Ⓖ They play dead.

mammal (n)
any animal that gives birth to live babies and feeds its young on milk

pouch (n)
a pocket

adaptable (a)
able to change in order to deal with new situations

immune (a)
that cannot catch a particular disease

rabies (n)
a deadly viral disease that makes one crazy

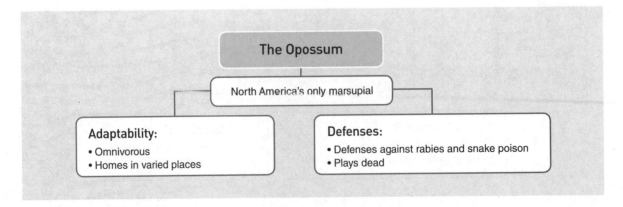

D Read the following passage, and answer the question.

The Mariana Trench
Time Limit: 1 min. 30 sec.

Trenches are long holes. They are formed when one tectonic plate slides under another. There are 22 great trenches under the sea. Three are in the Atlantic, and one is in the Indian Ocean. Eighteen are in the Pacific Ocean. The greatest is called the Mariana Trench. It is located in the Pacific Ocean not far from Japan.

The Mariana Trench is the deepest place on Earth. It is 542km long and 69km wide. It is 11,033 meters deep. The tallest mountain on earth still would not reach the top if it were inside. There would still be two kilometers of water above it.

The bottom is very different from near the surface. Down below, the pressure is one thousand times that of the surface. Man could not survive without a submarine. It is impossible to believe that anything could live in those conditions. But in fact, fish and shrimp do live at the bottom of the trench.

The water at the bottom is not heated by the sun. It does not freeze because of cracks that cut into the earth's crust. Heat comes out at 300 degrees Celsius. At the surface, the water is comparatively clear. Down below, the water is filled with the remains of tiny skeletons and skins of animals that once lived and also bacteria. This mix forms a thick mix.

Directions: Complete the table below by matching FIVE of the seven answer choices that describe the water of the trench.

Water at the Bottom
-
-
-

Water at the Surface
-
-

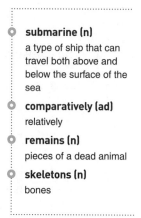

- submarine (n)
  a type of ship that can travel both above and below the surface of the sea
- comparatively (ad)
  relatively
- remains (n)
  pieces of a dead animal
- skeletons (n)
  bones

Ⓐ Animal particles change the texture.
Ⓑ Water is heated by the sun.
Ⓒ There are two kilometers of water above the bottom.
Ⓓ Animals are not capable of withstanding the pressure.
Ⓔ The water is clearer.
Ⓕ The pressure is enormous.
Ⓖ Water does not freeze.

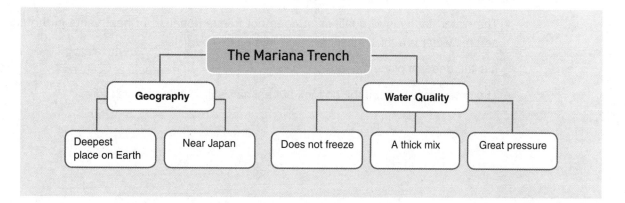

Building Summary Skills

Put the following sentences in order to make appropriate summaries based on the long passages you worked on earlier. The first sentence is already provided.

1. **Man's Perception of the Universe**

   Man has tried to understand the night sky for a long time, and he has created many stories about it.

   _____ Newton came upon the idea of gravity.

   _____ For years, it was believed that man was the center of the universe.

   _____ Copernicus and Galileo showed us information to the contrary.

   _____ This helped explain the motion of all the objects in our universe.

2. **Lewis and Clark and the Louisiana Purchase**

   The Louisiana Purchase was a great addition to the United States, but it posed a few challenges.

   _____ Some were concerned about relations with other countries, and others were concerned about how it would affect political power in the U.S.

   _____ Politically, many people did not like the idea.

   _____ After buying the land, information about the people, the resources, and the rivers was needed to make use of it.

3. **The Opossum**

   Opossums are the only marsupials in North America.

   _____ Opossums have a number of defenses.

   _____ They are adaptable in that they are omnivores and can find a home in lots of places.

   _____ They are mostly immune to rabies and snake poison, and they can also play dead.

   _____ They are mostly nocturnal and, despite having many teeth, are very gentle.

4. **The Mariana Trench**

   The Mariana Trench is a long hole at the bottom of the sea.

   _____ The water has unique qualities: it does not freeze because of heat vents in the earth, and the water is a thick mix of bacteria and animal particles.

   _____ It is the deepest place on earth.

   _____ The pressure is huge at the bottom, but animals still manage to live there.

B Fill in the blanks with suitable words or phrases to complete the following summaries. Do not look at the previous page until you are finished.

1. **Man's Perception of the Universe**

Man has tried to understand the (1)_____ for a long time, and he has created many (2)_____ about it. For years, it was believed that man was the (3)_____ of the universe. (4)_____ and (5)_____ showed us information to the contrary. (6)_____ came upon the idea of (7)_____. This helped explain the (8)_____ of all the objects in our universe.

2. **Lewis and Clark and the Louisiana Purchase**

The (1)_____ was a great addition to the United States, but it posed a few (2)_____. Politically, many people did not (3)_____ the idea. Some were concerned about (4)_____ with other countries, and others were concerned about how it would affect (5)_____ power in the U.S. After (6)_____ the land, information about the people, the (7)_____, and the rivers was needed to (8)_____ it.

3. **The Opossum**

Opossums are the only (1)_____ in (2)_____. They are mostly (3)_____ and, despite having many teeth, are very (4)_____. They are adaptable in that they are (5)_____ and can find a home in lots of places. Opossums have a number of (6)_____. They are mostly (7)_____ to rabies and snake poison, and they can also (8)_____.

4. **The Mariana Trench**

The Mariana Trench is a long (1)_____ at the (2)_____ of the sea. It is the (3)_____ place on earth. The pressure is huge at the bottom, but (4)_____ still manage to live there. The water has unique (5)_____: it does not (6)_____ because of (7)_____ in the earth, and the water is a thick mix of (8)_____ and animal particles.

1. **The word encircle in the passage is closest in meaning to**

   (A) hide   (B) divide

   (C) follow   (D) surround

2. **The word cling in the passage is closest in meaning to**

   (A) stick   (B) throw

   (C) move   (D) drag

3. **All of the following are mentioned in paragraph 2 EXCEPT:**

   (A) sun   (B) asteroid

   (C) gas   (D) dust

4. **The word this in the passage refers to**

   (A) having more than one moon

   (B) being made of rock or metal elements

   (C) moving around the sun

   (D) being more like gas and ice

5. **According to paragraph 4, what happens when an asteroid burns near our planet?**

   (A) It becomes dust.

   (B) It crashes into other asteroids.

   (C) We see it as a shooting star.

   (D) We try to shoot it down.

6. **Directions:** Complete the table below by matching FIVE of the seven answer choices that describe the features of the solar system. TWO of the answer choices will NOT be used. *This question is worth 3 points.*

   Answer Choices

   (A) They have metal elements.
   (B) They avoid our planet.
   (C) They can have moons.
   (D) They are no bigger than 10km across.
   (E) They have gaseous elements.
   (F) They have tails.
   (G) They are made of rock.

   Planets
   -
   -
   -

   Asteroids
   -
   -

The Solar System

The solar system is made up of the objects that move around our sun in a regular path. Things were not always this way. The sun and the objects that encircle it started out in a very different form.

It is believed that our solar system began as a large cloud of gas and dust. The cloud had a round shape and spun slowly. The spinning caused the gas and dust to flatten into a large disc. The mass of gas and dust at the center became the sun. The gas and dust were pulled together by gravity so that nuclear reactions started. The rest of the dust and gas outside of this moved so slowly that it started to cling together in places. Eventually, enough material stuck together to form planets.

There are many different objects in our solar system. Of course, there are planets. Each one is unique. Some planets are made of rock or metal elements. Mercury, Venus, Earth, and Mars are like this. Other planets are more like gas and ice. Jupiter, Saturn, and the others are like this. The planets have moons—sometimes more than one.

Our solar system has a major asteroid belt. An asteroid is basically a rock. The largest is about 10km across. Huge numbers of these rocks circle the sun between Mars and Jupiter. Sometimes the asteroids crash into each other and move towards Earth. When they pass near our planet, they heat up and burn. We see them as shooting stars.

Lastly, there are comets which are made of ice and gas. They also go around the sun but not with a normal path. When they are near the sun, they start to melt and form a tail. Far from the sun, where space is cold, the comets remain frozen solid.

7. **According to paragraph 2, what is the nature of the top layer of the Earth?**

    Ⓐ It is very hot at the center.
    Ⓑ It is fragmented into about 10 different plates.
    Ⓒ It is heated by forces at the center of the Earth.
    Ⓓ It moves when the seasons change.

8. **The word divergent in the passage is closest in meaning to**

    Ⓐ separating   Ⓑ moving
    Ⓒ squeezing   Ⓓ shaking

9. **In paragraph 3, why does the author mention plates can move in three different ways?**

    Ⓐ To describe what plates are
    Ⓑ To compare the movements of plates
    Ⓒ To set up a comparison of plate movement
    Ⓓ To contrast the Himalayas with the Andes

10. **The word shift in the passage is closest in meaning to**

    Ⓐ jump   Ⓑ break
    Ⓒ move   Ⓓ shake

11. **The word it in the passage refers to**

    Ⓐ liquid   Ⓑ earth's core
    Ⓒ rock   Ⓓ rift

12. **Directions:** Complete the table below by matching FIVE of the seven answer choices below that describe different types of plate boundaries. TWO of the answer choices will NOT be used. *This question is worth 3 points.*

Answer Choices

    Ⓐ The liquid core fills the space.
    Ⓑ They move towards each other.
    Ⓒ They slide against each other.
    Ⓓ One plate goes below another.
    Ⓔ The youngest mountains in the world form this way.
    Ⓕ They move apart.
    Ⓖ This happens at the ocean floor.

Convergent
-
-

Transform
-
-

Divergent
-

Plate Tectonic Theory

Plate tectonics is a theory of geology. It explains how the surface of the earth moves. It states that the surface of the earth is made of floating plates that move.

The earth is made of several different layers. The top layer is solid but broken into about ten different plates. They are about one hundred kilometers thick. These plates float on top of the layer below, which is liquid. The heat of the lower layer forces the plates to move. As the plates move, they create earthquakes, volcanoes, mountains, and trenches in the ocean along their edges.

Plates can move in three different ways. They can move apart. This is called a divergent boundary. There are a few such places at the ocean floor. When plates move this way, the liquid in the earth's core moves up to fill in the space, called a rift. The rock closest to the rift is younger than the rock further away from it. Rifts usually spread about 2cm per year. A transform boundary happens when two plates move side to side. This happens a lot in California. The Pacific Plate rubs against the North American Plate for nearly 1,300km. They shift at 0.6cm per year. It forms the San Andreas Fault, which is responsible for many earthquakes. Convergent boundaries form when two plates move towards each other. Usually one plate goes below the other. When this happens, the top plate rises up. Mountains can form this way. The Himalaya Mountains were formed this way. It is one of the youngest mountain ranges in the world. The plate underneath India continues to move into the plate under Tibet. These great mountains rise about 5mm each year.

Vocabulary Review

Choose the word with the closest meaning to each underlined word or phrase.

1. This kind of sand is made by grinding glass.
   - (A) setting
   - (B) mixing
   - (C) smashing
   - (D) shaving

2. The air environment plays a huge role in our health.
   - (A) material
   - (B) junk
   - (C) interest
   - (D) part

3. The director is in charge of the export division.
   - (A) keeps out of
   - (B) gets rid of
   - (C) is responsible for
   - (D) comes around

4. The noble is a full of imagination.
   - (A) disgrace
   - (B) dreams
   - (C) relationship
   - (D) journey

5. Almost every earth scientist agrees on the theory of continental drift.
   - (A) trouble
   - (B) beginning
   - (C) habit
   - (D) slow movement

6. Happiness is not achieved according to one's performance.
   - (A) failed
   - (B) intended
   - (C) accomplished
   - (D) determined

7. The new device squeezes the package under its bar.
   - (A) spreads
   - (B) blows
   - (C) succeeds
   - (D) compresses

8. There are many packaging boxes, bags, and pouches.
   - (A) sticks
   - (B) pockets
   - (C) pieces
   - (D) covers

9. The big pictures were stuck everywhere on the walls.
   - (A) attached
   - (B) loose
   - (C) relaxed
   - (D) completed

10. The accountant should keep track of the company's expenses.
    - (A) forget
    - (B) leave
    - (C) calculate
    - (D) monitor

This part provides lists of important vocabulary words in each unit. They are essential words for understanding any academic texts. Many of the words are listed with their derivative forms so that students can expand their vocabulary in an effective way. These lists can be used as homework assignments.

Vocabulary Wrap-up

→

Unit **1** • Vocabulary

⊙ Step A

☐ muscle	☐ nutritious	☐ prey	☐ physical
☐ brutal	☐ disastrous	☐ repair	☐ link
☐ illegal	☐ affect	☐ vanish	☐ shrink
☐ diagnose	☐ retire	☐ exotic	☐ worsen
☐ disable	☐ impact	☐ agriculture	☐ segment

⊙ Step B

Noun	Verb	Adjective	Adverb
☐ access	☐ access	☐ accessible	☐ accessibly
☐ affordability	☐ afford	☐ affordable	☐ affordably
☐ appreciation	☐ appreciate	☐ appreciative	☐ appreciatively
☐ attraction	☐ attract	☐ attractive	☐ attractively
☐ condensation	☐ condense	☐ condensed	
☐ decoration	☐ decorate	☐ decorative	☐ decoratively
☐ density	☐ densify	☐ dense	☐ densely
☐ detection	☐ detect	☐ detective	☐ detectively
☐ electricity	☐ electrify	☐ electric	☐ electrically
☐ courage	☐ encourage	☐ courageous	☐ courageously
☐ endangerment	☐ endanger	☐ endangered	
☐ evolution	☐ evolve	☐ evolutionary	☐ evolutionarily
☐ extremity		☐ extreme	☐ extremely
☐ identity	☐ identify	☐ identifiable	☐ identifiably
☐ improvement	☐ improve	☐ improving	☐ improvingly
☐ innovation	☐ innovate	☐ innovative	☐ innovatively
☐ invention	☐ invent	☐ inventive	☐ inventively
☐ pollution	☐ pollute	☐ polluted	
☐ preservation	☐ preserve	☐ preservative	
☐ sustenance	☐ sustain	☐ sustainable	

Unit 2 • Reference

⦿ Step A

- [ ] aim
- [ ] release
- [ ] hire
- [ ] publish
- [ ] concept

- [ ] persist
- [ ] divorce
- [ ] dine
- [ ] modernize
- [ ] crucial

- [ ] aware of
- [ ] recall
- [ ] customer
- [ ] trend
- [ ] financial

- [ ] knowingly
- [ ] economy
- [ ] intense
- [ ] continent
- [ ] loan

⦿ Step B

Noun	Verb	Adjective	Adverb
☐ achievement	☐ achieve	☐ achievable	
☐ assertion	☐ assert	☐ assertive	☐ assertively
☐ civilization	☐ civilize	☐ civilized	
☐ comparison	☐ compare	☐ comparative	☐ comparatively
☐ complaint	☐ complain	☐ complaining	☐ complainingly
☐ competition	☐ compete	☐ competitive	☐ competitively
☐ conquest	☐ conquer	☐ conquerable	
☐ depression	☐ depress	☐ depressing	☐ depressingly
☐ education	☐ educate	☐ educative	
☐ inclusion	☐ include	☐ inclusive	☐ inclusively
☐ inflation	☐ inflate	☐ inflated	
☐ influence	☐ influence	☐ influential	☐ influentially
☐ investment	☐ invest	☐ investable	
☐ maintenance	☐ maintain	☐ maintainable	
☐ measurement	☐ measure	☐ measurable	☐ measurably
☐ participation	☐ participate	☐ participatory / -tive	☐ participatively
☐ reflection	☐ reflect	☐ reflective	☐ reflectively
☐ reliability	☐ rely	☐ reliable	☐ reliably
☐ sacrifice	☐ sacrifice	☐ sacrificial	☐ sacrificially
☐ vision	☐ visualize	☐ visual	☐ visually

Unit 3 • Factual Information

⊙ Step A

☐ ancestor   ☐ volunteer   ☐ innocent   ☐ guilty

☐ flexible   ☐ method   ☐ expose   ☐ destination

☐ search for   ☐ address   ☐ privileged   ☐ mandate

☐ launch   ☐ permanent   ☐ evidence   ☐ meteoroid

☐ dissolve   ☐ cave   ☐ copper   ☐ instrument

☐ research   ☐ acid   ☐ architecture   ☐ astronaut

⊙ Step B

Noun	Verb	Adjective	Adverb
☐ announcement	☐ announce	☐ announcing	☐ announcingly
☐ apology	☐ apologize	☐ apologetic	☐ apologetically
☐ breath	☐ breathe	☐ breathing	☐ breathingly
☐ celebration	☐ celebrate	☐ celebratory	
☐ collection	☐ collect	☐ collective	☐ collectively
☐ composition	☐ compose	☐ compositional	☐ compositionally
☐ distribution	☐ distribute	☐ distributive	☐ distributively
☐ exploration	☐ explore	☐ explorative	☐ exploratively
☐ explosion	☐ explode	☐ explosive	☐ explosively
☐ liberation	☐ liberate	☐ liberated / -ting	☐ liberatingly
☐ performance	☐ perform	☐ performative	☐ performatively
☐ population	☐ populate	☐ populous	☐ populously
☐ protection	☐ protect	☐ protective	☐ protectively
☐ public	☐ publicize	☐ public	☐ publicly
☐ recovery	☐ recover	☐ recoverable	☐ recoverably
☐ reference	☐ refer	☐ referential	☐ referentially
☐ solution	☐ solve	☐ soluble	☐ solubly
☐ tragedy		☐ tragic	☐ tragically
☐ translation	☐ translate	☐ translatable	

Unit 4 • Negative Factual Information

⊙ Step A

- ☐ nomad
- ☐ planet
- ☐ purpose
- ☐ feature
- ☐ formula

- ☐ expert
- ☐ laboratory
- ☐ liquid
- ☐ presence
- ☐ essential

- ☐ submerged
- ☐ climate
- ☐ ensure
- ☐ basin
- ☐ efficient

- ☐ marine
- ☐ plantation
- ☐ consequently
- ☐ perspective
- ☐ eventually

⊙ Step B

Noun	Verb	Adjective	Adverb
☐ accomplishment	☐ accomplish	☐ accomplished	
☐ amusement	☐ amuse	☐ amusing / -sed	☐ amusingly / -sedly
☐ approximation	☐ approximate	☐ approximate	☐ approximately
☐ behavior	☐ behave	☐ behavioral	☐ behaviorally
☐ decrease	☐ decrease	☐ decreasing	☐ decreasingly
☐ destruction	☐ destroy	☐ destructive	☐ destructively
☐ equipment	☐ equip	☐ equipped	
☐ engagement	☐ engage	☐ engaged	
☐ equality	☐ equalize	☐ equal	☐ equally
☐ expansion	☐ expand	☐ expansive	☐ expansively
☐ flatness	☐ flatten	☐ flattening	
☐ flexibility	☐ flex	☐ flexible	☐ flexibly
☐ fluorescence	☐ fluoresce	☐ fluorescent	☐ fluorescently
☐ height	☐ heighten	☐ high	☐ high /-ly
☐ involvement	☐ involve	☐ involved	
☐ liquid	☐ liquidize	☐ liquid	☐ liquidly
☐ mistake	☐ mistake	☐ mistaken	☐ mistakenly
☐ normality	☐ normalize	☐ normal	☐ normally
☐ perfection	☐ perfect	☐ perfect	☐ perfectly
☐ threat	☐ threaten	☐ threatening	☐ threateningly

Unit **5** • Sentence Simplification

⦿ Step A

☐ hereditary ☐ environment ☐ replicate ☐ graduation

☐ debris ☐ lumber ☐ criminal ☐ cruel

☐ trait ☐ offspring ☐ unique ☐ aspect

☐ tablet ☐ plunder ☐ decay ☐ unconscious

☐ tumor ☐ barren ☐ carnivorous ☐ plunder

⦿ Step B

Noun	Verb	Adjective	Adverb
☐ contamination	☐ contaminate	☐ contaminative	☐ contaminatively
☐ conviction	☐ convince	☐ convincing	☐ convincingly
☐ deterrence	☐ deter	☐ deterrent	☐ deterrently
☐ donation	☐ donate	☐ donative	☐ donatively
☐ emphasis	☐ emphasize	☐ emphatic	☐ emphatically
☐ establishment	☐ establish	☐ established	
☐ injury	☐ injure	☐ injurious	☐ injuriously
☐ inspiration	☐ inspire	☐ inspirational	☐ inspirationally
☐ legality	☐ legalize	☐ legal	☐ legally
☐ moisture	☐ moisten	☐ moist	☐ moistly
☐ mutation	☐ mutate	☐ mutational	☐ mutationally
☐ prediction	☐ predict	☐ predictable	☐ predictably
☐ reduction	☐ reduce	☐ reducible	☐ reducibly
☐ reformation	☐ reform	☐ reformative	☐ reformatively
☐ response	☐ respond	☐ responsive	☐ responsively
☐ rotation	☐ rotate	☐ rotational	☐ rotationally
☐ selection	☐ select	☐ selective	☐ selectively
☐ suffocation	☐ suffocate	☐ suffocating / -tive	☐ suffocatingly
☐ suspicion	☐ suspect	☐ suspicious	☐ suspiciously
☐ transfer	☐ transfer	☐ transferable	☐ transferably

Unit **6** • **Rhetorical Purpose**

⊙ Step A

☐ flesh	☐ damp	☐ anxiety	☐ disorder
☐ entire	☐ stretch	☐ wreck	☐ sociolinguist
☐ fluid	☐ gender	☐ outgoing	☐ personality
☐ whereas	☐ aggressive	☐ oracle	☐ feat
☐ tend	☐ pollinate	☐ decade	☐ forensics
☐ psychology	☐ varied	☐ altitude	☐ avalanche
☐ geographical	☐ motion	☐ ruin	☐ chemical

⊙ Step B

Noun	Verb	Adjective	Adverb
☐ annoyance	☐ annoy	☐ annoying / -yed	☐ annoyingly
☐ argument	☐ argue	☐ arguable	☐ arguably
☐ determination	☐ determine	☐ determinative	☐ determinatively
☐ divination	☐ divine	☐ divine / -natory	☐ divinely
☐ embarrassment	☐ embarrass	☐ embarrassing	☐ embarrassingly
☐ generation	☐ generate	☐ generative	☐ generatively
☐ guidance	☐ guide	☐ guidable	
☐ instruction	☐ instruct	☐ instructive	☐ instructively
☐ invasion	☐ invade	☐ invasive	☐ invasively
☐ precision		☐ precise	☐ precisely
☐ pronunciation	☐ pronounce	☐ pronounceable	
☐ supervision	☐ supervise	☐ supervisory	
☐ type	☐ typify	☐ typical	☐ typically

Unit **7** • Inference

Unit **8** • **Insert Text**

◉ Step A

☐ military	☐ media	☐ conflict	☐ independent
☐ complex	☐ delicate	☐ incredible	☐ similar
☐ spread	☐ strict	☐ challenging	☐ obese
☐ budget	☐ flaw	☐ heal	☐ athlete
☐ defect	☐ clone	☐ geology	☐ humanitarian
☐ mental	☐ entomb	☐ warrior	☐ drain
☐ dope	☐ emotional	☐ jury	☐ mystique
☐ myth	☐ prefix	☐ archery	☐ bully
☐ capitalism	☐ charity	☐ dean	☐ leather
☐ lung	☐ element	☐ poet	☐ twist

◉ Step B

Noun	Verb	Adjective	Adverb
☐ advertisement	☐ advertise	☐ advertising	☐ advertisingly
☐ anger	☐ anger	☐ angry	☐ angrily
☐ delivery	☐ deliver	☐ deliverable	
☐ escape	☐ escape	☐ escaping / -ped	☐ escapingly
☐ femininity	☐ feminize	☐ feminine	☐ femininely
☐ insistence	☐ insist	☐ insistent	☐ insistently
☐ origination	☐ originate	☐ original	☐ originally
☐ production	☐ produce	☐ productive	☐ productively
☐ profession	☐ professionalize	☐ professional	☐ professionally
☐ rejection	☐ reject	☐ rejective	☐ rejectively
☐ relief	☐ relieve	☐ relievable	☐ relievably
☐ uniformity	☐ uniform	☐ uniform	☐ uniformly

Unit 9 • Prose Summary

⊙ Step A

☐ drunk	☐ property	☐ victim	☐ sue
☐ advance	☐ nutrient	☐ manure	☐ major
☐ throat	☐ force	☐ afford	☐ fair
☐ ideally	☐ fragile	☐ artificial	☐ border
☐ tissue	☐ lack	☐ curve	☐ spot
☐ mining	☐ surface	☐ extinguish	☐ crack
☐ solid	☐ selfish	☐ soil	☐ weed
☐ brief	☐ credit	☐ economist	☐ labor
☐ logical	☐ minor	☐ secure	☐ theory
☐ compost	☐ insomnia	☐ jurisprudence	☐ liability
☐ narcolepsy	☐ organic	☐ pesticide	☐ scurvy

⊙ Step B

Noun	Verb	Adjective	Adverb
☐ adaptability	☐ adapt	☐ adaptable	☐ adaptably
☐ adjustment	☐ adjust	☐ adjustable / -tive	☐ adjustably
☐ blood	☐ bleed	☐ bleeding	☐ bleedingly
☐ concentration	☐ concentrate	☐ concentrative	☐ concentratively
☐ fertility / -lization	☐ fertilize	☐ fertile	☐ fertilely
☐ reaction	☐ react	☐ reactive	☐ reactively
☐ removal	☐ remove	☐ removable	☐ removably
☐ specification	☐ specify	☐ specific	☐ specifically
☐ summarization	☐ summarize	☐ summary	☐ summarily

Unit 10 • Fill in a Table

⊙ Step A

☐ give off	☐ squeeze	☐ gravity	☐ benefit
☐ pottery	☐ grind	☐ drift	☐ float
☐ comet	☐ upset	☐ double	☐ pouch
☐ rabies	☐ submarine	☐ skeleton	☐ comparatively
☐ remains	☐ spin	☐ awareness	☐ core
☐ intelligence	☐ nuclear	☐ shift	☐ similarity
☐ abundant	☐ asteroid	☐ cling to	☐ cluster
☐ crust	☐ encircle	☐ glacier	☐ jet lag
☐ mammal	☐ marsupial	☐ nebula	☐ opossum
☐ physicist	☐ solar	☐ termite	☐ trench

⊙ Step B

Noun	Verb	Adjective	Adverb
☐ collapse	☐ collapse	☐ collapsible	☐ collapsibly
☐ colony	☐ colonize	☐ colonial	☐ colonially
☐ convergence	☐ converge	☐ convergent	☐ convergently
☐ cooperation	☐ cooperate	☐ cooperative	☐ cooperatively
☐ divergence	☐ diverge	☐ divergent	☐ divergently
☐ emission	☐ emit	☐ emissive	☐ emissively
☐ immunization	☐ immunize	☐ immune	
☐ internalization	☐ internalize	☐ internal	☐ internally
☐ location	☐ locate	☐ locatable	
☐ orbit	☐ orbit	☐ orbital	☐ orbitally
☐ perception	☐ perceive	☐ perceptive	☐ perceptively
☐ purchase	☐ purchase	☐ purchasable	
☐ radiation	☐ radiate	☐ radiate	☐ radiately
☐ storage	☐ store	☐ storable	☐ storably

Reading Section **Directions**

This section measures your ability to understand academic passages in English. It consists of three passages and a set of questions about each of them.

Most questions are worth 1 point but the last question in each passage is worth more than 1 point. The directions indicate how many points you may receive.

Some passages include <u>underlined</u> words or phrases in shade. You can see a definition or an explanation at the end of the passage.

While working on the questions, you can go to the next question by clicking **Next**. You may skip questions and go back to them later. If you want to return to previous questions, click on **Back**. You can click on **Review** at any time and the review screen will show you which questions you have answered and which you have not answered. From this review screen, you may go directly to any question you have already seen in the Reading section.

You may now begin the Reading section. You will read 3 passages. You will have 54 minutes to read the passages and answer the questions.

Actual Test

1. **According to paragraph 1, what is the best way of identifying a white-tail deer?**

   Ⓐ It is the most numerous of deer species in North America.
   Ⓑ It runs away from humans.
   Ⓒ It lifts its tail, showing its white underside.
   Ⓓ It weighs about 110 kilograms.

2. **According to the passage, white-tail deer live in all of the following EXCEPT:**

   Ⓐ Finland
   Ⓑ the continental United States
   Ⓒ South America
   Ⓓ Alaska

3. **Look at the four squares [■] that indicate where the following sentence can be added to the passage.**

   As a result, the fawn is safe while its mother looks for food.

   Where would the sentence best fit?

   Click on a square [■] to add the sentence to the passage.

The White-tail and Black-tail Deer

Of all of North America's large animals, the most numerous is the white-tail deer. This species of deer is known by its habit of raising and flopping its tail over its back, revealing its white underside and buttocks. People often observe this telltale marking as the deer runs away from them. When the tail is down, it is brown with a white fringe. Varying with the seasons, the color of the white-tail deer is reddish in summer and grayish in winter. An adult male, known as a buck, grows to over a meter at shoulder height and weighs about 110 kilograms. Males grow antlers, which occasionally become entangled with those of another male, dooming each animal to a slow death.

Also known as the Virginia deer, the white-tail deer inhabits most of the continental United States as well as southern Canada, Mexico, Central America, and the northern countries of South America. It has also been introduced into northern Europe, especially in Finland.

White-tails are highly adaptable. Though they most often live in densely forested areas, they can also adapt to open savannas, such as the plains of Texas or the Venezuelan llanos. Mating season is in the fall, and bucks will attempt to copulate with as many females (called does) as possible. ▪A Does give birth to one or two fawns in late spring. ▪B A doe leaves her fawn alone for hours at a time, as its natural camouflage—a spotted coat and the absence of scent—makes it invisible to most predators. ▪C The doe returns periodically to feed the fawn. ▪D

4. **The word nuisance in the passage is closest in meaning to**

Ⓐ competitor
Ⓑ obligation
Ⓒ attraction
Ⓓ annoyance

5. **What does this passage say about the white-tail deer's ability to survive in different environments?**

Ⓐ They can live in flat lands.
Ⓑ They can only live in forests.
Ⓒ They cannot adjust to cold weather.
Ⓓ They do not like hot weather.

6. **Which of the sentences below best expresses the essential information in the highlighted sentence in paragraph 4? *Incorrect* choices change the meaning in important ways or leave out essential information.**

Ⓐ As humans move into the deer's natural habitat, deer are able to adapt to the changing environment.
Ⓑ Humans have caused the white-tail species to become extinct.
Ⓒ The needs of the increasing human population take away the deer's sources of food and safe habitats.
Ⓓ Humans cut down forests in order to make it easier to hunt deer.

With sufficient food and shelter, white-tail deer populations grow rapidly, sometimes too rapidly for a locality. They often become a nuisance to farmers, whose crops serve as food for the deer. Also, they frequently collide with automobiles as they bound across roadways, causing their own deaths and injury or death to human drivers. Regulated hunts are scheduled to thin out an excessive population. Indeed, deer hunting is a significant cultural ritual in many areas, where it even serves as an important boost to the local economy. The cutting down of forests to make way for commercial development has deprived many herds of their natural habitat, leading to their starvation or increased vulnerability to highway collisions.

The black-tail deer descended from its white-tail relative millions of years ago. Scientists believe that the white-tail deer migrated down the east coast of the North American continent, across Mexico, and up the California coast, where it ultimately evolved into the black-tail deer. Their common ancestry explains why the two species resemble each other, both in physical appearance and psychological traits. Indeed, the two are often hard to distinguish. Though the black-tail's tail is, of course, black, it shares the white-tail's habit of raising its tail, displaying some white coloring underneath. And the males of both species have similar antlers. But the black-tail is found only along the western edge of the continent, extending from British Columbia in Canada to southern California. Moreover, the black-tail is slightly smaller than its white-tailed cousin.

Until recently scientists believed that the black-tail deer was a subspecies of the mule

241

Actual Test

7. **The word it in the passage refers to**

   - (A) mule deer
   - (B) black-tail deer
   - (C) white-tail deer
   - (D) subspecies

8. **Which of the following can be inferred about hunting black-tail deer?**

   - (A) It is too difficult to be very popular.
   - (B) It is better for the economy than white-tail hunting.
   - (C) It is permitted only in the daytime during hunting season.
   - (D) It occurs only during the winter.

9. **The phrase venture out in the passage is closest in meaning to**

   - (A) get into trouble
   - (B) manage to survive
   - (C) start a hunting business
   - (D) risk going outside

deer. But DNA testing has proved that it is a separate species. The mule deer evolved into a distinct species from breeding with the white-tail and black-tail.

Experienced hunters report that the black-tail is the hardest deer species to hunt. One reason is that black-tails inhabit a much hotter climate, with daytime temperatures around 100 degrees Fahrenheit in the summer, during archery season in California. In that heat, black-tail bucks stay quiet during the day and move only under the protective cover of darkness. In the rainy season the black-tail will be active during the day, but few hunters want to venture out in bad weather. Black-tail hunting is further complicated by the fact that the hunting season in western states ends before the mating season, when many bucks are most active while searching for females. Thus they are most accessible at a time when hunting is not permitted.

Despite the relative difficulty of hunting black-tail deer, hunters eagerly seek them out, often successfully. In fact, California hosts about 200,000 deer hunters each year, reaping about $450,000 for its economy.

10. Directions: An introductory sentence for a brief summary of the passage is provided below. Complete the summary by selecting the THREE answer choices that express the most important ideas in the passage. Some answer choices do not belong in the summary because they express ideas that are not in the passage or are minor ideas in the passage. *This question is worth 2 points.*

This passage describes two major species of North American deer.

-
-
-

Answer Choices

(A) A white-tail fawn has natural protection: its spotted coat and lack of scent.

(B) The white-tail and black-tail deer are difficult to distinguish from each other because of their common ancestry.

(C) Male white-tails sometimes die when their antlers get entangled with another's.

(D) White-tails inhabit most of the continental United States while the black-tail is limited to the west coast of North America.

(E) Deer hunting serves as a means of curtailing excessive populations and also stimulates the local economy.

(F) DNA testing shows that the black-tail is a subspecies of the mule deer.

Drag your answer choices to the spaces where they belong.
To remove an answer choice, click on it. To review the passage, click **View Text**.

Actual Test

11. The word hoax in the passage is closest in meaning to

(A) fake
(B) exception
(C) mirage
(D) copy

12. According to the author, each of the following is true about Magdalenian art EXCEPT:

(A) It is found as far east as Southeast Asia.
(B) Most of its themes involve animals.
(C) Artists signed their work with paintings of their hands.
(D) It is named after the inhabitants of a town in Spain.

13. The word their in the passage refers to

(A) cave paintings found in Spain
(B) sites around the world
(C) cave painters from Spain
(D) techniques of carbon dating

Ancient Cave Painting

Though pre-historic cave paintings have been extant since the Upper Paleolithic Era, from 40,000 to 10,000 BC, they were not rediscovered until 1879, in a cave in Spain. At first they were suspected of being a hoax. But their authenticity became accepted as cave art was found in other sites around the globe. Modern techniques of carbon dating have confirmed their ancient origin. Other impressive work has been located on the walls of caves in France, Italy, Africa, Australia, and Southeast Asia.

The 1879 find was the work of the Magdalenian people, so named after the nearby town of Magdalena, Spain. They lived from about 18,000 to 10,000 BC. Magdalenian art is distinctive, characterized by recurring themes and style. The most popular subjects were animals, especially bison, deer, horses, and the woolly mammoth, which is now extinct. Realistic human subjects were rare, limited to abstractions of human shapes. But recognizable human hands, which an artist might have included as his or her "signature," can be seen.

Cave paintings remained hidden as long as they did because of two factors. First, artists chose to do their work deep inside the caves, where their stone-wall "canvases" were protected from the weather. These locales were often inaccessible to modern searchers for signs of ancient civilizations. Second, once a cave's art is detected and announced to a curious public, excavations are made that expose the work to both people and the

14. The word it in the passage refers to

- Ⓐ excavations
- Ⓑ the public
- Ⓒ artwork
- Ⓓ painters

15. In paragraph 3, why does the author mention cave paintings found in France?

- Ⓐ To show that cave paintings are found all over the world
- Ⓑ To illustrate how cave art can disappear once exposed to the elements
- Ⓒ To indicate that some cave art is considered to be a "treasure"
- Ⓓ To give an example of cave paintings that are still preserved after being excavated

16. According to paragraph 3, one reason cave paintings were NOT discovered until the late 19th century was that

- Ⓐ carbon dating was not invented before then
- Ⓑ scholars did not search for them before then
- Ⓒ many were destroyed in World War I
- Ⓓ they were located on walls deep inside caves

elements, from which it had been protected for thousands of years. Thus, a treasure trove of paintings identified in France during World War I disappeared within six months of becoming open to the public. Air conditioning can preserve some sites for viewing, but most are closed to tourists. Scholars must apply for access, and then they are permitted to study the artwork for only short periods.

Despite cave art's relative inaccessibility, scientists have managed to infer much about the methods and materials used by ancient artisans. The earliest works were finger drawings in soft clay on the surface of rock, which depicted animals' claw marks. Artists then adopted engraving methods, using stone tools to carve figures into rock walls. Using their own skill as well as specialized implements, artists could alter the tone, color, and depth of a scene.

The last technique to evolve was wall painting. Few colors were available, as the Paleolithic people were limited to what they found in nature. They manufactured their colors from various minerals and trees. For example, red was extracted from oxidized iron and white from mica. From burned wood they obtained carbon to make a black pigment.

Even with their primitive resources, the artists nonetheless showed ingenuity in mixing and applying colors. Nearly 200 color-producing mineral fragments have been found in barnacle shells, in which the pigments were mixed. One artist used a human skull to mix his colors. Cave water containing calcium was used as a mixing agent, and animal and vegetable oils bound the pigments. Though

Actual Test

17. Which of the following can be inferred about the site of cave paintings found in France during World War I?

(A) It was destroyed by bombing during the war.

(B) It was first discovered in 1879.

(C) It was destroyed by exposure to weather and people.

(D) It is still visited by scholars today.

18. The word illuminating in the passage is closest in meaning to

(A) lighting

(B) covering

(C) finding

(D) coloring

19. Which of the sentences below best expresses the essential information highlighted sentence in paragraph 7? *Incorrect* choices change the meaning in important ways or leave out essential information.

(A) Cave painting was a form of entertainment practiced by all.

(B) Cave painting was done mainly by women because the men were occupied with hunting.

(C) Only a few people had the skill and means to devote their lives to painting.

(D) Cave painters gathered their materials during their hunting expeditions.

no paint brushes have survived, the finished works show telltale brush marks. Paint was sometimes sprayed onto surfaces covered by prepared stencils, with blow pipes serving as paint sprayers.

Painting was a profession. It was too difficult and expensive to be practiced by casual amateurs, who had to spend all their time hunting and inventing means of survival. One difficulty was illuminating the dark cave walls. Scientists theorize that ancient painters worked by torches fueled by animal fat. Another problem was the inaccessibility of some wall surfaces. Some scenes could only have been painted lying down in narrow openings, and others were so high from the floor as to have required elaborate scaffolding.

The locales chosen for painting offer anthropologists important clues about the lifestyles of the Upper Paleolithic people. Despite their popular label, they did not actually live inside caves. Cave walls served as their canvasses for the practical reason that open-air work quickly disappeared. So caves sheltered and preserved the art. They wanted the art to last, not simply for their own entertainment but also because of the cultural function it served. Art was the medium through which prehistoric civilizations passed on their history and honored their traditions and ancestry.

20. Directions: An introductory sentence for a brief summary of the passage is provided below. Complete the summary by selecting the THREE answer choices that express the most important ideas in the passage. Some answer choices do not belong in the summary because they express ideas that are not in the passage or are minor ideas in the passage. *This question is worth 2 points.*

This passage reviews the history of ancient cave painting.

-
-
-

Answer Choices

(A) Cave paintings have been studied by scholars ever since 1492.

(B) The authenticity of cave paintings was not established until the late 19th century.

(C) Cave art is viewable today because of the protection offered by its location deep inside the Earth.

(D) A frequent subject for cave painters was the human body.

(E) Cave painters used black pigments only; they had no way to make colors.

(F) Painting served as a means to communicate history and traditions.

Drag your answer choices to the spaces where they belong.
To remove an answer choice, click on it. To review the passage, click **View Text**.

Actual Test

21. **The word phenomenon in the passage is closest in meaning to**

   (A) abnormality
   (B) event
   (C) technology
   (D) destination

22. **According to paragraph 1, time zones became necessary when**

   (A) humans began to use written language
   (B) technology permitted long-distance travel and communication
   (C) longitude lines were invented
   (D) Earth began to rotate

23. **According to the author, each of the following is true about time zones EXCEPT:**

   (A) They are needed to adjust local times to Earth's rotation.
   (B) They led to standardized railroad schedules.
   (C) They are one hour long in every country.
   (D) They are measured by lines of longitude.

History of Time Zones

Time zones are necessary because of the rotation of the Earth as it revolves around the sun. Spinning around once every 24 hours, the Earth continuously moves each place on the planet toward the sun in the morning and away at night. As one traces the globe in a westerly direction, the sun reaches the overhead point—12:00 noon—at different times at each location. So one city's 12:00 noon would not be the same as that of a city just a hundred miles to the east, where the sun has already passed overhead.

This was not a problem in the pre-industrial age, before technology allowed rapid communication across long distances. Timekeeping was a local phenomenon. Each town would set its clocks so that 12:00 noon was when the sun reached its zenith in that particular place. One who traveled to another city would have to change his pocket watch to reflect the new local time.

In the nineteenth century, railroads were laid, and telegraph communications became widespread. For the first time, people could traverse many miles each day, and they could conduct cross-country business by telegram. The old system of irregular time keeping made commerce and communication difficult and confusing. Uniform train schedules were impossible, as each stop observed a different local time. Each railroad company used its own standard time, usually the time of its corporate headquarters or of an important stop. Some train

24. Why does the author mention in paragraph 3 that a train station in the 19th century might have 6 clocks with different times?

(A) To show that clocks were inaccurate in the 19th century

(B) To explain why time zones were not needed for early rail travel

(C) To argue that each major city needed six time zones

(D) To illustrate the need for the standardization of time

25. The word accommodate in the passage is closest in meaning to

(A) alienate

(B) modify

(C) denigrate

(D) satisfy

26. According to the author, Fleming's system could not be used worldwide until

(A) time was more accurately kept by atomic clocks

(B) railroad schedules were standardized

(C) Congress passed the Standard Time Act in 1918

(D) countries chose a line of zero longitude as a base line

stations had separate clocks for each railroad using that station. A traveler stopping in a major city, for example, might see six clocks on the wall of the train platform, each displaying a different time. Efficient operation of railroads demanded that time be standardized.

In 1878 a solution was proposed by a Canadian railway engineer, Sir Sandford Fleming. He suggested that the globe be marked by time zones separated by Earth's lines of longitude. Each zone should be 15 degrees wide, he calculated, so that Earth's 360 degrees would be sectioned into 24 zones of 15 degrees each. By this system, the rotation of the planet would move each zone 15 degrees, or one twenty-fourth of the globe, in one hour.

American railroads began using Fleming's system in 1883. But efficient use worldwide required that a beginning line of longitude be designated as a base line for measuring a day. In 1884, an international gathering, the International Prime Meridian Conference, met for that purpose in Washington, D.C. It chose the longitude line passing through Greenwich, England as the "Prime Meridian," or the line of zero longitude. The time at this longitude is known as Greenwich Mean Time, or GMT. Each of the longitude lines runs from the North Pole to the South Pole, perpendicular to the Equator. While the longitude lines are straight in theory, in practice many have been bent to accommodate the needs of local populations.

Not all countries adopted the system right away. Most of the United States did not do so until

Actual Test

27. **Which of the following can be inferred about time in a large city that is divided by a line of longitude?**

   (A) The time zone line normally dividing the time zones will be moved so that all parts of the city observe the same time.

   (B) Time in one part of the city will be an hour earlier or later than time in another part.

   (C) The city will always observe Daylight Saving Time.

   (D) Trains in the city will have schedules reflecting two different time zones.

28. **The word it in the passage refers to**

   (A) the United States

   (B) the Standard Time Act

   (C) Fleming's system of GMT

   (D) Daylight Saving Time

29. **Which of the following can be inferred about time zones?**

   (A) They were not needed during ocean voyages in the 15th century.

   (B) They are not needed now that atomic clocks have been invented.

   (C) The Internet has decreased their importance.

   (D) One who flies halfway around the world will arrive at the same time as when he or she left.

1895, and it was not mandated by Congress until 1918 with the Standard Time Act. Even today, some countries depart from its uniformity. Israel begins its day at 6:00 PM instead of at 12:00 AM. While China should have 5 time zones, in fact its government has chosen to have just one zone for the whole country. Some other countries employ half-hour time zones.

Another common manipulation of time zones is Daylight Saving Time, also called Summer Time in some countries. Those countries move their clocks ahead one hour in the spring and maintain that system until fall, giving an extra hour of daylight at the end of a working day. The main purpose is energy conservation. If darkness arrives an hour later, that equates to one less hour that consumers are awake to consume electricity. Another benefit is to lengthen the time that people can be outside during the warmer months.

Because GMT is based on the rate of the earth's rotation, which is not constant, it is subject to slight inaccuracy over time. Accordingly, in 1972 GMT was synchronized with super-accurate atomic clocks, which incorporate "leap seconds" that account for variations in planetary rotation. This new system is called Coordinated Universal Time, or UTC.

30. Directions: Fill in the table below by matching the appropriate statement to whether it refers 1) to the **problems** creating the need for time zones or 2) to the **solutions** to the problems. ***This question is worth 3 points.***

> Drag your answer choices to the spaces where they belong.
> To remove an answer choice, click on it. To review the passage, click **View Text**.

Problem

Select 2
-
-

Solution

Select 3
-
-
-

Answer Choices

(A) The Earth revolves around the sun every 24 hours.

(B) A base line of zero longitude passes through Greenwich, England.

(C) The rotation of the Earth causes variations in local time.

(D) Each country has one time zone.

(E) Local time differences complicated travel and communications.

(F) The globe is divided into time zones.

(G) Atomic clocks correct for variations in the Earth's rotation.

How to
Master Skills ^{for the}

TOEFL® iBT
Reading

Basic

Answer Book

Unit 1 Vocabulary

Skill & Drill

Definition Clues

Example: Ⓒ

在每一场棒球比赛中，球迷们都期望看到有选手打出一个本垒，也就是打出一个本垒打。球棒挥舞，球划过天空——这令球迷们兴奋不已。球有时落在场地，有时飞向坐席。

1. Ⓐ

伪装就是将自己掩藏起来，不被敌人找到。一些动物用伪装来保护自己免于敌人的伤害。一些动物用伪装来猎取食物。青蛙、蝴蝶和蛇就是这样的动物。它们改变颜色或形状将自己掩藏于周围的环境中。伪装后，它们看上去像草、树叶或石头。伪装提升了它们在野外生存的机会。

2. Ⓑ

一些野生动物冬眠，也就是睡过整个冬天。它们在深秋时节进入洞穴，并且直到春天才出来。在冬眠前，动物们吃东西以积累脂肪。这些脂肪支持它们度过冬天。春天时，动物们非常瘦，也非常饿。冬眠使许多野生动物在没有食物可吃的寒冬里得以生存下来。

Synonym & Antonym Clues

Example: Ⓒ

每一项生意都寻求创新。现在，即使是健身俱乐部都有做生意的新方式。他们使用 MP3 播放器和下载。健身爱好者们可以付很少的钱下载健身课程。这样，他们就不用每小时付 50 美金给健身教练了。通过这种方式，健身俱乐部也可以获得更多的顾客。

1. Ⓐ

视察员上周去了动物园。他们想要看看猴子是如何被饲养的。动物园的一些猴子很肥胖，另一些则瘦得像牙签。视察员想知道造成这种差异的原因。也许是一些猴子偷了另一些猴子的食物。

2. Ⓓ

绝大多数电视机都有遥控装置。它们运用了红外线技术。红外线是看不到的，而电视屏幕的光是可见的。遥控器

用红外线给电视机发送指令。电视机一定要有一个特别的接收装置才能够读取这些瞬间的光线。进而，观众能够变换频道并查看节目单。

Example Clues

Example: Ⓐ

在春天，许多人会受到咳嗽、瘙痒、打喷嚏、流鼻涕和迎风流泪的折磨。大家会认为这些是感冒的症状。如果这些症状持续很长时间，就要去看医生了。这也许是由灰尘、土壤和花粉导致的过敏。这会给人们带来很多不适。

1. Ⓑ

美国东北部降水很多。这个地区常常发生降雨、降雪和冰雹。有几年的降水甚至对农作物造成巨大破坏。这导致很多农民向银行借钱来填补损失。降水有时甚至也会导致对建筑物的破坏。

2. Ⓒ

狼獾是一种坚忍的动物。它非常强壮，能够在寒冷的环境中生存，也能够捕猎大动物。它生活在加拿大和美国的森林里。狼獾为了猎取食物每天能够走大约 100 英里。它足够强壮并具有进攻性，它甚至可以从熊的口中盗取食物。

Experience Clues

Example: Ⓒ

电子字典是非常有效的学习工具。它们可以检索单词的拼写和词义，并查找同义词。而且，它们还可以给出单词所在的例句，这有助于学生学习词汇的语法知识。这样，学生就可以在学习使用该词汇时少犯错误。通过这种方式，他们的写作水平也会得到提高。

1. Ⓐ

足球在美国的流行速度非常慢。这主要是因为绝大多数美国人喜欢看棒球、篮球和橄榄球。这些球类运动都是美国的发明。许多美国人认为足球是一项欧洲或南美的运动，而足球没有任何美国特征。他们也不喜欢足球比赛中的低比分。

2. Ⓐ

近地的空气被太阳加热就形成了云。热气在大气中上升是因为其密度比周围空气的密度小。最终，上升的空气冷却下来。最初以气体形式存在的水凝固并形成了肉眼可

见的水滴。此时，人们就能够看到云了。

Practice with Short Passages

A　1. Ⓑ　2. Ⓐ　3. Ⓒ　4. Ⓐ

软体动物

　　软体动物是海洋中一个重要的生命形式。几千年来，它们一直是人类的一个食物来源。软体动物包括贝类生物，如蛤、蚌类、牡蛎和蜗牛。它们在水中用鳃来获取氧气。它们常常选择生活在河流的淡水与海洋的咸水交汇的地方。这样的地方食物非常丰富。这些动物通过用一种被称作"足"的肌肉来打开贝壳，并让水从身体流过来获取食物。它们吃有营养的植物物质和住在它们周围的其他小动物。还有其他类型的软体动物，如鱿鱼和章鱼。它们只能住在咸水中。它们的"足"进化形成了叫"触须"的手臂，这些手臂用来抓捕大型猎物。

B　1. Ⓐ　2. Ⓓ　3. Ⓐ　4. Ⓒ

极限运动

　　"极限运动"是新的运动类别，包括蹦极、一些自行车运动和滑板运动。年轻人热衷于从事这些运动并以此来测试他们的体力、面对恐惧的能力和安全感。这些运动的特点是高速度或危险的绝技表演。这些运动在人们的头脑中创造出"精神冲动"———一种大脑在感受到压力时的感觉。许多人都喜欢这种感觉。极限运动现在已经发展成为年轻文化的一个重要部分。由于这些体育运动对年轻人的吸引力非常大，一些公司已经开始在这些体育赛事中销售如饮料和服装等商品。

C　1. Ⓓ　2. Ⓐ　3. Ⓒ　4. Ⓐ

魁北克的灾难

　　2003 年对魁北克来说是灾难的一年，主要是因为那儿的大火。这是最近几次火灾中最具破坏力的，同时也是加拿大这一地区自然灾害造成的经济损失最为严重的一年。三年的恶劣天气是火灾非常严重的一个主要原因。一些地区遭遇了百年一遇的最严重的干旱。土地干裂。2400 多起森林火灾烧毁了大片的土地。为了扑灭这些大火花费了近 5 亿美金。保险公司支付了 2.5 亿的赔付。三名消防队员牺牲。弥补这些损失将是一个漫长的过程。2003 年是十年中最糟糕的一年。

D　1. Ⓑ　2. Ⓒ　3. Ⓓ　4. Ⓑ

人脑和电脑

　　有一天，我们将能够用思想来控制电脑，而不需要用键盘或者鼠标。科学家正在研究用脑电波来控制电脑的方式。韩国科学家已经开发出软件用来测量人脑的活动。电脑发现，当一个人放松下来的时候，其大脑活动不太活跃。进而，电脑改变屏幕上的图案。工程师们将其称之为电脑—人脑接合。这是人脑和电脑的直接连接。麻省理工大学的另外一名科学家用猴子来描绘出人脑的信号。当一只猴子抓食物的时候，其大脑向手臂发出电信号。研究者们用这些信号来控制一只机器手臂。这只机器手臂能够比猴子更快地抓到食物。

Practice with Long Passages

A　1. Ⓐ　2. Ⓑ

野生动物贸易

　　每年，全球非法的野生动物贸易达到几十亿美元。这个问题已经同毒品买卖和武器贸易一样严重了。受到这一问题影响的有包括犀牛、象、老虎、蛇、鸟类和海龟等很多物种。许多物种濒临灭绝，这意味着这些物种将要在地球上消失。

　　这些动物，或它们的肢体，常常被用来当作战利品、特别的食物和珍奇的药材。许多动物失去了它们的自然家园。原因有如下几种。城镇的不断扩展使丛林面积变小，野外地区越来越容易受到影响。森林中的动物很容易被偷猎者捕杀。这个问题由于警察对非法偷猎的打击不力而变得更加严重，因为警察在处理这一问题上的人手非常有限。最严重的问题还是需求。世界各地的人们想要这些动物，他们很愿意为这些特别的东西付高价。

　　只要人们想要买这些商品，偷猎者的捕杀就会继续。警方一定要打击偷猎。各国应该更加努力地保护丛林。最后，文化习俗应该改变，人们应该认识到野生动物贸易是错误的。

B　1. Ⓐ　2. Ⓒ

魔术师约翰逊

　　魔术师约翰逊是体育界最知名的运动员之一，他也是历史上最伟大的篮球运动员之一。现在，他的生活已经不一样了，但他仍然很有影响力。

　　他的名字已经进入了篮球名人堂。他被提名为全球最伟大的 50 名篮球运动员之一。他也是一个伟大的投手，很长时间内他保持了最多的助攻记录。这是因为他出色的传球技术。他的一个队友说他似乎是如同变魔术般地将球穿过其他球员的身体来传球。他整整 13 年的篮球运动生涯都在为洛杉矶湖人队效力。在 1991 年，他被诊断出患了艾滋病。他退出了篮球场并很快转行。利用他的声望，魔术师约翰逊周游全国，拜访教堂和学校。他对年轻人讲述艾滋病，并鼓励他们负责任地生活。同时，他还为艾滋病医疗机构募集捐款。他自己已经捐赠了近一千万美元。

虽然他现在的生活已经发生了变化，但他仍然是一个重要人物。他不再打球。他现在的任务是保证年轻人以最好的方式生活。

C   1. Ⓐ   2. Ⓒ

天气的影响

今年，加拿大东部的冬天非常寒冷。去年冬天不是很寒冷，所以今年冬天的到来有些让人惊讶。寒冷对许多人而言是非常糟糕的，但对一些人来说却是一件好事。

今年的低温持续创造最低纪录。大约有 25 天的气温达到零下 20 摄氏度以下。持续的寒风使这种情况变得更加糟糕——它使人们觉得温度更低。当学校因为下雪而关闭时，下雪天实际上变成了"冷冻天"。一些学校因为水管被冻、供热系统瘫痪而不得不关闭。寒冷也影响到了农业。在一些地区，百分之四十的葡萄藤不得不被其他作物取代。

然而，对一些人来说，严寒也是一件好事。能源供应商为了满足不断增长的供热需求而增加了销售。服装供应商也很快从中看到了商机。他们卖出了很多的冬衣。寒冷也为冬季运动创造了理想的条件，进而促进了旅游，并让人们得以享受寒冷。除了寒冷负面的影响，人们也能从中有所获益。

D   1. Ⓓ   2. Ⓑ

数码录像机

数字视频记录机（数码录像机）正在改变人们看电视的方式。虽然价格昂贵，但它们相对于过去看电视和录电视节目方式的优势也是非常明显的。

数码录像机是能够记录多达 30 个小时电视节目的硬盘驱动器。人们可以在看一个节目的同时录另外一个节目。观众不用再看电视中的商业广告了。他们可以快进到节目的下一个部分，并跳过广告。他们甚至可以实时按暂停键、倒退键，并重放他们刚刚看过的一段。与此同时，数码录像机一直将节目录到结束。

使用录像带的录像机并不是很方便。首先，你得买 15 盒录像带以达到同数码录像机同等的容量，它同时还需要许多存储空间。其次，由于录像机没有像数码录像机一样的选择菜单，因此，使用录像机来寻找录制的节目不会像使用数码录像机那么快、那么容易。一些数码录像机有很强大的搜索功能。观众可以按节目名称、导演甚至主题来搜索。

Building Summary Skills

A & B

1. The Wildlife Trade

The [1] illegal wildlife trade is a big business and puts many animals [2] in danger. The places where they live are getting [3] smaller, which make them [4] easier to catch. Police cannot stop people from [5] hunting. The greatest problem is that people continue to ask for [6] animal products. They feel [7] special when they have [8] rare animal parts and are happy to pay for them.

2. Magic Johnson

Magic Johnson is a famous [1] basketball player who received many [2] awards. He contracted HIV, so he decided to [3] retire. Now he talks to [4] the public about HIV and AIDS. Magic goes to [5] schools and churches because he wants [6] young people to make [7] good choices. He also [8] raises money for charities.

3. Effects of Weather

Canada had [1] the coldest weather in a long time. The [2] temperatures caused a lot of [3] damage and caused schools to [4] close. However, it was good for suppliers of [5] electricity and gas because there was a great [6] demand to heat homes. Retailers sold a lot of [7] warm clothing, and winter sports helped [8] tourism.

4. DVR

DVRs are a [1] better way to record [2] television shows than VCRs because they can record [3] for longer. It is easier to view other shows while [4] recording, and you do not have to watch [5] commercials. You can also [6] rewind something you have just seen. VCRs cannot [7] search as well as DVRs because DVRs have better [8] menu controls.

Mini TOEFL iBT

1. Ⓑ 2. Ⓓ 3. Ⓐ 4. Ⓒ 5. Ⓒ 6. Ⓐ
7. Ⓑ 8. Ⓑ 9. Ⓒ 10. Ⓐ 11. Ⓒ 12. Ⓐ

走私野生动物

最近，走私野生动物的增长势头令很多机场警员非常吃惊。有时，他们在旅客随身携带的包里发现活的海龟、蜥蜴、青蛙和蛇。走私者用各种各样的方法将走私的野生动物带过海关。他们将活蛇放在胶卷盒中，把鸟放在网球罐里。警察甚至发现一个人将鬣蜥用胶带粘在自己的胸前。然而，不是所有走私的动物都是活的。许多动物都会在途中死亡。动物的部分尸体也被发现，包括鹿茸、皮毛、晾干的器官、蹄或腿等。

走私野生动物的原因是由于人们对稀有物品的兴趣。人们相信拥有一些稀有物品能够令他们显得很特别。为了装饰，人们将动物的头挂在墙上。人们购买动物的毛皮使自己的房间看起来更华丽。而另一些人相信吃动物的某部分能够令自己更强壮。无论死的还是活的，老虎从来不愁没有买家。虎皮、虎骨、虎胆和虎牙都可以被利用——老虎的全身都有价值。虎骨被认为能够治疗风湿。有些老虎是在野外被猎捕的，有些则不是。老虎被囚禁后是很容易饲养的。它们被关在一些小型动物园里，也被当作私人宠物来饲养。被捕获的老虎会被卖给那些为了得到老虎身上的部件而愿意出大价钱的人。

从 1975 年起，稀有物种的交易被禁止。这个禁令得到了全世界 136 个国家的认同。但走私野生动物仍然是一个很大的问题。它是继毒品走私后第二个最赚钱的行业。但它伤害了个别的动物物种，并破坏了自然的平衡。生物物种的多样性应该是下一代人优先考虑的事。

会飞的汽车

你是否曾经梦想过驾着自己的汽车在天空中飞行？这样随意的飞行将非常激动人心。你不需要每天花费几个小时在路上，你还可以在很短的时间内就飞越很长的距离。自从 1903 年莱特兄弟发明了飞机，一些先驱者已经为了发明一辆会飞的车而作出了很多的努力。一些汽车产业的专家认为，会飞的汽车这一梦想将会很快实现。

一个叫保罗·莫勒的天才工程师最近就发明了一辆这样的车。莫勒用了近四十年的时间，花费了几百万美元来开发这辆样车。这辆车可以容纳四个人。它被设计成可以在小范围内起飞和降落，最高可以飞行到一万米的上空。它用四个外部引擎来上升、下降和转弯。然而非常不幸，这辆汽车并不节能，所以不能飞很远的距离。莫勒的这辆车靠计算机和卫星来导航。为了防止坠毁，车里还安装了

安全气囊和降落伞。他向人们证明，汽车是可以飞的。

一个拥有"会飞的汽车"的社会将面临很多有待解决的问题。第一个问题是安全。如果没有了路，怎么才能防止人们撞车呢？一辆车在天上飞很容易，但是成千上万辆车在天上飞会怎样？另一个问题是价格。当前，一辆车大约要几百万美金。人们如何才能买得起呢？第三个问题是燃料。满足这些车需要很多燃料。而且，使用的燃料也要比我们目前使用的更环保。但是，科学是不断进步的。这些问题很有可能会在几年内得以解决。到那时，快速而便捷的飞行就会变为现实。

Vocabulary Review

1. Ⓓ 2. Ⓑ 3. Ⓓ 4. Ⓒ 5. Ⓑ
6. Ⓑ 7. Ⓒ 8. Ⓓ 9. Ⓐ 10. Ⓒ

Unit 2 Reference

Skill & Drill

Personal Pronouns

Example: Ⓓ

拍卖是一种流行的买卖方式，也是给物品定价的一个有用的方式。E-Bay 网就是一个很好的例子。在互联网上，买家互相竞价来购买他们想要的商品，而卖家也可以以买家付出的最高价格卖出物品。

1. Ⓓ

安妮·弗兰克是第二次世界大战的受害者。为了躲避纳粹，她藏在一个小屋里，写下了她的日记。她在那里躲藏了两年。她的日记表现了纳粹统治下的悲惨生活。在她逝世后，她的父亲出版了她的日记，很快这本日记成为了全世界最被广为阅读的书之一。

2. Ⓐ

在 20 世纪 20 年代，爵士乐还不太被白人所熟悉。路易斯·阿姆斯特朗是那个让白人知道爵士乐的黑人音乐家。在十四岁时，路易斯开始学习吹小号。很快，他开始在酒吧里工作。他独特的嗓音和出色的小号演奏吸引了很多黑人和白人爱好者。很快，爵士乐对大众来说变得越来越流行。

Demonstratives

Example: Ⓑ

这是一个动荡的时代。南方各州试图从联邦中分离出去。亚伯拉罕·林肯总统非常气愤。这意味着国家将一分为二。他需要找到一个能够使各州都满意的解决奴隶制问题的方法。总统保证他会维护美利坚合众国的统一。

1. Ⓑ

一天,艾萨克·牛顿坐在一棵树下。他正在思考世界上的物体是如何相互联系的问题。这没什么新鲜的,牛顿经常思考这些问题。他是个物理学家。突然,一阵风吹来,一个苹果从他头顶的树枝上落了下来,正好砸在他的头上。虽然受到惊吓,但这使他陷入了一系列的思考,并很快形成了他的万有引力理论。

2. Ⓐ

1929年10月29日这一天,股价暴跌,投资者陷入了恐慌。他们尽快将股票卖出。这是三十年来美国经济第一次出现问题。人们担心他们的钱会亏掉,而更糟糕的是,投资银行也亏了钱。一夜之间,富人变成了穷人。

Relative Pronouns

Example: Ⓓ

科学家一直在寻找可以替代石油的其他能源。他们已经研究了风能、乙醇和核能,现在开始再次研究煤炭了。作为最便宜的能源,煤炭在全世界很多地方都出产。然而,开采煤矿是很危险的,而且它也污染环境。

1. Ⓑ

吉他,又被称为穷人的钢琴,被多个文化所珍爱。西班牙对吉他文化的发展作出的贡献最大。这个国家有着许多经典的吉他乐曲。巴西的吉他音乐也很有名,它演绎出Bossa Nova舞曲风格,将古典与爵士乐风格融合在了一起。

2. Ⓒ

税收对一个社会来说非常重要。税收被用来资助学校和修建公路。去年的税率是百分之二十五,这引起了人们的不满。人们感觉税收太高。人们想要多存点儿钱。他们认为政府是无能的。

Indefinite Pronouns

Example: Ⓐ

交响乐团有许多成员。每一个成员都有他或她负责演

奏的部分。第一小提琴通常演奏基本旋律。大提琴和中提琴演奏和声。当然,低音提琴和大号演奏低音。黑管和笛子常常演奏乐曲的配乐部分。音乐家们一起演奏出美妙的曲调。

1. Ⓒ

三哩岛危机几乎是一次巨大的核灾难。这个发电厂为宾夕法尼亚州成千上万的人提供电能。一天,一个阀门没有关,反应堆芯连续加热了三天,差一点爆炸。电厂周围处在极度危险中。在方圆20英里范围内的绝大多数人都有可能死去。死亡人数将高达几千人。

2. Ⓑ

《绿野仙踪》是一部非常有名的电影,它的配乐非常出色。每年都有几百万人在电视上看着这部电影长大。当然,其中的许多人还能够唱出其中的歌曲。最让人记忆深刻的歌曲开头是一句简单的歌词"彩虹之上的某个地方"。许多美国人都能说出这首歌接下来的歌词。虽然不是所有人都能把剩下的歌词唱出来,但这首歌已经成为美国文化的一个重要部分了。

Practice with Short Passages

Ⓐ   **1.** Ⓑ   **2.** Ⓓ   **3.** Ⓐ   **4.** Ⓒ

镭射笔不是玩具

德克萨斯的一个中学生被带上了法庭,因为在几周前,这个学生在自然课上将镭射笔对准了老师的眼睛。愤怒的老师要求他停下来,但他继续照射,因此,老师的眼睛出现了问题,将学生告上了法庭。

一般认为,直视镭射光如同直视太阳一样危险。镭射光会损害位于眼睛后部的视网膜。当时,老师已经使学生认识到了这一点。学生也知道他可能会伤害到老师。法官说,"镭射笔不是玩具。它们会很危险"。学生因为明知故犯伤害了老师而被罚款。

Ⓑ   **1.** Ⓐ   **2.** Ⓓ   **3.** Ⓑ   **4.** Ⓑ

"嘿,朱迪"

根据流行音乐排行榜,"嘿,朱迪"是1960年到1969年最受欢迎的歌曲。它1968年首次发行,随后连续九周稳居流行音乐排行榜第一的位置。该歌曲的唱片卖出了四百万张,是20世纪60年代最畅销单曲之一,它同时也是"甲壳虫"乐队最成功的作品之一。

保罗·麦卡特尼在一次长途汽车旅行中写下了这首

歌。他是为了约翰·列农的儿子朱利安而创作的。朱利安因为父母的离异而感到失落。保罗试图向他传达一个充满希望的信息，让他高兴起来。歌曲开始时唱到，"嘿，朱迪，别把事情想得太坏。唱一首感伤的歌，让它变得快乐起来。"朱利安回忆说，在很多方面，他与保罗的关系比他与父亲的关系更亲密。

C 1. Ⓐ 2. Ⓐ 3. Ⓑ 4. Ⓒ

新政

新政在 20 世纪 30 年代由罗斯福总统提出。他想要帮助那些遭到大萧条影响的人们。贫穷的人数以百万计。银行系统也不是很可靠。罗斯福想要帮助穷人，同时他也想提升经济。最重要的是，他想要防止未来可能发生的问题。

新政政策包括工作计划。它在城市或者乡村为人们提供工作。新政也包括社会保险。这种保险在穷人因年纪太大而无法继续工作时给他们提供补助。如果一个工人失去了工作，他会获得失业保险。为保障银行系统的安全，新政也提供了储蓄保险。如果银行亏损，人们可以从政府领到钱。这些措施帮助美国人民再次站了起来。

D 1. Ⓓ 2. Ⓒ 3. Ⓑ 4. Ⓐ

神秘顾客

几星期前，凯特在百货商场偶然遇到了她的朋友简。简说她很喜欢她的新工作。"我每天逛街、看电影、去好饭馆吃饭就能挣钱。"这听起来像是开玩笑。

很快，凯特就明白简的意思了。简是一个神秘顾客。她就像商场里的一个秘密特工。商场主雇用她来检测商场对顾客的服务质量。神秘顾客逛不同的商店、饭店、酒店和影城。他们看上去与普通顾客没什么差别，然而，他们为商场主收集信息，以使商场持续为顾客提供高品质的服务。

Practice with Long Passages

A 1. Ⓓ 2. Ⓒ

激光

激光是 20 世纪的主要成就之一。激光发明于 1958 年，阿尔伯特·爱因斯坦的理论使它成为可能。激光在社会的多数领域被广泛使用，并且是最重要的科技之一。

激光与普通电灯泡的光线很不同。激光的光线是一种向一个方向发射的单一光线，而普通电灯泡的光线是一种向各个方向发散的宽光谱。一支小小的激光笔的光线比普

通灯泡要亮得多。这种密集的能量有许多用途。

每年，几百万的激光发射器被售出。这些激光发射器被纤维光学用来发送信息。它们也被用来刻录 DVD 碟片和 CD 碟片。在电脑的 CD 和 DVD 只读驱动器中，它们也被广泛应用。激光还被用来进行切割和灼烧。医生用激光来矫正视力。工业方面，激光用来切割金属。建筑工人用激光来测量并创造水平表面。警察用激光来测速。最后，激光也用来创造剧场中的视觉效果。激光改变了我们的生活、工作和娱乐方式。在未来，激光也将是一项前途无限的科技。

B 1. Ⓑ 2. Ⓑ

《流行音乐排行榜》杂志

《流行音乐排行榜》是一本著名的音乐杂志。其影响力非常大。该杂志收集音像店和广播电台的销售数据，接着，对最受欢迎的音乐作品进行排榜。排行榜每周出版一次。

《流行音乐排行榜》出现在 1894 年。当时的售价是 10 美分，并且只有 8 页。最初，它与音乐没什么关系，而主要是为了推动当地的演出和活动。现在，其中的文章都与音乐专业人士有关，然而这些排行榜受众广泛。音乐排行榜最热百首单曲在 1958 年左右首次出现，这是最著名的排行榜。人们能够在其中找到美国最流行的百首单曲。这份排行榜提供了关于最新流行单曲的新闻、视频发行和流行音乐趋势。

(杂志)公司的业务涉及了音乐的许多方面，包括销售 CD 和 DVD 碟片，并在互联网上提供付费音乐下载。几年前，流行音乐排行榜热门手机铃声被推出，这使得手机用户可以下载音乐排行榜的任何歌曲。杂志紧跟发展趋势，不断寻找方法使自己与时代同步，并保持成功。

C 1. Ⓐ 2. Ⓑ

亚美利加·韦斯普奇

每个人都知道克里斯托弗·哥伦布发现了美洲。然而，他坚信他所到达的地方是印度。当然，事实并非如此。亚美利加·韦斯普奇是第一个肯定这个地方并不是印度的欧洲人。由于这个原因，美洲以他的名字命名。

亚美利加于 1454 年出生于意大利。他的前半生是一个商人。在他四十几岁的时候，他移居到了西班牙，当上了一个船舶公司的主管。他帮助哥伦布准备了到达新大陆的第二次航行。这使得他有机会航行到"新大陆"去。

在 1502 年，亚美利加发现了陆地。他相信这是一个新的大陆，而并非亚洲的一个部分。在 1507 年，一个地图制

图师提议用"America"来命名新发现的大陆，以此纪念亚美利加。他的名字被用来命名北美洲和南美洲两个洲。亚美利加在 1512 年死于疟疾，然而他的遗赠将永存于世。

D 　 1. Ⓒ 　 2. Ⓓ

自主创业

自主创业很不容易，它要求辛勤的工作和大量的时间。它要求创业者作出牺牲，如牺牲与家人在一起的时间。但是对很多人来说，这些牺牲是值得的。他们喜欢自己当老板。他们喜欢按自己的想法行事。对于创业来说最重要的是要有计划。

第一步是要有创意，一个独特的想法。你能创造一个新的产品或服务以新的方式帮助别人吗？或者你要复制别人的东西，只是比别人做得更好？发展一个理念帮助你将精力和金钱集中到你事业的重要领域。第二步是决定你在公司中最希望扮演什么角色。你喜欢和人一起工作？还是喜欢面对数字？抑或是喜欢与商品一起工作？记住，你将在这个工作上花很多时间。重要的是你要尽量享受这份工作。第三步是制订一个经济计划。你需要为你的事业贷款。你也需要明确在公司开始运营之前，你拥有的钱能够维持多长时间。

Building Summary Skills

A & B

1. A Laser Pointer Is Not a Toy

[1] Albert Einstein's theories made the laser possible. Lasers are different from [2] light bulbs because laser light only goes [3] one way with only [4] one color. The laser has many [5] applications. It is used in [6] computer drives, in factories, in doctors' offices, and in police departments for [7] measuring. It is also used for [8] visual effects in shows.

2. *Billboard* Magazine

Billboard magazine writes charts about [1] music sales, and it posts the [2] most popular songs in the United States. The magazine started in [3] 1894, but it just [4] advertised shows and events. Then it started [5] writing about music. Even now, the company continues to [6] modernize, and it sells [7] music downloads. Also, it started a new feature, *Hot Ringtones*, so your [8] phone can sound like your favorite song.

3. Amerigo Vespucci

North and South America was [1] named after Amerigo Vespucci because he learned that this land was not [2] India. Amerigo moved to [3] Spain to work for a [4] shipping company, and he decided to sail to the [5] New World. A mapmaker suggested calling the New World [6] "America." This was to [7] honor Vespucci's efforts. Even though Amerigo died in [8] 1512, his name is remembered forever.

4. Starting Your Own Business

It is difficult to start your own [1] business. You must [2] work a lot, and sometimes you cannot spend time with your [3] family. You need a [4] plan to do this, and you need a [5] good concept that will make your company interesting. It will also make your company [6] efficient. You have to decide what [7] work you want to do, and you also need a plan on how to [8] budget your money.

Mini TOEFL iBT

1. Ⓓ 　 2. Ⓑ 　 3. Ⓑ 　 4. Ⓒ 　 5. Ⓐ 　 6. Ⓑ
7. Ⓒ 　 8. Ⓑ 　 9. Ⓑ 　 10. Ⓓ 　 11. Ⓐ 　 12. Ⓑ

希腊文明史

希腊是南欧的一个魅力国家。在古时候，它也被称作"Hellas"。希腊被认为是欧洲文明的诞生地，其文化对欧洲和中东具有深远的影响。

希腊的历史可以追溯到几千年前。希腊文化始于公元前 3000 年的克里特。希腊文化的黄金时代从公元前 600 年持续到公元前 400 年。许多著名的思想家，如苏格拉底和柏拉图，都生活在这个时代。希腊具有强大的实力，它的殖民地遍及地中海周围，包括法国南部、西班牙、北非和意大利。

从公元前 500 年到公元前 336 年，希腊由三百多个小的城邦构成。雅典和斯巴达是其中最强大的两个。他们的政府非常相似，但是生活方式却大不相同。斯巴达热衷于战争但却乐于独善其身，而雅典关注艺术和教育却想要统治这个国家。当然，这导致了了多场战争，特别是对斯巴达的战争。而最终，斯巴达在战争中取得了胜利。

此后，罗马军队和希腊军队常常发生战争。在公元前 146 年，罗马人入侵了希腊。这使得希腊人改变了罗马的生活。希腊人影响了罗马的艺术和思想。这种文化的融合最终形成了欧洲文化的基础。当罗马人占领整个欧洲时，他们也将希腊文化带到那里。一千年后，希腊思想再次在欧洲复兴。这是一个艺术家和思想家研究希腊和罗马思想的时机，其主题涉及建筑，还有文学和艺术。政治学也在研究的范围之中。"民主"这个名词就来自希腊语，它意味着人民的权力。今天，绝大多数欧洲国家是民主制。这一强大的政治体制就源自希腊。

欧元：统一的货币

在欧洲，欧元极具争议性。所有欧洲国家都要使用同一种货币吗？统一货币是统一文化的象征。许多欧洲人并不赞同这一点。他们关注的是国家特征的丧失。他们也担心一个国家的经济会影响另一个国家。意大利的通货膨胀是否会影响法国的经济呢？

在 1999 年，十二个欧洲国家联合在欧元这面旗帜下。这个联合给普通百姓和企业带来了益处。当百姓在欧元通用区域中旅行时，他们不需要再兑换货币了。他们能够更容易地对比价格，而且不用担心汇率。统一货币促进了商业贸易的增长，在欧洲单一市场的形成方面也扮演了重要的角色。依此，欧洲得以与美国和亚洲竞争。

欧元由欧洲中央银行统一管理。欧洲中央银行发行纸币和硬币。所有的纸币都采取同一种设计，而不考虑国别差异，只是在纸币的一面上印有国家代码。每一枚硬币有一面是一致的，而另一面则体现出各国的特点。体现各国特点的一面由每一个成员国用一个表示国家特征的符号进行设计。这些设计依据公众调查来选定。

欧元在 2002 年 1 月 1 日开始使用。比利时、德国、希腊、意大利、西班牙、法国、爱尔兰、卢森堡、荷兰、奥地利、葡萄牙和芬兰批准了该统一货币的使用。英格兰选择冷眼旁观。现在，欧元是三亿欧洲人每天生活的一部分。他们的联合使他们有足够的经济实力与更大的国家展开竞争。

Vocabulary Review

1. Ⓑ **2.** Ⓓ **3.** Ⓐ **4.** Ⓓ **5.** Ⓒ
6. Ⓑ **7.** Ⓒ **8.** Ⓑ **9.** Ⓐ **10.** Ⓓ

Unit 3 Factual Information

Skill & Drill

Example: Ⓒ

流星体是太空中漂浮的大天体。这些天体大于宇宙尘埃，而直径小于十米。当一个流星体进入地球大气时，它的温度快速升高，周围的气体开始燃烧。我们在地球上看到这种现象，就将其称为流星。科学家称每天都有一千吨到超过一万吨的流星体落在地球上。

1. Ⓐ

古埃及人相信人死后会到另一个世界去。因此，他们要为死去的人准备好来生。他们尝试用各种各样的方法使尸体保存得更长久。一种方式是把尸体制成木乃伊。埃及人将尸体风干并裹上麻布。这种方式防止了细菌和真菌的滋生。

2. Ⓑ

奥地利作曲家弗朗兹·舒伯特是一个音乐天才。他是一个写短曲的大师。在十三岁时他便开始作曲。他最著名的一些作品写于他十几岁的时候。他在三十一岁时逝世，但却留下了六百多部美丽的作品。在生前，鲜有人认同他的天才，一生始终贫困潦倒。

3. Ⓑ

伽利略是意大利的天文学家，也是物理学家和哲学家。他喜欢凝视夜空，是第一个造出望远镜的人。他设计了超过六十架望远镜。最初的一些不太实用，很难用它们来观测。他总是试图用它们看得更清楚、更远。他的发明极大地促进了我们对太空的理解。

4. Ⓐ

亚洲是地球上最大的陆地，占全世界土地的三分之一。世界上很多土地都是无人居住的，但超过世界人口百分之六十的人都居住在亚洲大陆。亚洲有四十八个国家，包括中国和印度。这两个国家是世界上人口最多的国家。亚洲也是世界五大宗教——印度教、佛教、犹太教、基督教和伊斯兰教的发源地。

5. Ⓑ

现代世界始于文艺复兴。在法语中，这个词的意思是"再生"。文艺复兴始于 14 世纪的意大利。这是一个文化和思想发生巨大变化的时期。思想家们将旧的希腊和罗马思想现代化。这改变了许多人的信仰。这些思想通过艺术、文学和建筑得以表达。

Practice with Short Passages

A　**1.** Ⓑ　**2.** Ⓓ　**3.** Ⓓ　**4.** Ⓐ

大屠杀幸存者

密歇根大学的礼堂座无虚席。学生们聚集到这里聆听大屠杀幸存者的故事。讲述者是一个七十四岁的犹太老人。他在一个犹太中心做志愿者。他开始讲述他的悲惨回忆。"在经历了纳粹集中营后，我觉得把我知道的关于大屠杀的事实告诉别人是我的责任。我是我全家六口中唯一幸存下来的。这让我感到悲伤。"他的故事刚刚讲完，一个德国学生站了起来。他是一个交换学生，他想要为德国人对犹太人的伤害道歉。然而，犹太老人说："你需要了解你的前人对几百万无辜的人所做的事。但是你不需要为他们的所作所为有负罪感。"

B   1. Ⓐ   2. Ⓒ   3. Ⓑ   4. Ⓐ

机器人宇航员

机器人正在代替人做很多工作。机器人被用在汽车产业中。人们抱怨说机器人抢走了人的工作。但是有一个工作非常适合机器人做。

美国国家航空航天局发明了名叫"Robonaut"的机器人宇航员。它们看上去很像人。但是，它们的胳膊和手比人类更灵活。它们可以在太空中做很艰难的工作。机器宇航员在未来会和人类宇航员一起工作。它们在太空中生存不需要太空服、氧气和食品。人类则需要空气来呼吸，并且需要保护从而免受极度温度变化的影响。最重要的是，机器宇航员可以被送到人类宇航员无法到达的危险地带。

C   1. Ⓓ   2. Ⓓ   3. Ⓒ   4. Ⓒ

印刷

在 17 世纪有两种非常流行的印刷技术——雕刻印刷术和蚀刻印刷术。雕刻印刷术是比较老的方法。它是指用一种叫凿的工具在铜板上刻画出线条。凿是一个头很尖的钢条。人们从铜板上刮起金属的细长条，并小心地移除。接着，铜板将被涂墨，并将纸覆盖到上面进行印刷。印刷出来的东西线条非常清晰。蚀刻印刷术与此不同。首先，用树脂或蜡包裹住铜板。接着，印刷匠用针在树脂上刮出图画。这样，只有树脂刮除的地方铜板才会显露出来。最后，将铜板浸在酸中。这样酸就腐蚀了铜板，产生出更不规则的线条。接下来就可以在铜板上涂墨和印刷了。

D   1. Ⓐ   2. Ⓒ   3. Ⓓ   4. Ⓐ

失踪女孩

肯塔基州警方希望市民提供帮助来寻找一个失踪的十一岁女孩。她与另外十九名中学生一起在猛犸洞国家公园探险时失踪。那是一个很受欢迎的旅游地。她最后被看到是在第一天早上在猛犸洞穴的入口处。老师说："我让学生分成两组。几个小时后，两组重新会合。那时我们发现她失踪了。"老师立即将情况汇报给公园巡逻员。她失踪时穿着一件绿色的短袖衬衫，头戴黄色帽子，脚穿白色旅游鞋，背一个背包。孩子的父母请求尽一切努力寻找他们失踪的女儿。公园发言人说："她也许在公园里。但是，公园太大，因此我们需要广大市民的帮助。"他们寻找了三天，但没有任何结果。

Practice with Long Passages

A   1. Ⓑ   2. Ⓓ

大屠杀

在大屠杀中，几百万犹太人被纳粹杀死。这是世界历史上最恐怖的事件。当阿道夫·希特勒在 1933 年执政后，他计划灭绝全欧洲所有的犹太人。他秘密建造了死亡集中营。到战争结束时，大约六百万犹太人被屠杀。

许多人试图通过艺术、文学和电影来表现大屠杀这一悲剧。当年的犹太囚犯冒着生命危险尝试用艺术来表达自己。他们不得不隐藏他们的作品和画稿以免被看守发现。他们被禁止记录看到的恐怖，被禁止表达他们的人性。现在，人们用日记、诗歌和小说的形式记录这一切。大屠杀也已经成为了电影的一个主题。《辛德勒的名单》和《美丽人生》是其中最出名的。

铭记这场悲剧非常重要。这样的悲剧不应再次发生。全世界已经建起了许多博物馆，用来提醒未来的人们这段悲惨的过去。许多欧洲国家已经将 1 月 27 日指定为"大屠杀纪念日"。1945 年的这一天是著名的死亡集中营——奥斯威辛集中营被解放的日子。

B   1. Ⓒ   2. Ⓓ

美国国家航空航天局

从 1958 年起，美国国家航空航天局在科学和技术上已经取得了许多进步。它是航空研究的领袖。它给我们提供了观测地球和太空的新视角。

1961 年，肯尼迪总统宣布美国将把宇航员送上月球并把他安全带回地球。他想要打败俄国人。美国国家航空航天局成功地用阿波罗十一号完成了肯尼迪的命令。阿波罗十一号是一艘著名的火箭。1969 年 7 月 20 日，美国国家航空航天局将人类送上月球。第一个登上月球表面的人是尼尔·阿姆斯特朗。那是一个伟大的时刻。他的第

263

一句话是："这是人迈出的一小步，却是人类迈出的一大步。"

在 20 世纪 80 年代，航天飞机成为一个大众关注的新焦点。美国国家航空航天局在 1981 年发射了第一架航天飞机。他们开发的航天飞机是可以重复使用的，而火箭只能使用一次。美国国家航空航天局也执行了许多使用机器人的无人任务。宇宙飞行器被发射到其他几个星球，如木星、土星、天王星和海王星。它们将科学数据和彩色图片传回地球。

C   1. Ⓓ   2. Ⓓ

艺术品大盗和他的母亲

2002 年，一个法国艺术品大盗被捕入狱。他偷遍了全欧洲的 170 多家博物馆，藏品价值共计 25 亿美金。警方最终将其抓获。但不幸的是，警方没能找回所有被盗的艺术品。大盗的妈妈用一种"永久的方式"将它们储存起来。

警方在他的公寓里发现了乐器、兵器和花瓶，还有 60 幅画。大盗斯蒂芬和他的女友安妮每周末都去偷盗艺术珍品。他热爱艺术，但也非常享受偷盗给他带来的快感。他们经常在保安松懈的时候去博物馆。安妮负责望风，而他则把艺术品从框里切出来。

警方发现了他们，并且逮捕了斯蒂芬。安妮跑回家里告诉了他的妈妈。他妈妈因为儿子的问题非常恼火。她将除了画作的所有东西都丢入了河里，然后，又将 60 幅画都切成了碎片，扔进垃圾箱。这些 17 和 18 世纪的名画被永远毁坏了。他的妈妈不想警方找到任何证据。她担心她会因为将这些画藏在自己的公寓里而失去工作。她说，以她现在的年纪，不太可能再找到其他工作了。如此珍贵的历史因为一个不起眼的原因而丢失，让人感到非常遗憾。

D   1. Ⓒ   2. Ⓐ

猛犸洞穴

猛犸洞穴拥有超过 579 公里的隧道，是全世界最长的洞穴。"猛犸"这个词用来形容它的大小。这个洞穴由于其长度和丰富的历史而闻名于世。

猛犸洞穴是一个石灰岩洞穴，它掩藏在肯塔基中部的森林和群山之下。洞穴由地表下面一系列小洞穴构成，至少有五层。许多的隧道和通道还没有对游人开放。这个洞穴形成的过程非常缓慢。起初，这里是大海。经过几百万年，动物的壳和骨头在海底逐渐堆积成厚厚的几层。这些层后来在水中形成石灰岩。后来，海水逐渐消失。雨水穿过岩石并逐渐将它溶解。猛犸洞穴的形成共经历了两亿五千万年的时间。

在 1941 年 7 月 1 日，这个洞穴成为国家公园。这使得洞穴得以免于房地产商的开发。土地不是最重要的。最重要的是这个公园是几千种动植物的家园。1981 年，这里成为世界遗产。猛犸洞穴是全世界人类的财富。

Building Summary Skills

A & B

1. The Holocaust

The [1] Holocaust resulted in the death of approximately [2] 6 million Jews in Europe. In the camps and ghettos, Jews tried to express themselves through [3] art and writing. In many cases, this was [4] dangerous because they were not permitted to show their [5] humanity. There have been [6] books and films about the Holocaust. There are also [7] museums and [8] national holidays in Europe to pay tribute to those who died.

2. NASA

NASA is an [1] organization that explores [2] space. It helps with [3] scientific discoveries. It was [4] responsible for putting Neil Armstrong and other men on the [5] moon. They were the [6] first human beings to go there. Now, NASA has a [7] space shuttle program and [8] robot missions to other planets.

3. The Art Thief and His Mother

A [1] French art thief went to jail for stealing [2] 2.5 billion dollars in art. His girlfriend, Anne, watched for [3] guards and people while he was taking the precious objects in the [4] museums. He loved art, but he also loved [5] stealing. After the police [6] arrested him, Anne told Stephane's mother. The mother then threw the big objects in the [7] river and the paintings down the [8] drain.

4. Mammoth Cave

Mammoth Cave is the world's [1] longest cave. It has many [2] chambers and [3] tunnels though some are [4] not open to the public. The cave took [5] 250 million years to form. It is a typical [6] limestone formation. In [7] 1941, it became a [8] national park to ensure its preservation.

Mini TOEFL iBT

1. Ⓓ 2. Ⓐ 3. Ⓑ 4. Ⓒ 5. Ⓐ 6. Ⓑ
7. Ⓒ 8. Ⓒ 9. Ⓐ 10. Ⓐ 11. Ⓓ 12. Ⓑ

著作权

著作权是一种控制思想使用的方式。他人的思想不能被随意使用。印刷、拷贝、贩卖或发行他人作品是非法的。改编、翻译、录像或表演一个作者作品的任何一部分都是不可以的。这样做需要得到许可。而且,拷贝和粘贴其他人的电子邮件信息也是非法的。没有授权的拷贝等同于犯罪。

著作权涉及的不仅仅是思想,也涉及事物的表达方式。著作权存在于广泛的创造性工作中,包括书面作品、设计和音乐,也包括绘画、照片和电视广播。著作权在作品中用ⓒ这个符号来表达。然而,即使没有任何符号标记,作品从完成创作之日起就受到法律保护。

《安妮法案》是最早的知识产权法。英国在1710年通过该法案。在此之前,创造的权力被少数人和行会所掌握。这一法案适用于全体公民,而非少数人。该法案保护的是作品的作者,而非行会。同时,该法案也为著作权限定了时间。个人享有独有权的时间是21年。

毫无疑问,著作权在创造中扮演了重要角色。如果作家能够掌控自己的作品,他们会感到安全并创造更多作品。对绝大多数创作者来说,作品和作品的法律权利同等重要。这种法律保护有助于经济、文化和社会的发展。

罗马式建筑

"罗马式"这个词指的是欧洲11世纪和12世纪的建筑时期。这一时期的建筑样式和材料与古罗马非常相似。罗马式意味着"用罗马人的方式"。在11世纪以前,人们忙于战争,经常没有足够的食物。人们没有时间和精力来建造巨大而漂亮的房子。大约在975年,欧洲社会逐渐稳定下来。到1050年,国王们开始命令建造大的石头建筑。

罗马式建筑的主要成就是拱状的石头建筑。弯曲的屋顶取代了木屋顶。木头很容易着火。拱状的石头为建筑工匠提出了难题。什么样的形状有效呢? 石头的重量如何被支撑呢?

建筑工匠发明了一些解决方法,包括圆形屋顶和圆尖头。为了支撑沉重的石头,工匠们使用了厚墙和墩。为了保持墙的支撑力,窗户不得不被设计得很小。这使得教堂里面比较暗。这种情况直到几个世纪后哥特式设计被广泛采用才得以改变。

罗马式建筑是从罗马时代起第一个流行于欧洲的建筑风格。这一风格的广泛传播主要是因为那个时期的人旅行主要是出于宗教目的。他们会看到大的建筑并将建筑方法带回家。罗马式建筑在法国、英国、意大利、德国和西班牙北部到处可见。

Vocabulary Review

1. Ⓓ 2. Ⓓ 3. Ⓑ 4. Ⓐ 5. Ⓑ
6. Ⓒ 7. Ⓐ 8. Ⓓ 9. Ⓑ 10. Ⓒ

Unit 4 Negative Factual Information

Skill & Drill

Example: Ⓑ

在19世纪末,一个澳大利亚人开始用女性的名字来命名飓风。他们希望不要有会给人和房子带来巨大破坏的飓风。从1979年起,男性的名字也被用来命名飓风。当人们给飓风命名时,有一件有趣的事。如果一个热带风暴导致了许多人伤亡和建筑物毁坏时,这个名字将不再被使用。然而,如果不是,这个名字会被再次使用。卡特里娜飓风造成了美国几千人伤亡,这个名字将不会再用。绝大多数风暴非常可怕,但是它们也能够给人带来好处。因为强风暴会带走肮脏的空气,并给我们带来新鲜的空气。

1. Ⓑ

原子是构成物理世界的基本单位。然而它们体积非常小,必须用高倍望远镜才能看到。一个原子由三部分构成:质子、中子和电子。中子和质子是原子的中心,被称为核子。质子带有正电荷,中子没有电荷,而围绕核子运行的电子具有负电荷。

2. Ⓓ

文化被定义为人类群体赋予他们所处世界意义的方式。文化以一种系统的方式成就了这一定义。它影响了我们的衣着、行为、甚至是思想。在一种文化中,人们也许会相互对视。他们认为这是为了表达友好。而在另一种文化中,直视某人的眼睛被认为是一种不尊重的表现。由于有这些相应的信仰体系,人们常常依此行事。

3. Ⓓ

查理·卓别林是无声电影时代最著名的电影明星。他生于伦敦。在他的戏剧电影中，他是导演，同时也是制片人和剧本创作人。当然，他也是一个演员。他的星途始于1914年在电影《小流浪汉》中的首次出镜。他的形象包括一件很小的夹克衫和一条很肥大的裤子。许多人称他为世界上最滑稽的人。

4. C

引力是一种将所有事物牵引在一起的自然力量。地球的引力使得我们能够站在地上。由于这个力量，我们才没有在地球上漂浮。这是由于我们的星球体积巨大。引力也同样将整个太阳系连接在一起。它使得月亮绕着地球转，而地球绕着太阳转。

5. A

星系是由星星、星尘和气体构成的。所有这些物质都围绕一个引力中心运动。我们所在的银河系非常巨大。它拥有三千亿颗星星。这些星星之间的距离非常远，我们只能用时间和光速来表示。光穿过我们的星系要花几千年。

Practice with Short Passages

A   1. Ⓒ   2. Ⓐ   3. Ⓓ   4. Ⓑ

海上吉普赛儿童

在泰国的西海岸居住着一些小的游牧群体，被称为海上吉普赛人。他们住在那里几百年了。他们的语言、文化和生活方式与泰国社会的其他人群截然不同。他们靠海而居，因此这些游牧儿童都是游泳好手。他们可以在水中潜伏很长时间。他们在水下拥有很强的视觉能力，可以在不戴潜水镜的情况下在水中看到很小的东西。他们过人的能力与他们对大海的依赖是分不开的。他们的眼睛已经适应了水下的环境。而且，他们也有非常丰富的海洋知识。在2004年的大海啸中，由于他们对大海的了解，海上吉普赛人得以幸存下来。

B   1. Ⓐ   2. Ⓒ   3. Ⓐ   4. Ⓓ

红色星球

我们都知道火星上没有生命。海盗机器人在这个红色星球上执行的任务证明了这一点。这一任务主要是由一个人来完成的。一个富有的美国商人珀西瓦尔·洛厄尔提出火星上有生命。他对火星着迷，花了23年来研究火星。他对火星生命研究非常痴迷，还因此建立了一个自己的实验室。实验室里有一个巨大的天文望远镜。在海平面以上

7000英尺（2.13公里）的地方，在干燥的气候下，就是观察火星的最佳地点。洛厄尔相信他看到了一个穿越火星的线条网络。他认为这些线条是有智慧的生命建造的。火星上也可能有水。他在笔记本上画了很多图。他的想法引起了公众的关注。很快，人们相信火星上有生命存在。

C   1. Ⓐ   2. Ⓓ   3. Ⓑ   4. Ⓒ

《乱世佳人》

《乱世佳人》是一部美国经典电影。故事发生在美国南北战争时期。这是一个关于斯嘉丽·奥哈拉———一个住在南方种植园中的漂亮女人的故事。她深深地爱上了一个男人，阿什利。但他已经与另一个女人订婚，因而不会与她结婚。斯嘉丽非常生气。在经历了战争和他死亡的威胁后，斯嘉丽才认识到他们友谊的珍贵。斯嘉丽希望保护她的朋友不被军队捉到。在这个过程中，她与瑞德，一个戏弄她但却爱她的男人相爱了。这部影片是一个经典的战争背景下的爱情童话。历史使得故事成为可能，其角色所处的环境也被观众所信服。

D   1. Ⓐ   2. Ⓓ   3. Ⓒ   4. Ⓐ

重力

重力在各种机械操作中被使用。其中之一是用来制造圆形的被称作炮弹的圆球。军队使用这一方法已经几百年了。它的操作需要一个很高的火炮塔。液态铅被带到塔顶，并被灌过一个金属格栅。这将以一种统一的方式将铅液分开。随着铅液下落，就形成了圆的铅球并迅速冷却。接着，铅球落在水池中避免变平，并保证其冷却。接下来，铅球将会被确认大小和形状，以满足枪炮的需要。

Practice with Long Passages

A   1. Ⓑ   2. Ⓐ

吉普赛人

罗姆人居住在欧洲、北非和美洲各地。他们常常被称为吉普赛人。由于他们传统上具有深色的皮肤和头发，所以常常被误解为来自埃及。这一误解解释了他们为什么被称为"吉普赛人"。事实上，他们称自己为罗姆人。一千年前，这一族人从北印度来到了欧洲。他们的语言罗姆语是印度雅利安语的一种，但他们常常说他们所在国的语言。

令人感到悲哀的是，他们在自己居住的地方从没有过好的生活。罗姆人的生活始终与种族主义相伴。例如，在

匈牙利，学校往往将他们隔离到单独的教室上课。有时，学校甚至把他们和有问题的学生放在一起学习。因此，许多人没有接受完整的教育。获得大学学位的罗姆人不到百分之一。这使得他们不能找到好的工作。所以，许多罗姆人的生活非常贫穷。在他们中间，社会问题和犯罪问题非常突出。

B　1. Ⓒ　2. Ⓐ

火星

　　火星是太阳系的第四大行星。从地球上可以观测到火星，这使得它成为几个世纪来研究的中心。它的地质特点令人难以置信。

　　火星的体积只有地球的一半，但是火星的表面与地球的陆地大小几乎相同。其表面的红颜色来自于表层的一些矿物质，如氧化铁（铁锈）。火星的密度没有地球大，大约是地球的十分之一。火星的北半球和南半球有很大差异。北半球由于火山熔岩的流动而非常平坦。那儿有一个叫奥林匹斯的巨大平坦火山。该火山高 26 千米，是太阳系的最高峰。

　　火星的南半球有最大的峡谷系统，长 4000 公里，深 7 公里。其中的一部分是几十亿年前由流星冲击而成的。与之相比，美国的大峡谷就像是一个沙盒。有一个叫做希腊斯冲击盆地的巨大陨石坑，那是由流星形成的，其宽度为 2100 公里。

C　1. Ⓒ　2. Ⓑ

独立电影

　　独立电影产业正在不断发展。独立电影这个称谓是由好莱坞大型电影公司向其投入的资金数量来定义的。预算的百分之五十为独立的最低限。增长的部分原因是由于内容。好莱坞所承担的风险比独立电影公司承担的风险小得多。另外一个原因是较低的技术成本。

　　电影观众了解好莱坞的套路。来自于大型电影公司的许多影片有着同样的故事。其原因非常明显：他们制作观众想看的电影，而且人们总是想看同样的东西。然而，这并不完全正确。许多观众已经厌倦了看同样的东西。他们想要看有新鲜情节和有趣视角的故事。他们想要看有独特主题的电影。独立电影制作有能力实现这些想法。

　　摄像机和剪辑设备的价格正在下降。这些制作电影的工具一度非常昂贵，只有好莱坞能买得起。现在，对于绝大多数人来说，大型摄像机的价格都在承受范围内，而且绝大多数剪辑可以在家用电脑上完成。市场上有许多类似的软件。在互联网上，甚至有免费的电影编辑软件。

D　1. Ⓓ　2. Ⓒ

热力学

　　热力学对于我们了解科学是非常必要的。"热力学"这个词在 1894 年由凯尔文爵士提出。这个词来自于拉丁文，意思是"热的力量"。这个理论陈述了四个法则，其中的两个表述如下：

　　当能量移动的时候，我们能够感觉到。第一法则表示一个系统中的所有能量都可以被解释。当移动时，能量一定会发生转移。能量不能被创造也不能被摧毁。它只是在移动。一个例子是一只普通白炽电灯泡和一只普通荧光灯泡的差异。荧光灯炮的使用效能更高，因为能量被保留在灯泡中并创造光。而在一只普通白炽灯泡中，一些能量被用来产生光，但是很多能量都转化为热的形式了。

　　第二法则表示热能的差异最终会平衡。当冰块融化时，水会升到与房间等温；当河水凉下来的时候，空气也会相对凉下来。这种平衡的程度称为熵。所有的能量差异均通过一定时间来达到平衡。

Building Summary Skills

A & B

1. The Gypsies

[1]Gypsies originally came from [2]northern India, not from Egypt. Some speak [3]Romany, but most speak the language of their [4]home country. They have [5]bad experiences in schools, like in Hungary for example. Because they do not get well [6]educated, they cannot find good jobs. Their communities are often [7]poor and have social problems and [8]crime.

2. The Planet Mars

Mars, our neighboring planet, has some fascinating [1]land features. The [2]north is characterized by large [3]lava plains, and it also has the highest [4]volcano in the solar system. The [5]south is characterized by [6]canyons and craters. These were formed millions of years ago. One crater, the [7]Hellas Impact Basin, is over [8]2,000km wide.

3. Indies

The number of [1]independent films is increasing, but

[2]Hollywood is funding films less and less. This means that movies can be [3] different from the Hollywood formula. Many viewers are [4] tired of the same stories and find [5] indie films refreshing. These films are [6] flexible enough to address interesting or unpopular topics. The [7] cost of cameras and other equipment is [8] decreasing, which gives many people the power to make their own film.

4. Thermodynamics

Thermodynamics describes the relationship between [1] heat and power. The first law states that [2] energy in a system [3] stays in a system. It only moves, [4] never to be lost. Efficient [5] light bulbs do not allow energy to be lost in heat. The second law states that different [6] temperatures try to equalize. This means that hot temperatures "try" to [7] cool down and cold temperatures "try" to [8] warm up.

Mini TOEFL iBT

1. Ⓐ 2. Ⓐ 3. Ⓑ 4. Ⓓ 5. Ⓒ 6. Ⓒ
7. Ⓒ 8. Ⓐ 9. Ⓑ 10. Ⓑ 11. Ⓑ 12. Ⓓ

蒸汽机

蒸汽机是人类的一项伟大进步。它使得现代工业成为可能。突然，需要几百人来做的工作用一部机器就可以代替了。"工作"被一种叫"能量"的新肌肉来完成。这依赖于热力学的基本理论，特别是波义耳定律。

波义耳定律认为气压是其体积和温度的变量。当气球中的气体被加热时，其体积增加，压力减小。如果体积不变，则热量会导致压力增加。

蒸汽机基本上就是利用了这些事实。能量，以热的形式，可以被转化成物理力量。如果控制得当，能量可以被用来移动物体。存储下来的热能可以被用来做物理工作。首先，水被加热到产生蒸汽。以此方式，水可以如气体一般，加热时可以膨胀。随着膨胀，蒸汽进入像管子一样的汽缸。汽缸底部的活塞随着气体膨胀而逐渐下降。然后，活塞推动金属手臂，进而进行各项操作。

在纺织厂、农场和矿山，蒸汽机被广泛使用。蒸汽机带动用来纺织的巨大机器转轮，还可以为将棉花与籽或谷粒与梗分开的机器提供动力。蒸汽机也用来将水排出矿坑，并将人和煤提升到地表。当然，蒸汽机也用于将货物和人运载到各个大陆的火车。

过山车的历史

第一架过山车在 17 世纪始创于俄国。然而，它与现代的过山车差异还很大。早期过山车更像是大雪橇。人们坐着它从陡峭的冰坡上滑下。这些雪橇需要很好的操控技术才能安全滑下，而且出过很多事故。

在 19 世纪末，美国的铁路公司引进了过山车。当人们还很少出游时，他们建立了游乐园在周末赚钱。在 1884 年，第一架真正意义上的过山车出现了。它是一部重力驱动的火车。乘客爬几段楼梯进入车厢。接着，过山车被推出车站顺山而下，途中经历几个颠簸。在山下，乘客走出车厢，工人们将车厢抬到第二站。

在 20 世纪初，过山车有了巨大的进步。与之前不同，新的过山车采用了机械轨道。第一座过山车轨道建于 1912 年。这是一个伟大的跨越。它使人们能够体验更快的速度和更陡峭的山脉，而其安全性较以往有很大提高。在 20 世纪 20 年代，人们又建造了很多过山车，但是在第二次世界大战后，过山车的数量锐减。

1955 年，美国第一个主题公园迪士尼公园成立了。它开创了游乐园的新时代。1955 年，迪士尼采用了管状钢轨过山车。在此之前，过山车总是被建在木头框架上。钢轨不仅仅提供了更好的稳定性，同时也打开了翻转和螺旋车道的大门。

Vocabulary Review

1. Ⓒ 2. Ⓐ 3. Ⓓ 4. Ⓒ 5. Ⓑ
6. Ⓐ 7. Ⓓ 8. Ⓒ 9. Ⓑ 10. Ⓐ

Unit 5 Sentence Simplification

Skill & Drill

Example: Ⓒ

全球变暖受到了普遍的关注。有证据证明全球的温度正在上升。例如，在北极地区，几千年来都没有出现过像现在这样的冰层快速融化。过去，人们可以像北极熊一样步行穿越北极冰覆盖的部分地区，但现在出现了明显的融化带。

1. Ⓐ

查尔斯·达尔文发表了《物种起源》一书。他写到生命的形式根据环境而变化。他的自然选择理论引发了科学界的重要变革。但这一观点挑战了宗教信仰。他的理论认为生命是进化的。上帝对于我们今天所看到的生命没有任何责任。

2. Ⓒ

雪花的形状令人惊叹。没有任何两片雪花是完全一样的。雪花通常都是扁平的六边形。当灰尘微粒上结了冰，雪花就形成了。雪花的形状是由温度决定的。雪花在大气中落下，并穿过不同的温层。这使得水冻结成独特的形状。雪花最大的直径超过 28 厘米。

3. Ⓒ

气象学者需要收集来自全世界的数据。他们用很多方法收集数据。一种方法是使用卫星——它们永远改变了气象研究。卫星检测地球的表面，寻找水蒸气和热能。最后，卫星将气象情况的数据传回。通过使用这些数据，气象学家能够更准确地预测天气。

4. Ⓒ

细胞是构成人体的基本组织结构。人体由大约一亿个细胞构成。然而，并非所有的细胞都一样。它们各自发展出特殊的功能，形成器官、肌肉、神经、皮肤和骨骼。身体的每一部分都有特别的细胞种类。然而，一种叫干细胞的细胞能够变成其他任何种类的细胞。

5. Ⓐ

杰里米·本瑟姆是一位英国哲学家。他提出了许多具有重大影响的社会和法律改革的提议。他认为宗教和政治应该分离。他提倡女性应获得与男性平等的权利。他同时也是言论自由的坚定支持者，并倡导终结奴隶制。本瑟姆也相信针对穷人和富人的健康保险制度。

Practice with Short Passages

A　**1.** Ⓐ　**2.** Ⓒ　**3.** Ⓑ　**4.** Ⓐ

变异的细胞

癌症源自于一个细胞的变异。这个细胞的 DNA 发生变化。这种 DNA 变异只有百分之十是遗传的。这意味着只有百分之十的癌症基因来自你的家族。绝大多数的变异源于环境，例如吸烟或生活在污染的环境中。随着年龄的增长，我们身体中变异的细胞也在增多。由于这个原因，癌症经常发生在我们年纪较大时。当细胞复制时，变异的DNA 被复制到了新细胞中。最后，细胞发生巨大的变化，以至于它们不再遵循身体的常规信号。变异细胞不加节制地增长，最终变为肿瘤。

B　**1.** Ⓐ　**2.** Ⓓ　**3.** Ⓐ　**4.** Ⓒ

一名英勇的龙卷风受害者

十八岁的苏没有出现在她的高中毕业典礼上。但是校长却说，她活在班级所有同学的心里。在一次四级龙卷风中，她严重受伤。龙卷风以时速 400 英里的速度抛撒碎片。令人惊讶的是，苏挽救了她两个小弟弟的生命。当她看到龙卷风逼近她家时，她将两个弟弟保护在了身下。当龙卷风经过时，她拼命保护着他们，忍受着伤痛的冲击。乱飞的碎片穿过她家的房子击中了她，她的两个弟弟基本没有受伤，但她现在已经失去了意识。她的勇敢感动了她的邻居、朋友和家人。

C　**1.** Ⓐ　**2.** Ⓐ　**3.** Ⓓ　**4.** Ⓑ

穆尔森林

长期以来，原木产业有着非常强的政治力量。利用这个力量，该产业得到了美国的许多大森林。在世纪初，该产业的公司砍伐了加州海岸森林的绝大多数树木。地球上许多最大的树木生长在这里。红杉树和美洲杉被用来造木材和纸。绝大多数的森林消失了。一个叫做肯特的人目睹了这一切，于是他将土地买下来以保护森林。起初，他以为森林得到了保护。接着一个水利公司想要通过将水引入峡谷来发电。该公司将肯特告上法庭。为了拯救这片森林，肯特将其捐献给联邦政府。现在这里已经成为国家公园。这个公园被命名为穆尔森林，以纪念著名的自然主义者约翰·穆尔。这个峡谷是第一个由私人捐赠而成立的国家公园。这为未来的森林保护铺平了道路。

D　**1.** Ⓑ　**2.** Ⓐ　**3.** Ⓑ　**4.** Ⓒ

死刑

一千多年来，死刑备受争议。这种"公正"来自于《汉穆拉比法典》。这个古老的法律称，"以眼还眼，以牙还牙"。一些人坚信死刑是公正的。触犯了最严重罪行的罪犯应该付出最大的代价。维护社会文明的唯一方式是去除坏的成分。一些人认为死刑是一种威慑。如果罪犯知道自己将要付出生命的代价，他们将不会犯罪。而另一些人认为死刑是野蛮社会的标志。他们坚信我们的社会已经非常进步，这种原始的刑法已经没有必要了。没有任何正当理由进行杀戮。

Practice with Long Passages

A   1. Ⓐ   2. Ⓒ   3. Ⓐ

DNA

DNA 是一个打击犯罪的有力方式。侦探用它来抓捕罪犯，他们用在犯罪现场找到的 DNA 来判定真正的凶手。这是最可靠的查出罪犯的方式之一。

DNA 是一个包含生命蓝图的分子，它控制着身体如何生长。它将父母的基因特点传给后代。在一百万亿人体细胞中，DNA 存在于每一个细胞。每个人都有完全独特的 DNA 排列方式。

侦探经常在受害者身上或犯罪现场发现一些 DNA 的线索。这些线索可能是一根毛发、一滴血，甚至是皮屑。警方收集这些样本并对其进行分析。如果幸运，他们会在嫌疑人中找到相匹配的样本。然而，一些因素可能会影响这一进程。DNA 样本是能够被污染的。样本可能与他人的样本混合，或部分遭到破坏，例如被热量。

B   1. Ⓓ   2. Ⓑ   3. Ⓑ

龙卷风

龙卷风是一个猛烈旋转的气体柱。它从暴风云顶端一直延续到地面。最猛烈的龙卷风能够造成巨大的破坏，最高时速可达每小时 500 公里。龙卷风能够对生命和财产造成巨大威胁。

龙卷风经常光顾美国，特别是在春季和夏季。每年，全美报道的龙卷风能够达到 800 次。它们导致 80 人死亡，1500 人受伤。受到破坏的地区达到 1 英里宽，50 英里长。

有一个地区被称作"龙卷风走廊"。这个地区在俄亥俄州和德克萨斯州之间。在这里，猛烈龙卷风的发生比全国其他地区更加频繁。这一地区的独特性源于落基山脉的干冷空气。这些干冷空气与来自墨西哥湾的湿热空气汇合，而这正是龙卷风形成的绝佳条件。

C   1. Ⓐ   2. Ⓑ   3. Ⓐ

约翰·穆尔

约翰·穆尔帮助建立了全世界最大的国家公园之一。他 1838 年生于苏格兰，1849 年移居美国。虽然没有大学毕业，他却获得了一份工业工程师的工作。很快，他决定探索野外环境。他徒步几千英里从印第安纳到佛罗里达州，感受美好的大自然。穆尔本打算去南美旅行，但是因为疟疾而没有成行。于是，他转而去了加州。

他在 1868 年到了旧金山。很快，他从那里去了约塞米蒂——一个他只从书本里读到过的地方。他在第一次看到那个伟大地方的时候就被深深震撼了。他写到，"没有任何人造的神庙能够与约塞米蒂相比。约塞米蒂是自然界所拥有的最宏大的神庙。"

1903 年，罗斯福总统与穆尔一起参观了约塞米蒂公园。穆尔告诉总统州政府对这个峡谷的管理非常落后。他强调了保护自然的重要性，并说服了罗斯福总统通过联邦控制和管理来保护山谷。

D   1. Ⓑ   2. Ⓒ   3. Ⓓ

《汉穆拉比法典》

汉穆拉比是古巴比伦的第六位国王。他生于公元前 1810 年。从公元前 1792 年他开始统治他的王国直至公元前 1750 年逝世。也许，他最著名的事迹是创造了《汉穆拉比法典》。

对于现代人来说，法典中的惩罚似乎过于残忍，但该法典在两个方面是领先于时代的。首先，他将法律条文付诸笔头，而不仅仅是他的话。其次，他试图系统地应用法律。这是向文明进化的重要一步。"疑罪从无"的观点就来自于该法典。

该法典的条款被写在石板上面，并被摆放在公开的场合。人们可以看到，但很少有人能够读懂并理解它们。数年后，石板被掠夺到了埃兰的苏萨。1901 年，它们被再次发现。现在这些石板被保存在法国巴黎的卢浮宫。

Building Summary Skills

A & B

1. DNA

DNA is used to [1] catch criminals because it is a very [2] reliable method. All of our cells contain [3] DNA. When [4] investigators find traces of a person, they [5] analyze them. If the DNA in the sample [6] matches the DNA of someone they know, police have [7] identiied the criminal. DNA can be [8] contaminated however.

2. Tornadoes

Tornadoes are violently [1] rotating columns of air, and they usually occur during [2] spring and summer. In the U.S., [3] 800 tornadoes are reported each year. They result in [4] 80 deaths and over [5] 1,500 injuries. They most frequently occur in an area called [6] Tornado Alley. It stretches from [7] Ohio to [8] Texas.

3. John Muir

John Muir, a [1]naturalist, was born in [2]Scotland in 1838. In his twenties, he decided to explore the [3]American wilderness by walking from Indiana to Florida. After this journey, he went to [4]Yosemite. He was [5]fascinated by this great park but was [6]worried by how the state was managing it. He asked the [7]president of the U.S. to [8]protect this beautiful place.

4. The Code of Hammurabi

[1]Hammurabi was the [2]sixth king of the [3]Babylonian dynasty. He created the Code of Hammurabi. These [4]laws became famous because they were [5]written down for the first time and [6]publicly placed. Another importance of these laws was that the concept of "[7]innocent until proven [8]guilty" comes from the Code of Hammurabi.

Mini TOEFL iBT

1. Ⓑ　2. Ⓒ　3. Ⓐ　4. Ⓐ　5. Ⓓ　6. Ⓐ
7. Ⓐ　8. Ⓐ　9. Ⓑ　10. Ⓑ　11. Ⓑ　12. Ⓒ

食肉植物

食肉植物通常生长在土壤非常贫瘠的地方，包括沼泽和湿地。这些植物需要潮湿的环境和充足的光照。但是它们必须通过吃小动物或昆虫来获得养分。这些植物捕获猎物的方法十分高明。

1875 年，查尔斯·达尔文写下了第一篇关于食肉植物的著名论文。他描述了五种陷阱。掉落式陷阱用一个底部有细菌的卷曲的叶子来捕捉昆虫；捕蝇纸陷阱使用的是一种黏稠的液体；突击陷阱利用快速的叶片运动；口袋陷阱用一个类似真空的口袋将昆虫吸入；最后一种方法是利用植物内部向内生长的尖刺，这种尖刺迫使昆虫只能向内行走，而无法后退。

食肉植物的发展是很难研究的，而且鲜有化石记录。绝大多数现存的化石都只是种子和花粉的化石。然而，通过当前陷阱的结构，我们能够学到很多。掉落式陷阱非常明显是从卷曲的叶子演化而来的；捕蝇纸陷阱也是通过简单的演化从有黏性但不致命的叶子变成现在的致命武器。

捕蝇草是一种有趣的植物。每片叶子的中间都有三根毛发。在被昆虫触及到两根毛发后，叶子快速收拢。接下来，植物就可以享用美食了。

科学家认为所有这些叶子种类都是从简单的、有毛发的叶子变异而来的。植物可以通过收集雨水来滋生细菌。

落在叶子上的昆虫会被水裹住。在昆虫窒息时，细菌开始腐化昆虫并将养分传送到植物体。现在已知的食肉植物大约有五百种。

沙漠化

撒哈拉沙漠每年以 10 公里的速度扩大。每年全球的沙漠增长 60 平方公里。这一进程被称为"沙漠化"。这一名词在 20 世纪 50 年代开始使用。

在 20 世纪 30 年代，沙漠化这一概念首次被提出。由于干旱和落后的农业技术，许多大平原地区变得非常干旱。这被称为"沙窝"。数百万人被迫放弃他们的庄稼和生活。从那时起，大平原地区的农业耕作得到了很大提高。这使得"沙窝"这个灾难不会再次发生。

放牧是一件让人担心的事。牛群对土壤的影响有两方面：首先是牛群将吃掉用来固沙的草和植物；其次，它们的蹄子也会破坏土壤的表层。结果是好的土壤被风刮走，而留下的灰土不适合植物生长。

一些人认为干旱是沙漠化的原因，而事实上，沙漠化是由人导致的。它已经成为全球最严重的问题之一。旱灾在干旱和半干旱地区比较普遍。在雨水丰沛时，养护良好的土壤可以恢复生机。人类活动对于自然的影响是问题的关键。几年前，在西非，持续五年的旱灾由于落后的土地管理而变得更加严重。这直接导致了十万人和一千两百万头牲畜的死亡。

沙漠化是政治中的常见问题。对此，我们还有许多不了解的地方。沙漠化是一个复杂的退化过程。为了加深对该问题的了解，还需要进行更多的研究。

Vocabulary Review

1. Ⓒ　2. Ⓐ　3. Ⓒ　4. Ⓑ　5. Ⓒ
6. Ⓒ　7. Ⓓ　8. Ⓐ　9. Ⓑ　10. Ⓓ

Unit 6　Rhetorical Purpose

Skill & Drill

Example: Ⓑ

萤火虫是有趣的昆虫。它们将发出的光作为信号。它们可以精确地控制光的关闭和打开。萤火虫用这种方式来求偶。萤火虫中某些种类的雌性喜欢发长亮光的雄性；而另一些种类的雌性喜欢能快速闪光的雄性。某些种类的萤火虫还可以发出红色和绿色两种不同颜色的光。

1. D

雪崩非常危险。从山顶滑下的大片冰和雪会摧毁眼前的一切事物。没有冻结在一起的雪很容易滑落。滑雪者可能受伤甚至死亡。科学家通过研究雪花来更多地了解雪山。他们关注冰晶如何形成。某些形状能使雪冻结在一起，而另外一些形状会导致雪的滑落。

2. C

马尔代夫是印度洋中的一个群岛，由超过一千多个小岛构成。这些小岛由堆积在水下火山上的珊瑚礁形成。珊瑚通常以环形生成。当珊瑚长至海面时，小岛就形成了。通常，在小岛的中心有一个部分是没有珊瑚的。这就使得岛中央形成了一个海水孕育的湖。

3. A

饮食不规律是一种影响人健康的吃饭方式。一些人吃得过多，从而导致体重增加；而另一些人吃得太少；还有一些人患有贪食症——他们通常一次吃得非常多直到感觉疼痛。他们常常因此感到尴尬，所以尽量不与别人共食。饮食不规律的一个方面是人无法控制他们吃东西的方式。

4. B

贫困是一个主要的社会问题。导致贫困的原因有很多。某些群体被剥夺了基本权利。他们由于种族或宗教而找不到工作。另一个原因是缺乏自由。有时，上司阻止手下按照他们自己的方式生活和工作。他将所有的金钱和权力都掌控在自己手中。第三个原因是战争。战争可以摧毁一个国家的经济基础。人们将大部分精力用于生存，而非改善生活。

5. C

印度的乞拉朋齐是地球上最潮湿的地方。有时，那儿会连续下两个月的雨。令人奇怪的是，降水不会停留在一个地方。那里曾经长满了绿色植物，但是人的介入使那里被彻底改变了。人类破坏了土地。现在，那里一下雨，水就会流过坚硬的土地，将尘土和植物冲走。

Practice with Short Passages

A　**1.** A　**2.** C　**3.** A　**4.** D

提供线索的小虫

当有人死去时，警方一定要弄清楚事件发生的具体时间和地点。这有助于解答人是如何死亡的。死亡原因也许是意外，也许是犯罪。犯罪专家可以从昆虫身上获取答案。飞蛾、螨或甲虫等昆虫有不同的生活周期和觅食习惯。一些种类的螨只吃刚刚开始腐烂的尸体上的肉，而另一些种类的螨吃更腐烂一些的肉。甲虫通常情况下吃在潮湿环境中已经比较腐烂的肉，而飞蛾吃干燥环境下的腐肉。专家可以观察现场有哪些昆虫，以及这些昆虫的卵是在何时产下的。这些线索能够帮助判断一个人死亡的时间和地点。

B　**1.** B　**2.** C　**3.** A　**4.** B

焦虑症

焦虑症使人无法做自己想做的事。焦虑的人的情绪通常通过身体症状表现出来。他们的心跳可能加快，开始出汗，甚至可能遭到极度恐惧的侵袭。这种病症使人无法控制他们的担忧，即使是约会或打扫房间，甚至是书桌杂乱这样的小事也会令他们忧心忡忡。医生说如果人们长时间地担忧就会产生这种紊乱情绪，这样的人总是因为担忧而感觉疲劳和苦恼。有时，他们无法正常入睡及饮食。通常来说，担忧是他们生活的中心。

C　**1.** C　**2.** B　**3.** A　**4.** C

麦哲伦海峡

从大西洋到太平洋的旅行曾经是危险的。那是在巴拿马运河建成之前的一段时间。航船不得不开到世界的最南端。有时，他们还要绕过非洲。他们也可以选择德雷克海峡——这是在南极和美洲之间的一条水路。那里的海况和天气都非常恶劣。巨大的冰块威胁着船只的安全。1520年，麦哲伦发现了另一条路线。这个通道被称为麦哲伦海峡，北起南美大陆，南至一个叫火地岛的小岛。这条狭长的水路被岛屿保护。这样船只就能够安全航行了。

D　**1.** D　**2.** B　**3.** A　**4.** B

我们说话的方式

我们说话的方式能够告诉别人有关我们的许多背景。我们能够猜出一个人是来自北方还是南方。如果一个孩子有南方口音但却使用北方的词语，这是怎么一回事呢？我们可以猜测出孩子的家是从北方搬到南方的，他的口音受到朋友的影响，但却习惯使用只有父母才用的某些词语。社会背景也会影响我们的说话方式。著名的社会语言学家威廉·拉博夫试着在口音和社会等级之间找到联系。他去了纽约三家不同的商店，第一家是上层社会经常光顾的，第二家是中产阶级常常光顾的，而第三家是下层社会常常光顾的。他发现，上层社会商店中的人读字母"R"的方式通常与其他商店的顾客不同。

Practice with Long Passages

A 1. Ⓓ 2. Ⓐ 3. Ⓐ

法医学

法医学是司法体系中的一个科学分支。"法医"意味着"与法庭有关"。这一领域回答了我们周围世界的法律问题。

法医学常常用于打击犯罪。警察试图证明罪犯的罪行，在房间中寻找嫌疑犯的指纹或鞋印。他们需要体液形式的证据，同时也关注皮肤上的抓痕和毛发。他们甚至可以通过咬痕锁定嫌疑犯。

警方也研究毒药如何对人体发生作用。犯罪专家记录一种化学品的使用量，并猜测出该化学品使用了多长时间。他们试图找出在现场有什么化学品。血液样本可以暴露出一种药品或毒药的短期使用，而毛发样本可以暴露出其长期使用。头发每月增长一厘米，这使专家能够了解药物或毒药的使用时间。

这些只是法医学关注的一些方面。这门科学涉及面非常广泛。科学在法律体系中非常有用，可以用来回答很多难以解答的问题。

B 1. Ⓑ 2. Ⓓ 3. Ⓐ

害羞

许多人会感到害羞。这是一种与他人在一起时试图隐藏的感情。当感觉害羞时，我们不希望有他人在场，这常常发生在陌生的场合或与我们不认识的人在一起的时候。有时这是一个性别问题。男性和女性在一个男女都有的场合下会感到害羞。当男人和男人、女人和女人在一起时，他们不容易感到害羞。

害羞的成因很复杂。有时，一个人会因为生活中一件糟糕的事情而变得害羞。例如，如果你被自己爱的人伤害，这可能会使你在将来变得害羞。一个人也可能天生就害羞。在某些家庭中，如果一个孩子很外向，那么另一个就会很害羞。两个孩子的家庭环境是一样的，但每个孩子有不同的人格特点。科学家甚至开始讨论害羞的基因。

害羞也可能是一个文化问题。美国文化看重开朗、大胆的人，它鼓励人们积极进取，因此人们认为害羞是消极的。而其他一些文化并不崇尚特立独行的人。因此，在这些文化中，害羞的人会感到非常适应。

C 1. Ⓒ 2. Ⓐ 3. Ⓑ

一个著名的绿洲

锡瓦是一个著名的绿洲。这里是穿越非洲沙漠的军队和商旅休息的地方。它位于开罗以西 560 公里处，已经存在了超过一万年。

这个绿洲也因其强大的神喻而出名。人们会从几百公里外赶来寻求指引。即使今天，那里的神庙依然挺立，诉说着其重要地位。

据说，亚历山大大帝在入侵埃及时曾经在这里休息。据说，他和他的大军在沙漠中饮水耗尽。众神派了两只乌鸦指引他来到锡瓦，并拯救了他的军队。亚历山大拜见了神使。神使告诉他，他是神圣的，并将成为埃及的统治者。

锡瓦依赖农业。这是沙漠中的一项伟绩。一些人认为绿洲出产全世界最好的枣和橄榄。农民们精心照顾庄稼，确保水流以正确的方式流入并流出他们的土地。他们甚至用手给海枣树授粉。

D 1. Ⓒ 2. Ⓐ 3. Ⓓ

延长的青春期

三十年前，年轻人在二十岁左右就被认为是成人了。这是一个做出人生重要决定的年龄。孩子不再是孩子了。他们要找地方生活，找工作，并计划结婚。在 20 世纪 70 年代，结婚的平均年龄是二十四岁，现在则接近三十岁，许多做出重大决定的时间都比以前要晚。

难道这只是一个没有长大的问题吗？人们真的只是将"青春期"延长至二十几岁？他们是否仍然依赖父母呢？许多二十多岁的人在大学毕业后仍与父母住在一起。他们喜欢过去的舒适生活。他们想要偿还借来交大学学费的钱，同时也想要得到快乐。

但这些不足以解释这一发展趋势。人们的寿命更长了，他们想要晚点再做出这些重大的决定。他们看到老人退休得更晚了，工作的年头增加了。年轻的一代相信他们将长年照顾年迈的父母和自己的孩子。他们不希望急于进入人生的这一阶段。

Building Summary Skills

A & B

1. Forensic Science

Forensic science helps collect [1] information that is useful for [2] police work and the law. Police look for [3] small clues that can identify the [4] criminal. The clues can come from someone's body （blood, skin, or [5] fingerprints） or they can be [6] chemical （drugs）. The field is very [7] broad. Many things are studied for [8] forensic purposes.

2. Shyness

When we are [1] shy, we wish to [2] avoid other people. It often happens in [3] new situations. Sometimes, [4] men and women feel shy around each other. Things can happen in your life to make you [5] shy. Sometimes you are [6] born that way. In some cultures, shyness is not [7] valued, and in other cultures, it is a [8] good quality to have.

3. A Famous Oasis

[1] Siwa is a famous oasis, and it has sheltered people who cross the [2] desert. A powerful [3] priest lived there in ancient times. [4] Alexander the Great stopped in Siwa to consult him while conquering [5] Egypt. Siwa has a [6] water source, it depends on [7] farming, and it has some of the best [8] dates and olives in the world. Farmers must be very careful to manage the land and plants.

4. Extending the Teen Years

Children are taking on adult [1] responsibilities later in life. But are they just trying to keep living their [2] teenage lives? It is true that they owe a lot of money for [3] college, but they want to [4] enjoy their lives as well. People are also [5] working for many more years, and they are living longer, too. Children realize they will have to [6] take care of their aging [7] parents for longer periods of time, so children are not [8] in a hurry to begin this long phase of their lives.

Mini TOEFL iBT

1. Ⓐ 2. Ⓑ 3. Ⓐ 4. Ⓓ 5. Ⓑ 6. Ⓒ
7. Ⓐ 8. Ⓒ 9. Ⓐ 10. Ⓓ 11. Ⓐ 12. Ⓐ

世界的终点

从地理学的术语来看，火地岛也许就是世界的终点。它是位于南美洲最南部的一个小三角形岛屿。岛的名字表示"火的土地"。一个著名探险家看到了岸上的土著人所生的火，小岛由此得名。这个小岛属于阿根廷和智利共有。火地岛由于其独特的地理特征而闻名。

然而，这个岛并没有火。它位于南美洲的最南端，全年的平均温度只有5摄氏度。在冬天，这里变得更加寒冷。温差的主要原因是纬度。安第斯山脉往西形成冰河。冷雨和冷风使东北平坦的土地变得寒冷。

谈论火地岛的土地很容易。环绕小岛的河海也很独特，也许它们是世界上最重要的。它们是各种鸟类的家园。那里的信天翁是最出名的，还有鲸鱼、鱿鱼和许多其他种类的鱼。夏天的一些日子，成群的沙丁鱼游到这里。当地人可以走到水里用购物袋轻易地抓住它们。到处都是鱼群。没有饵，人们也能抓到鱼。这些鱼对当地和全世界都具有巨大的经济价值。

火地岛是一个少有的地方。在这样一个小岛上，有各种各样的地形面貌：山脉、森林和草原。两大洋在岛的两面交汇。这些特点使得这里成为很多野生动物的家园。这里的白昼夏天较长而冬天较短。这是地球上一个独一无二的地方。

家庭和金钱

现代世界正在改变家庭的关系。生活的开销正在影响美国家庭的行为。这也许不是什么好事。

几十年前，父亲出去工作。他的工资缴纳各种账单。母亲待在家里。她也许会去当地教堂或社区做义工。孩子们去上学。在十几岁时，有时孩子们在周末还有工作要做。

在美国的许多地方，事情发生了变化。生活开销正在增加，这其中最主要的是房价和健康保险。一般来说，一份工资已经无法购买或租一间房子并缴付账单。因此，父母都要工作。这使得家庭能够维持生计，并在需要时可以去看医生。

当父母都工作时，他们与孩子在一起的时间也发生了变化。许多父母把孩子送到日托的托儿所，这保证了孩子们受到照顾，但也减少了孩子在早期发育阶段与父母在一起的时间。此外，日托也是一项额外支出。父母双方要做更多的工作。

在学校读书时，通常都是孩子比父母回家早。由于要自己开门，他们常常被称为"钥匙儿童"。妈妈没有等在家里给孩子开门。这段时间可能会使他们接触到毒品或犯罪。孩子会因为缺乏监管而陷入很多麻烦。

逐渐增加的支出正在改变家庭生活。为了更好地生活而不断努力工作的同时，他们也面临着不同的危险。

Vocabulary Review

1. Ⓐ 2. Ⓒ 3. Ⓑ 4. Ⓓ 5. Ⓐ
6. Ⓑ 7. Ⓓ 8. Ⓐ 9. Ⓑ 10. Ⓓ

Unit 7 Inference

Skill &Drill

Example: Ⓑ

身体质量指数(BMI)能够告诉我们一个人的体重是否健康。这是一个身高和体重的比率。身体质量指数低于20的说明体重偏轻,指数为25说明健康,如果高于30说明体重超重。这个指数不是绝对的,它只是用来大致估计一个人的健康体重。

1. Ⓐ

在夏季,人们需要当心。炎热能使人生病,其中最严重的是中暑。中暑有一些基本症状:其中之一是高体温,第二是行为变化,而皮肤干燥是第三个症状。在许多情况下,身体无法出汗来冷却自己,这有可能导致晕厥。

2. Ⓒ

新闻有"硬新闻"和"软新闻"之分。硬新闻指的是那些严肃和时效性强的主题,包括政治、犯罪和战争。软新闻指的是那些不太严重的主题,时间不是新闻报道的重要因素,这包括体育新闻和名人的新闻。

3. Ⓒ

州权利关注的是州独立于国家之外的权利。各州有权决定自己的重要事务。一个州也许不批准死刑,而另一州却批准。只要与国家政府的法律没有冲突,各州可以自行作决定。现在,国家没有关于死刑的规定。各州可以按自己的意愿来决定。

4. Ⓑ

风湿使人的关节胀痛。随着人年龄的增大,包裹骨头的组织对骨头的保护变弱了,关节增大并变得疼痛。这常常发生在上了年纪的人身上,而且女性患病的概率高于男性。近三分之一的美国人或多或少地有这一疾病的症状。在一些例子中,病人的关节非常疼痛,医生不得不对关节进行替换。

5. Ⓐ

真人秀电视节目近几年很受欢迎。观众们喜欢看普通生活中的普通人。他们认为每天的生活中会发生很特别的事。但这真的是现实吗?有时一个电视节目会将普通人置于特别的情况中。他们会去特别的地方,而且节目并不完全播出。编导来选择播放哪些镜头。这改变了我们如何看待这件事。

Practice with Short Passages

A 1. Ⓓ 2. Ⓐ 3. Ⓑ 4. Ⓐ

成为记者

成为一名记者有一些条件。首先是良好的教育。广泛的知识是很重要的。但是就读于一所好大学有另一个优势。由于学校与新闻公司之间的关系,你可以受益找到第一份好工作。有时,你受的教育越多,工资就越高。其次是术业有专攻。可写的东西非常多,而且每个人都有自己独特的风格。第三是工作经验。找一家能够帮你学习你所需技能的公司,这份工作也许没有工资。第四是了解好的新闻记者是怎样工作的。他们知道如何找到好的新闻素材,明白事实和观点之间的区别。他们知道如何保护自己的新闻来源免受伤害。有了适当的背景、技能和努力的工作,新闻可以成为一个大有可为的事业。

B 1. Ⓐ 2. Ⓓ 3. Ⓐ 4. Ⓒ

白内障

白内障非常普遍,其症状是人眼的晶状体变模糊。一半以上的六十岁老人患有白内障。眼睛受伤也是一个可能的原因。最普遍的原因是太阳的紫外线。一项研究表明飞行员患白内障的风险很高,这很有可能是因为在高处,太阳光具有危险性。一些疾病也能导致白内障。当然,年龄也是一个原因。随着时间的推移,眼睛的一些部分也变弱了。医生过去用针将模糊的部分移除。现在,他们经常用塑料晶状体来代替人眼的晶状体。在绝大多数情况下,病人在手术当天就可以回家。

C 1. Ⓐ 2. Ⓒ 3. Ⓑ 4. Ⓐ

麦卡锡

美国的20世纪50年代是一个让人恐惧的时代。一个叫约瑟夫·麦卡锡的人想要获得政府的权力。他决定使用恐惧作为武器。那时,美国非常害怕与俄国交战,害怕俄国的侵略。当然，俄国人是共产主义者。麦卡锡利用了这种对共产主义的恐惧。如果没有任何证据，他就宣称某人为共产主义者。这导致了一系列的调查、审判和监禁。很多公众人物的生活被麦卡锡毁了。他们知道麦卡锡想要拥有更大的权力。他们抱怨说他很不公平。但他还是利用恐惧毁了他们的名誉。

D 1. Ⓑ 2. Ⓒ 3. Ⓑ 4. Ⓐ

斗牛中的马

每年，许多马在斗牛中受伤。牛和斗牛士往往是观众关注的中心，他们钦佩双方的勇敢和技能。有时，斗牛士是骑马的，他的马也要有技能。那是一匹经过高度训练的能够和斗牛士一起战斗的马。通过简单的指令，马和骑士可以向四个方向快速移动。这样可以躲避愤怒的公牛。公牛不知道是人给它带来疼痛。它只看到了马。观众不知道马的眼睛是被蒙上的，并且耳朵被棉花堵住。这样马就看不到也听不到公牛了。如果不这样的话，马将会被吓倒。在斗牛场上，马将生命托付给了斗牛士。有时，斗牛士不够快，因此公牛就杀死了马。

Practice with Long Passages

A 1. Ⓐ 2. Ⓑ 3. Ⓒ

新闻报道的标准

新闻是电视新闻和报纸新闻等的消息来源。人们可以自由选择、投票和思考。新闻推动了信息的流动。为了这个系统的运转，标准是必要的。好的新闻报道能够通过四个角度来解释：负面影响、真实、隐私和平衡。

报纸的新闻记者一定要想到负面影响。记者应该注意提出的问题可能会伤害他人的感情。例如，儿童非常敏感，所以一定要小心对待。在收集事实时，新闻记者一定要想到对儿童的影响。

真实是另一个方面。记者在报道事实时要尽量不犯错误。事实应该与观点明确区分开。这能够帮读者做出更好的判断。

隐私是另一点需要关注的。新闻记者一定要平衡公众的知情权与个人的隐私权。公众人物，比如政治家，不具有与普通大众一样的权利。

平衡也是很必要的。如果可能，一个故事的双方都应该被告知。当只有一方被告知时，记者似乎就是在偏袒一方。

B 1. Ⓐ 2. Ⓒ 3. Ⓓ

色盲症

色盲症更多困扰男性。患色盲症的人眼中的红色和绿色看起来一样——这一观点其实是错误的。实际上没那么简单。色盲有很多种。

眼睛的一个部分，视网膜，帮助我们分辨颜色。视网膜中有两种细胞：视杆细胞和视锥细胞。视杆细胞帮助我们在光线暗时看事物。视锥细胞使我们在正常光线下看事物。视锥细胞有三类，每一类分别对不同类型的光线敏感。我们能看到不同颜色是这三类视锥细胞共同作用的结果。当一种或多种视锥细胞不能正常工作时，就产生了色盲症。虽然少见，但还是有三种视锥细胞同时出现问题的时候。

色盲有时是由眼伤引起的。然而，绝大多数情况下，是由于基因遗传。基因位于 X 染色体。由于女性有两个 X 染色体，所以只有两个染色体都出现问题时色盲才会产生。而男性的两个染色体分别是 X 和 Y，只要 X 染色体受到影响就会出现色盲。

C 1. Ⓐ 2. Ⓒ 3. Ⓓ

国家分裂时期的林肯

亚伯拉罕·林肯促成了美国未来的命运。他帮助美国渡过了南北战争。奴隶制也随着战争一起终结。但是，这并非战争的目的。战争主要是为了维护政府下的国家统一。

在林肯时代，许多州还没有形成。美国政府拥有许多土地，但是这些土地还没有形成州。这些地方被称为准州。南方各州认为在准州成为州的时候应该推行奴隶制。这有利于他们在国家政治中的作用。而北方各州不希望南方因为拥有奴隶制而获得更多的国家政权。林肯意识到奴隶制正在分裂国家。他认为结束现状的最佳方法是结束全国的奴隶制。

林肯个人的种族信仰不得而知，但他坚信统一的思想是非常明显的。他相信"美利坚合众国"。所以他决定，在他上任的时候，就是奴隶制结束的时候。这会改变南方各州的经济体系，使其与北方各州一致，从而实现全国的统一。

D 1. Ⓒ 2. Ⓐ 3. Ⓒ

斗牛

斗牛是许多拉丁国家文化的一部分。葡萄牙、西班牙和法国保持了这一传统。美洲国家也是如此。古罗马和古希腊有人和牛的角斗。一些角斗要比另外一些更暴力。

勇气和风格是斗牛中最重要的。这不仅适用于人，也适用于牛。公牛被认为是一个值得尊重的对手。一头意志薄弱、体型较差的公牛会让牛的主人和整场斗牛盛会都很没有面子。如果斗牛士缺乏技巧，观众会为公牛喝彩。斗牛士一定要通过一击杀死公牛并站在公牛的两角之间来表现技巧。

这种对动物的残忍做法一直受到人们的关注。许多人认为让动物遭受痛苦是不对的，出于娱乐的目的而杀死它们更是不恰当的。为保持这一传统，法国和美国等国家有不致死的斗牛表演。法式斗牛必须要从公牛的角上抓下花朵。美国的斗牛使用维可牢（粘带）将矛粘在公牛身上。

Building Summary Skills

A & B

1. Standards in Reporting

TV news and [1] newspapers are examples of the [2] press, and they give information that helps people choose, [3] vote, and think. There are [4] standards for a good press. [5] Reporters must be careful not to harm the person they are writing about. He or she must try to report the [6] facts as closely as possible. A reporter must also consider a person's [7] privacy and try to tell [8] both sides of a story.

2. Colorblindness

Colorblindness is mostly found in [1] men. The parts of the eye called [2] cones help us see certain [3] colors of light. When the cones do not [4] work properly, it results in [5] colorblindness. Sometimes colorblindness happens because of an [6] injury. Most of the time, this condition is [7] genetic, and it is passed on to children through the [8] X chromosome.

3. Lincoln in a Divided Land

Lincoln came to [1] power at a time when the United States was trying to decide on [2] slavery. Many [3] southern states wanted any new states to have slaves. It would help increase their [4] political power, but [5] northern states did not want this. This issue [6] divided the North and South. Lincoln thought it was best to [7] end slavery in the whole country because he believed that the country should be [8] united.

4. Bullfighting

Bullfighting is an old [1] tradition in some countries. [2] Courage, form, and style are very important in this sport for both [3] man and bull. If the man has [4] poor skills, the crowd will cheer for the bull, so the man must show his skill by killing the bull [5] quickly. Some people think this sport is [6] cruel because it is not [7] fair to make animals suffer. Some countries have bullfights that do not [8] hurt the bull.

Mini TOEFL iBT

1. Ⓐ　2. Ⓑ　3. Ⓑ　4. Ⓐ　5. Ⓓ　6. Ⓒ
7. Ⓑ　8. Ⓒ　9. Ⓐ　10. Ⓒ　11. Ⓓ　12. Ⓓ

美国食品及药物管理局

FDA 是美国食品及药物管理局的简称。这是一个保证消费者商品安全的政府机构。该机构管理食品和食品供应。同时，它也控制食品增补剂。食品及药物管理局也要保证药品和医疗设备的安全和效用。

药品和医疗设备要获得批准，一定要经历一个较长的过程。这一过程中有许多严格的测试。首先，适用于人的药物一定要先在动物身上试验，这一阶段要经过六年的时间。接下来，要有一些人试用。在 15 到 20 个人身上的试验要持续一年半。第三阶段，一个中型人群（100 到 500 人）需要接受试验，这需要大约两年的时间。再接下来，一个更大的人群要接受超过三年的试验。在接受测试的 5000 种药品中，只有 5 种能够进入预选阶段；在这之中，只有 1 种被投放到市场。

食品增补剂，如人参，一般遵循不同的流程。食品及药物管理局不会进行如同药品一样的前期试验。他们只负责控制已经开始出售但不安全的产品。婴儿食品和医疗食品是两个例外。食用这些东西的人都不是很强壮，所以药管局对这些产品非常小心。

标签是一个重心。标签一定要标明商品的用途。对药品来说，标签应该包含药品名称和用途，还应详细标明该产品的使用人群和副作用。同时，标签上要对孕妇、儿童和老人使用该药物做详细的说明，还要写有详细的有关安全使用的信息。

食品及药物管理局保护公众免受伤害。该机构通过控制和标签来实现这个目的。它制定医疗产品的效果标准和信息共享的标准。

被剥夺的机会

机会可以表现为选择。人们到美国来就是因为如此。他们感觉有更多的选择。但是选择是有限的，机会没有想象的那么容易得到。

正如统计数字表明的，情况并不乐观。工资是一个关注的重点。女性每挣八十一美分，男性就挣到一美金。这种差异在受教育的男性和女性之间更大。第二，富人的工资增加了百分之二十七，而穷人的工资仅仅增加了百分之一。白人获得的最多。贫穷的少数族裔男性的数量正在增加。

拥有家庭是拥有一个成功生活的关键。在过去的二十年里，越来越多的穷人失去了他们的家。更多的中产阶级和上层社会拥有家庭，但是他们没有风险。拥有家庭，在有麻烦时就能借到钱。对于经常有麻烦的穷人来说，这是一个严肃的问题。

最后，银行和保险业拒绝机会。穷人因为自身的背景而很难得到贷款。即使得到贷款，他们也不得不支付更高的利息，因为他们属于高危人群。而他们恰恰是最付不起额外费用的人。同时，四千五百万人没有保险。他们中的绝大多数是移民、少数族裔和穷人。他们不能得到医疗保证。没有保险的保护，他们更有可能失去全部。许多穷人没有高价保护。当事件发生时，他们不得不为了支付账单而变卖全部财产。

Vocabulary Review

1. Ⓒ **2.** Ⓐ **3.** Ⓑ **4.** Ⓒ **5.** Ⓐ
6. Ⓓ **7.** Ⓑ **8.** Ⓒ **9.** Ⓐ **10.** Ⓓ

Unit 8 Insert Text

Skill & Drill

Example: Ⓐ

著名的摇滚明星博诺因为他其他方面的工作而出名。他是个人文主义者。他努力提高最贫穷国家人民的生活。他认为尊重人权是帮助他人的第一步。博诺想要帮助人们自助，也就是说他试图改变导致人们贫穷的社会结构，这也意味着要改变一个国家的经济规则，意味着帮助人们用一种现实的方法借钱还钱。他想要改变伤害穷人的不公平的贸易规则。

1. Ⓐ

欺凌弱小是一种卑鄙的行为。它指的是一个人恐吓和伤害比自己弱小的人。当欺凌发生在孩子们身上的时候，通常家长并不在身边。欺凌弱小者会谩骂受害者并取笑他们所做的事情。他会对受害者的朋友说受害者的坏话，甚至还会偷受害者的东西。欺凌弱小的行为一定要在早期得到制止，这样，孩子就不会养成这种行为习惯了。

2. Ⓐ

威廉·巴特勒·叶芝是一名爱尔兰诗人。他描写爱情、爱尔兰传说、魔术和精神。叶芝是现代最重要的英语诗人之一，但是他喜欢用传统的形式进行诗歌创作。他喜欢使用古代诗人所使用的韵律和节奏。他的诗歌给人印象深刻、永恒。叶芝对人类经验有独到的理解。他的思想被广为推崇，其影响甚至涉及到政治领域。

3. Ⓑ

克隆人类产生了一些问题。首先，我们必须考虑独一无二的意义。这对我们的社会重要吗？事实上，这对所有的生物来说都是一种必须的特质。作为独一无二的人，我们对自我的感觉是对所有事物感觉的中心。如果我们是从他人克隆来的，我们对自己身份的想法将发生变化。这也许不太好。同时，我们必须要考虑关系。当我们克隆其他人的时候，我们不是在影响被克隆的人，而是被克隆的人周围的人。

4. Ⓑ

共同法是英国的一个法律体系。全世界许多国家都使用该法。法庭的判决依据于以往案例的结果。共同法的一个特点是陪审团审判制。一群人来决定嫌疑人是否有罪。另一个特点是，没有任何人可以凌驾于法律之上，即使是总统。他或她一定要像普通人一样遵从法律。

5. Ⓑ

对于亚历山大城在埃及的重要性始终有一些争论。其文化中心和商业中心的属性难道不更为重要吗？有些人说其作为文化中心的作用最为重要。那里有著名的图书馆，并一度是全世界最大的；它吸引了世界各地的许多学者。该城对于当前学术发展的贡献不容小觑。埃及的很多粮食贸易都集中在该城。它为陷入饥荒的国家提供粮食并使自己变得富裕。这个城市因此拥有非常强大的力量。

Practice with Short Passages

A 1. Ⓑ 2. Ⓐ 3. **D**

温斯顿·丘吉尔

温斯顿·丘吉尔是大不列颠的一位伟大领袖。他来自一个培养了很多政治家和战争英雄的家族。小时候，他的学业不佳。但是随着年龄的增长，他对于军事学习非常着迷。他在皇家军事学院毕业时的成绩是班级的第八名。接着，他加入了英国驻印度的军队，学习士兵的技能。这对他来说是一段很有益的经历。后来，他从军队退役，作为一名新闻记者去了南非。他想要报道英国和荷兰之间的战争。虽然不再是一名士兵，但丘吉尔仍然坚持战斗。他被敌人抓到了。但在一个月后，他成功逃脱并来到几百英里外一个安全的地方。他作为一个英雄回到了英国。之后，丘吉尔竞选议员并顺利当选，他的政治生涯自此揭开序幕。

B 1. Ⓓ 2. Ⓐ 3. **C**

女性的社会压力

女性为了变得美丽和成功承受着很大的社会压力，这也导致了她们的紧张。媒体使她们认为自己应该像电影明星一样漂亮。她们认为美丽是由他人而不是自己来定义的。这种电影明星般的美丽与另一个信息相冲突，即女性应该有独立、成功的事业。基本上，她们应该坚强、聪明并善于工作。在许多情况下，她们会变得情绪低落。这些女性说她们不想太在意这些，但却不得不如此。到了三十岁，压力变小了。女性学会了不过于在意别人的想法。

C 1. Ⓒ 2. Ⓓ 3. **B**

埃兹拉·庞德

埃兹拉·庞德是一个著名的美国诗人。他在美国长大，但却在欧洲旅居多年。他受视觉艺术家和中国古典诗歌影响很大。他的诗歌复杂而精细。他在伦敦住了一些年，并遇到了他心目中的英雄——威廉·巴特勒·叶芝。他们一起进行诗歌的创作，彼此之间的影响也很大。庞德也与詹姆斯·乔伊斯和艾略特一起工作过。在第一次世界大战后，他搬到了意大利。他认为在那个时候，意大利是良好的、有道德感的社会。那里没有遭到资本主义的破坏。在第二次世界大战期间，他被美国人逮捕。他们说他犯有叛国罪，并将他送进了监狱。在监狱服刑的十二年中，他创作出了一批极其美妙的诗歌，这些诗歌表现了他对于周围生活的理解。

D 1. Ⓑ 2. Ⓓ 3. **C**

体育流氓

体育流氓是那些在体育赛事中捣乱的人。他们是喜欢惹是生非的体育迷，经常破坏体育比赛场馆周围的地区。"体育流氓"这个名词第一次出现在 1898 年伦敦警察的报告中。这些暴力有很长的历史。在公元 532 年，数千人在一次持续一周的暴力冲突中死亡。这次冲突是由一次田径比赛的体育迷们引起的。在现代，足球是引起球迷暴力的最主要原因。从 20 世纪 50 年代起，这个问题就频繁出现在英国。意大利也有类似的问题。这一体育暴力也扩展到了其他的国家。这直接威胁到了其他非暴力球迷安全地欣赏体育比赛，也使得足球场周围的商店很难安全地经营。各国都制定了严格的法律惩罚那些制造麻烦的球迷。

Practice with Long Passages

A 1. **1A** 2. **2A**

贝蒂·弗里丹

贝蒂·弗里丹在美国为女性争取权利。她的人生经历和教育赋予了她强大的影响力。她能够改变社会对女性的看法。

弗里丹生于 1921 年。她在史密斯学院学习心理学，同时为学院的报纸工作。弗里丹后来去了加州大学伯克利分校读研究生。

弗里丹婚后育有三个孩子。最初，她为女性居家杂志写稿。对此，她感到厌倦也很不开心。她的能力在家庭生活中毫无用武之地。1957 年，弗里丹问史密斯学院的毕业生们是否觉得自己生活幸福。她发现许多人觉得不幸福。她们的生活就是为了孩子和丈夫的成功。弗里丹写下了社会如何强迫女性生活在家里，她们就是为了家庭生活而存在，没有任何有趣、具有挑战性的职业。《女性的奥秘》一书变得非常出名。十二年后，弗里丹与丈夫离婚。她为了一个新的女性形象而努力工作。女性应该在更多领域参与社会而不仅仅是家庭主妇。她说，女性应该成为男性的搭档。

B　1. **1** B　2. **2** D

儿童肥胖症

肥胖是很多人在童年的必经时期。然而，肥胖症意味着体内脂肪过多。有这种问题的孩子在成年后也会有肥胖问题。它导致持续时间很长的健康问题。

从 20 世纪 70 年代起，患儿童肥胖症的人数逐渐增加。一些儿童属于高危人群。有超重问题的家族是一个危险因素；吸烟和生活懒惰则是另一个危险因素。

肥胖症不是一个个人问题，而是一个社会问题。当然，一个肥胖的人会有健康问题。但是当有太多肥胖的人时，社会一定会付出代价。健康保险的耗资会增加，学校会有更多的问题，而且，劳动力素质下降。

社会是导致肥胖的诱因之一。学校没有提供健康的生活选择。食品公司被批准在学校做垃圾食品的广告并进行销售。更糟的是，许多学校由于经费问题而削减体育课的课时。在家里，孩子们看太多的电视或玩太久的游戏。父母也有不良的饮食习惯。他们应该表现出良好的生活习惯，不应该购买太多不健康的食品。在孩子小时候就教给他们健康的行为是很重要的。

C　1. **1** A　2. **2** C

悲剧的文学形式

悲剧是戏剧类型的一种。这一戏剧形式在西方文化中已经存在几千年了。

悲剧是关于发生在一个主人公身上的悲惨事件的戏剧。这一悲惨事件与主人公的行为有关。这是由于主人公身上被称为"悲剧性缺陷"的人格弱点造成的。在许多情节中，诸神因为主人公而愤怒，并使他历经磨难。这种惩罚非常残忍，而主人公必须忍受。观众通过这一事件以及他的悲惨遭遇来理解主人公的缺点。

在一些时候，主人公会认识到自己的错误。他经历了某种学习的过程。接下来，诸神会决定停止对他的惩罚。在戏剧中，神会下界来传达信息，并将主人公从悲惨的遭遇中解救出来。

观众经历了从恐惧到欣慰的感情转变过程。这被称为心理疏泄，也就是情感的治疗。这些简单的想法已持续数千年之久。

D　1. **1** B　2. **2** A

残奥会

残疾人奥林匹克运动会与夏季奥林匹克运动会同年举办。这一赛事给运动员提供了展现能力的机会。他们的身体在一定程度上都是有缺陷的。

残疾人奥林匹克运动会在夏季奥林匹克运动会结束的三星期后开始。残奥会的运动员与奥运会的运动员使用同样的场地和场馆。前缀"para"在希腊文中意思是"在……旁边"。这一运动会是在其他运动会之外额外举办的。

参加这一体育赛事的运动员必须是残疾人。一般分为五类：一些残疾人没有胳膊或腿；一些人脑部有残疾，平衡感较差；一些运动员需要坐轮椅；有一些是盲人；还有一些有遗传缺陷。这一体育赛事的伟大之处在于对残疾人能力的关注。他们的残疾并不是重点。

残奥会始于英国，当时主要是为了从第二次世界大战战场上受伤归来的士兵而举办的。第一届官方残奥会于 1960 年成功举办，共有 400 名运动员参加。最近的一次残疾人奥林匹克运动会有来自 136 个国家的近 4000 名运动员参加。

Building Summary Skills

A & B

1. Betty Friedan

Betty Friedan was a [1] feminist, and she argued for women to be treated [2] fairly in society and in marriage. Friedan had a family, but she was not [3] happy with her life as a [4] housewife. She asked other female [5] college graduates how they felt. Friedan discovered that they felt the same way, so she wrote [6] a book about it. She said women should take part in society more [7] actively and be seen as [8] equal to men.

2. Child Obesity

Children with [1] obesity might have long lasting health risks. There are more children today with this problem than in the [2] 1970s. Some children are more likely to be [3] obese than others. Obesity also affects [4] society because it affects the cost of [5] health care and creates social problems. We can change how [6] schools and companies operate to decrease the risk of obesity, and we should allow better [7] food choices and promote good [8] behavior.

3. The Literary Form of Tragedy

A [1] tragedy is a traditional form of [2] theater. It has a hero who, because of his [3] personality, gets put into a [4] bad situation where he must [5] suffer. The hero learns from his ways, and the gods stop his [6] punishment. The audience experiences a range of [7] emotions while watching the play. This emotional change is a [8] key part of tragedy, and this form of drama has lasted for thousands of years.

4. Paralympics

The Paralympics give [1] disabled athletes the chance to show their [2] skills. Only certain kinds of [3] disabilities are permitted in the games. The important thing is that the disability is not the focus, but [4] excellence in sports is the focus. The games first started in [5] England after [6] World War II with just a few people. Years later, there are [7] four thousand athletes and [8] 136 countries competing.

Mini TOEFL iBT

1. Ⓐ 2. **D** 3. Ⓒ 4. Ⓑ 5. Ⓑ 6. Ⓓ
7. Ⓓ 8. Ⓓ 9. Ⓑ 10. Ⓐ 11. **D** 12. Ⓑ

威廉·史密斯

威廉·史密斯生活在 17 世纪末，是一名工程师。他的一个简单发现成就了他一生的事业。他想要勾画出英国的地质概况。

史密斯来自英格兰西部的一个农民家庭。他的父亲在他很小的时候就去世了。史密斯被叔叔抚养长大。他接受过一些基本的教育，但通过读书自学地理知识。他很早就对在住处附近找到的化石产生了兴趣。

史密斯长大后成为了一名工程师。他在煤炭公司做检测土地质量的工作。他需要从一些地方抽水以探测挖掘工作的难易。

史密斯要为煤炭公司挖一条隧道。挖的时候他发现土地有很多层。他注意到每一层都有某些种类的化石。当他穿越英国时，他发现了同样的特点。史密斯相信英国北部的土层与南部的是相联系的。他认识到这些土层讲述着土地的古老历史。很快，史密斯就走遍了英国。有时他每年骑

马或乘坐马车穿越几千英里观察土壤的层次。

史密斯尽一切努力和别人分享他的知识。他绘制地图，标记英国的不同地区分别产哪种石头、土壤和植物。他在农民的聚会和晚餐会上讲述这一切，还写了几本书。

史密斯才能卓越。他许多观察土地特点的方法沿用至今。他绘制的地图非常精确，即使在今天仍然被人们使用。他创造的许多地理学名词也被广为应用。

古埃及体育

古埃及的很多体育项目今天仍然存在。事实上，许多体育的基本因素，如规则和统一服装，首先是由埃及人创造的。体育有着重要的社会功能。一些体育运动可以给参与者带来快乐和健康，还有一些可以用来产生强壮的勇士和领袖。

第一类以乐趣为目的的体育项目包括划船、狩猎和跳高等。狩猎和捕鱼是国王和普通百姓都可以参与的。此外还有划船。划船比赛需要很多力量。成队的人坐在船上听一个领导的指挥。他将用规则的高声呐喊来告诉其他人何时划船。这一技巧即使在今天仍然在划船运动中使用。

另一项流行的运动是拔河。参赛的两支队伍要把对方拉过界。如果一队向前扑倒，裁判则判其输掉了比赛。这项运动在今天的埃及仍然流行。

第二类体育运动为军队和神庙训练人员，其中包括拳击、马术、赛跑和射箭。这些都是训练战斗技能的方法，也是磨练人精神力量的训练。马拉松就是一个很好的例子。

曲棍球是另一种埃及运动。在埃及人的陪葬中发现的图画就记录了这种运动。选手们手持如同今天的曲棍球棒的带弯把的树枝，并击打颜色鲜亮的皮质球。

这些运动都是埃及文化的一部分，它们给人带来了愉快和健康。其基本规则几千年前就形成了，而在今天，它们中的一部分仍然可见。

Vocabulary Review

1. Ⓑ 2. Ⓐ 3. Ⓓ 4. Ⓒ 5. Ⓑ
6. Ⓐ 7. Ⓒ 8. Ⓑ 9. Ⓑ 10. Ⓓ

Skill & Drill

Example: (A), (B)

农民在雨水不足的时候需要以其他方式浇灌庄稼。短期来看，这是一件好事，然而从长远来看，这种做法对土地极为不利。多数情况下，灌溉庄稼的水中含有少量的盐。通常，这没有什么问题，但假以时日，土壤中的盐分就会积聚。最终，盐分堆积到一定程度后，土壤就会变得不利于耕种。农民需要小心控制流过土壤的水量来掌控土壤中盐分的水平。

1. (B), (C)

稀少意味着不足。如果需要稀少的东西，你就得决定如何去做。例如，如果燃油稀少，油价就会上升，你就得决定是否要付这个价钱。如果你不想付怎么办？你可以去其他地方看看，但是不得不走很远。或者，你也可以学习在生活中不使用它。就燃油这个问题来说，你可以少开车，改为骑自行车或与别人搭车。

2. (A), (C)

法律的哲学被称为法学，意思就是"有关法律的知识"。研究法学的人尝试理解某些法律的原因、这些法律的构成以及如何使用。了解法律对我们的社会有非常重要的影响。法学学生可以学习当前正在使用的法律。除了好处之外，也会有一些意外的结果。学生们也可以研究新法律的理念。随着犯罪发生变化，新法律的出台也成为必然。

3. (A), (B)

流通中的美元钞票的数量一定要得到控制。如果政府印刷了太多的钞票，物价就会上涨。最开始，这看上去有些不符合逻辑。但是更多的钞票意味着人们有更多的钱可以花。在此情况下，由于人们能够偿付，因此物价很容易上涨。但是也会出现另一种结果。如果流通中的钞票增长了一倍，那么所有流通中的钞票的价值就下降了一半。那么你将必须付给工人一倍的工资以使他们得到同样的价值。这些新的花销推动了物价的上涨。

Practice with Short Passages

A   **1.** (C)   **2.** (A)   **3.** (A), (B)

酒后驾车的义务

酒后驾车是交通事故的一个主要原因。当一个醉酒的司机发生交通事故时，一系列事情便相应地发生。如果司机撞伤了某人，或导致某人财产的损坏，受害者将会起诉肇事者。这是因为肇事司机要对他的行为负责。从法律的角度来说，义务意味着责任。但是义务并不止于肇事司机。在美国，交通事故的受害者也能够起诉为肇事司机提供酒的酒吧。他们甚至可以起诉酒保。这是因为人们认为酒吧"帮助"司机喝醉，所以酒吧在交通事故中也有错。这意味着这些地方一定要小心，他们不能让客人喝醉。

B   **1.** (A)   **2.** (C)   **3.** (A), (C)

轮作的优点

轮作是中世纪社会的一个巨大进步。特殊的耕种技术使得种植粮食比以前更容易。因此，人口得以增长。轮作的概念很简单。每一种植物从土壤中获得不同的养分，吸引一些特别种类的昆虫。因此如果一直在同一个地方种植同一种植物，最终，土壤就会变得不具有庄稼生长所需的条件，而长出来的庄稼会被昆虫吃掉。

在中世纪，人们认识到如果每一季在同一块地种植不同的作物，第二种作物就会代替第一种作物从土地中得到的养分。如果农民种植一种牛喜欢吃的作物，那么它们的粪便会给土壤增加更多的养分。这是一个新的发现。因此，人们在每一季种植不同的作物。土地变得更适合耕种，就会产出更多的粮食。

C   **1.** (A)   **2.** (C)   **3.** (A), (C)

睡眠紊乱

睡眠紊乱主要有三种：无法入睡、嗜睡和呼吸影响睡眠。第一种被称为失眠，这意味着你无法睡好。也许你很难入睡，或你始终睡不着。在白天，你也许会感觉很困倦或压力很大，很难集中注意力。第二种是嗜眠，被称为睡眠疾病。你无法控制自己何时入睡，即使是在白天。事实上，如果你很兴奋，你的身体就会试着入睡。当醒来时，你无法移动或说话。第三种被称为呼吸暂停。这是一种睡眠中的呼吸问题。通常，入睡时你的喉咙开始闭合。导致这种问题的原因可能是酗酒或体重过重。肌肉无法有效地控制。还有一些时候，大脑不发出呼吸的信号，那么你就醒了。

D   **1.** (B)   **2.** (A)   **3.** (B), (D)

博弈论

经济学家研究选择的作用，他们称之为博弈论。其结果依赖于所有被研究者的选择。有时，我们不得不做出自私的选择。这样的选择可以使我们的生活变得更好，但不会对我们周围的人有任何帮助。不但没有帮助，甚至可能会给他们带来伤害。还有些时候，我们做出对其他人最有利而对我们自己不利的选择。例如，假设城里到处是垃圾，那么城市就会变得非常丑陋。游客也不愿来观光。商店的店主认为对城镇最好的做法就是走出家门，清理垃圾。如果一个店主清理了，那么大家都受益，然而，那个店主在使用自己的时间。他的工作没有任何回报，也没有人帮助他。

Practice with Long Passages

A   Ⓐ, Ⓑ, Ⓔ

米兰达权利

根据美国法律，一个人在被警察问询时有权保持沉默。如果他因为一项犯罪而入狱，他也有权请律师。这些权利的原因非常简单：警察不能强迫一个人说出任何致使他有罪的话。被逮捕的人一定要了解他的权利。

米兰达权利是警察在逮捕嫌疑犯时所说的话。他们说："你有权保持沉默。如果你放弃这一权利，你所说的任何话都将在法庭上被用作证据。你有权在问询期间请律师，如果你请不起律师，法庭将为你免费指定一位。在问询期间，你有权选择不回答。"警察要保证嫌疑犯了解这些。他们必须用犯人所使用的语言来陈述米兰达权利。

曾经发生过因警察没有很好地陈述嫌犯的权利而使嫌疑犯被释放的事例。在任何社会中，嫌疑犯了解法律并了解他们的权利都是非常重要的。这是一种保证社会对每一个人都公平的方式。

B   Ⓐ, Ⓓ, Ⓕ

如何种茶

茶是在多个文化中都颇受青睐的饮品。它历史悠久。过去，茶主要出产于中国的南方和印度的北部。现在，全世界都在种植茶叶。

茶树大约需要四年的时间才能长出能够用来制成好茶的叶子。在野外，茶树常常可以长到五到十五米。对于农业种植来说，一般将其高度控制在两米。这个高度保证了茶树能经常长出新叶。采茶季从三月一直持续到十一月。

茶树喜水，最理想的情况是在夜里下雨。这使得茶树能够获得足够的水分并为第二天的阳光做好准备。白天应该较长，并比较温暖，有很充足的阳光。阳光和水分给植物长出新叶提供所需的养分。

最好的茶叶是手工采摘的。绝大多数情况下，应采摘树冠顶部的两层最鲜嫩的叶子。茶树的高度使得人们从各个角度采茶都很容易。采摘下来的茶叶放进篮子中，准备进入下一个环节。

C   Ⓐ, Ⓓ, Ⓕ

维生素

维生素对人体的成长具有帮助作用。人体需要十三种维生素，其中的四种可以通过脂肪吸收，另外九种需要通过水吸收。这些维生素维系人体内发生的化学反应，使人体吸收摄入的食物。这在儿童的成长期是非常重要的。成年人需要维生素来保持健康。

儿童需要维生素来生长骨骼和组织。如果儿童缺乏维生素 D，他的骨头就会变软，从而导致腿骨弯曲。

成年人需要维生素来保证神经系统的运转。缺乏维生素，他们就会得病，例如视力下降或心跳不正常。他们可能总是感到虚弱。

早在一百多年前，人们就认识到饮食中的维生素是健康的主要原因。饮食不调也会导致一些疾病。英国水手曾经得过一种叫做坏血病的疾病。他们的皮肤出现斑点，嘴开始流血。这是因为他们没有摄入足够的维生素 C。一个医生发现了这个原因，并确保所有的船上都要备有柠檬和酸橙。

D   Ⓑ, Ⓓ, Ⓕ

宾夕法尼亚的煤矿

煤炭是一种重要的能源。各国都花费大量金钱来获得其所拥有的煤。美国东部有开采煤矿的传统，宾夕法尼亚州就是这样的一个地方。其产煤量巨大，但也是煤矿事故的高发区。

开采地下的煤炭有两种方式，第一种方式是在地表下挖洞。矿工们开出的隧道能达到几英里长。第二种方式叫做露天采矿。矿工们把地表的土层挖开很大的一个区域，直到挖到煤为止。

宾夕法尼亚州的森特罗利亚出产高质量的煤。其燃烧产生的热量比其他种类的煤更大。那里有许多露天煤矿。不幸的是，城市的垃圾倾倒场在一个古老的露天矿坑附近。1962 年，垃圾自燃，并引发了露天煤矿的火灾。火首先在地下燃烧，而想要扑灭地下的火几乎是不可能的。煤炭良好的质量使这场灾难更加严重。火在地下燃烧了四十多年。没有人知道如何将火扑灭。有人说这场火灾将持续 250 年。

Building Summary Skills

A & B

1. Miranda Rights

The [1] Miranda Rights remind people that they have the right to [2] silence and a [3] lawyer if police question them about a crime. This is because people do not have to [4] say anything that will make them [5] guilty of a crime. Criminals have been [6] set free because police failed to give them this [7] warning. All people must know their rights，even if they are [8] criminals.

2. How to Cultivate Tea

[1] Tea is drunk all over the world. The tea plant takes [2] four years to mature and is kept [3] small to ensure lots of leaves and easy [4] picking. It grows well in climates that are [5] warm and [6] wet. The best tea is picked [7] by hand. The delicate [8] top leaves are picked and carried in baskets to the next stage of processing.

3. Vitamins

Vitamins are [1] necessary for the body to build itself and stay [2] healthy. Some are taken in through [3] fat and others through [4] water. Children need vitamins to grow strong [5] bones and organs，and adults need them for strong [6] nervous systems. People have learned that their [7] diets are the key to getting enough vitamins. Some [8] diseases occur if you do not eat well.

4. Pennsylvania's Coal

Pennsylvania has provided a lot of [1] coal，which is an important [2] fuel. There are many [3] coal mines there. Open mining was used in a town called [4] Centralia，where there is high-quality coal. One of the coal mines caught [5] fire and started burning [6] underground. It is impossible to [7] put out the fire，and it may burn for [8] 250 years.

Mini TOEFL iBT

1. Ⓓ 2. Ⓐ 3. Ⓓ 4. Ⓓ 5. Ⓐ, Ⓒ, Ⓓ
6. Ⓒ 7. Ⓐ 8. Ⓒ 9. Ⓑ 10. Ⓑ, Ⓒ, Ⓔ

有机农业

有机农业背后的理念是不使用任何化肥。农民一定要使用天然的方式来促进植物茁壮成长，并保护植物免受害

虫的破坏。有人认为，没有化肥，这些植物将成为人类更好的食物。但是这个理念并非如此简单。有机农业关注环境中所有的作物和昆虫，旨在提升自然的健康状态。

化肥是促进农作物生长的化学物质。如果农民在一个地方一遍一遍地种植同一种农作物，土壤将会失去为农作物提供所需养分的能力。农民必须给土地施肥以达到这个目的。有机农业的农民不添加任何化肥。他们将采用轮作技术，并使用动物粪便和从分解到土壤中的植物成分做的植物堆肥使土壤变得肥沃。这样农作物生长所需要的所有养分就都能够满足了。

杀虫剂的使用也应尽量避免。杀虫剂是杀死害虫和有害动物的化学物质。有机农业的农民有其他方式来解决害虫问题，因为杀虫剂也会杀死对农作物有益的昆虫和动物。狐狸和蛇吃老鼠。一些昆虫，如瓢虫，会吃掉害虫。当然，还有杂草的问题。杂草是农民们不需要的，因为它们会抢夺农作物的生长空间。为了除去杂草，有机农业的农民可以多挖几次土壤，最终，杂草就会死掉了。

有机农业通常需要许多人力来达到施化肥起到的作用。这就是有机食品的价格更高一些的一个原因。但是，当我们考虑到土地、农作物和动物的健康的时候，这一切也许就物有所值了。一个健康的地球最终也意味着我们的健康。

世贸组织

世界贸易组织(简称世贸组织)有 149 个成员国。他们的目的是促进贸易。贸易意味着商品的买卖。世贸组织为这些国家提供了一个能够讨论所需商品的地方，它的目标是通过克服国家间的法律壁垒来促进贸易增长。

世贸组织在几个方面推进贸易发展。首先，它要求各成员国平等相待。各成员国不得为某一个国家提供特殊贸易交易而拒绝别国享有同等待遇。同时，成员国也不得阻止来自另一国的进口商品。这个理念就是商品和服务应该能够轻易地穿越国界。第二个促进贸易的方式是降低关税。关税是对买卖货物所征收的特别费用。第三种加强贸易的方式是保证规则不变。为了促进投资，有必要使投资者感到未来操作的安全。第四种方式是允许国家间更大程度上的竞争。其核心理念是竞争可以促进经济的发展。最后一种推动贸易的方法是帮助贫困国家。贫困国家需要帮助才能达到现代国家的水平。这可以通过给予他们更多的时间调整各项体制来实现。在与别国进行贸易时，他们应被给予优先权。

世贸组织的目标是自由和便捷的贸易。该组织支持富国，并帮助穷国前进。这是改善更多人生活状况的一个方法。它要求成员国制定法律来推进这一进程。每年，越来越多的国家申请加入世贸组织，他们认为这是一件好事。

1. Ⓓ   2. Ⓐ   3. Ⓑ   4. Ⓓ   5. Ⓒ
6. Ⓐ   7. Ⓑ   8. Ⓓ   9. Ⓐ   10. Ⓒ

Unit 10   Fill in a Table

Skill & Drill

Example: Liver Ⓓ / Brain Ⓑ

我们的体内有一个生物钟。我们感觉饥饿、睡觉和醒来都有一个固定的时间周期。体内的细胞也根据这一生物钟来自我修复。生物钟位于两个地方。首先，肝脏中的细胞在我们吃东西的时候发挥影响。其次，大脑中的一小部分细胞控制身体的生物钟，它们对阳光发生反应，这样，我们的身体就与太阳的运转有相似的时间表。如果乘飞机环球旅行，我们的身体会根据当地时间自行调整。当然，这要花上几天，这样我们的身体就经历了时差。

1. Interplate Quakes Ⓑ / Intraplate Quakes Ⓒ

当地球表面的板块移动时，地震就发生了。有时，板块互相摩擦，这被称为板间地震。当板块之间发生突然滑动时，能量以震荡波的形式被释放出来。这时，两个板块都如同吉他的琴弦一样波动。地震也会因为板块中间发生断裂而产生，这被称为板内地震。这种地震常令科学家们措手不及，因为它们发生在从未发生过地震的地方。

2. Gaseous Nebula Ⓓ / Dust Nebula Ⓑ, Ⓔ

"星云"这个词用来指任何既非行星又非流行的星体。这意味着星河和星群也属于星云的类别。星云实际是指宇宙中的尘埃和气体。事实上，"星云"这个词在拉丁文中的意思是"云"。一种星云是由气体构成的。当热气冷却，光亮就被释放出来。通常，这些星云是红色的。另一种星云由尘埃构成。它们反射附近星体的光。还有一种尘埃星云阻挡其后面物体发出的光。

3. Before Ⓑ / After Ⓓ, Ⓔ

伊利运河是一条连接纽约哈德逊河与五大湖的水上高速公路。在运河开掘之前，旅游和贸易都非常不便。人和货物不得不靠马车运输。虽然有时也使用河流来运输，但这对天气的要求很高。旅行和贸易非常昂贵、缓慢而且危险。在运河开掘之后，情况变得好了起来。首先，货物运输

的成本降低了，而且节约了时间。这促进了贸易的发展。在西部种植的农作物可以被卖到欧洲。其次，人们能够向西移动，美国的领土得以扩大。

Practice with Short Passages

Ⓐ   1. Ⓑ   2. Ⓓ
3. First Way of Formation Ⓐ, Ⓓ
   Second Way of Formation Ⓒ

黑洞

黑洞很难观测到。它们既不发光，也不反射光，因为其引力将所有东西都吸入其中。物理学家得以了解黑洞存在的唯一方式是通过观察事物被其吸入。在这一过程中，被吸入的物体受到挤压并释放出光和热。这种能量的释放是可以被看到的。黑洞有时由一颗死亡的星星形成。只有大的星星才能形成黑洞。星星在其中心碎裂、变小，但仍然有引力。这样就形成了黑洞的中心。有时，黑洞是由一大团气体形成的云形成的，它因为气体分子之间产生的引力而缩小。哈勃天文望远镜曾拍到过一张这种黑洞的照片。科学家认为这种黑洞就在我们所处的星系中心。

Ⓑ   1. Ⓑ   2. Ⓓ
3. Agriculture Ⓒ, Ⓔ / Military Ⓓ

苏美尔文明

苏美尔人取得了很多进步。他们首先改善了农业。后来，他们建立了一支军队。人们认为苏美尔人发明了轮子，并将之首次应用于对储存粮食非常重要的陶器制造。接着，轮子被用于研磨谷物。最后，用于农耕和军事车辆。苏美尔人甚至是在埃及人之前最早使用文字书写和数学的人。这帮助他们形成了他们的社会。这些体系被用来记录粮食储存和贸易，而军队用它来掌握人员、武器和给养的情况。苏美尔人是最早认真研究群星和太阳的人。这些研究帮助他们确认时节并依此决定何时开始农业种植。研究星相的方法也能够告诉他们何时开始对敌人发起进攻。他们相信，星相可以预知胜利或失败。

Ⓒ   1. Ⓓ   2. Ⓐ
3. Queen Ⓑ / Soldier Ⓐ / Worker Ⓒ, Ⓓ

蚁巢

白蚁成群地居住便形成了蚁巢。蚁巢里可能有几百万只这样的昆虫。蚁巢得以存在是从事不同工作的白蚁相互

合作的结果。每个蚁巢中至少有一个蚁王和一个蚁后。它们的任务是繁衍更多的白蚁，而不是指挥蚁巢的生活。一个蚁后每天可以产几千个卵，怀孕时身长能达到十厘米。从卵中孵化出的小白蚁被称为若虫。工蚁是看不见的。它们负责寻找食物，喂养兵蚁和小白蚁，并照管蚁巢。兵蚁要保卫蚁巢。它们的头上有一种保护性的外层。然而，它们的下颚太大，因此一定要由工蚁来喂食。有了这种组织结构，蚁巢的维护才能如此井井有条，而这是任何一个个体都无法独立完成的。

D　1. Ⓐ　　2. Ⓒ
　　3. Continental Drift Ⓑ, Ⓔ
　　　Plate Tectonics Ⓒ, Ⓓ

大陆漂移理论

大陆漂移理论是一个古老的地质学理论，甚至比板块构造理论还要古老。早期的科学家发现不同的陆地板块有相互适应的形状，也注意到板块间的地质特点是相似的。非洲和南美洲有很多相似性，在这两个地方还发现了同样的化石。即使是今天，在两个地方还发现一种同样的蚯蚓。科学家认为，在过去，地球的板块是连接在一起的。整个巨大板块被称为"泛古陆"。随着时间的推移，整个板块逐渐分裂。问题是要解释板块如何分离。科学家无法解释整个大陆是如何穿过海床上的岩石的。最终，他们发现，即使是海床也向某些方向延伸。这进一步推动了板块漂移和板块构造理论的发展。

Practice with Long Passages

A　Corpernicus Ⓒ, Ⓔ / Newton Ⓐ, Ⓑ, Ⓖ

人类对宇宙的感知

人类已经仰望夜空几千年了。人类对夜空抱有无限遐想，同时也满足了其对知识的追求。

我们的祖先首先认识到星星以同一种模式穿过夜空。他们将星星以熟悉的形状归类。这些形状为人们的旅行提供导航并告诉人们何时开始种植庄稼。这些形状也是故事和信仰的关注重心。几百年来，人们一直相信地球和人类是宇宙的中心。在 1543 年，哥白尼证明这个想法是错误的。事实上，地球是围绕太阳旋转的。这个观点开启了更深刻了解宇宙的大门。后来，伽利略使用天文望远镜来更多地了解太阳和行星。

最终，引力创造宇宙的观点出现了。这主要归功于艾萨克·牛顿。引力使得小的物体向大的物体运动。这解释了太阳系是如何形成的，行星如何围绕太阳运动，以及彗星是如何在太阳系中运动的。我们对于引力的了解帮助我们探索太空。

B　Pros Ⓑ, Ⓖ / Cons Ⓐ, Ⓔ, Ⓕ

刘易斯和克拉克以及路易斯安那购地

1803 年，杰斐逊总统从法国统治者拿破仑的手中买下了密西西比以西的土地。在当时，这对美国这个新兴国家提出了一些挑战，但是其益处是非常巨大的。

当时，许多人不赞同这一举动。一些人认为没有必要从法国手里"购买"。法国在北美洲没有军队，所以可以很轻易地将其占领。还有一些人认为总统没有权力购买土地。而其他人觉得购买这块土地会得罪他们的西班牙邻居。而且，还有人担心新的州会夺走旧州的权力。

尽管有上述疑虑，1803 年，这项收购还是将美国的土地扩大了一倍。然而，在最开始，杰斐逊总统和其他美国人对这片土地可以说是一无所知。他们不知道那里有什么可以使用的资源，但他们很快就会知道那里资源丰富。大片的土地可以用来进行农业生产。在地下有丰富的矿藏。最重要的是，那里的巨大河流可以促进经济的增长。总统派出了以刘易斯和克拉克为首的考察队来探索这片土地。考察队在二十八个月中行进超过八千英里。考察队绘制了很多地图，并记录了很多笔记。这些信息被用来计划美利坚合众国的未来。

C　Adaptability Ⓐ, Ⓕ
　　Defenses Ⓑ, Ⓒ, Ⓖ

负鼠

有袋动物是指身体上有袋的哺乳动物。雌性动物将幼崽饲养在袋中直到它们能够在袋外生存。北美洲唯一的有袋动物是负鼠。

负鼠的体积与一只大猫差不多。它有灰色的毛皮、粉色的鼻子、四肢和尾巴。它们有大大的黑眼睛，在活动最频繁的夜晚也能看得很清楚。虽然有五十颗非常尖利的牙齿，但它们的性格非常温顺。它们避免任何争斗。

负鼠适应力很强。它们可以在许多地方生存，如树上或地下。它们既吃植物也吃动物，如昆虫、老鼠、小蛇、草、树叶和浆果。

负鼠有一套防卫机制。它们对绝大多数毒蛇的毒液具有免疫力。由于它们血液的温度，它们通常不会得可怕的狂犬病。它们最著名的防卫是装死。绝大多数动物不吃死亡的动物，所以这种防卫方式很有效。负鼠会翻过来，露出尖利的牙齿，还会在它们的尾部产生出很难闻的味道。通常，其他动物会离开。

D **Water at the Bottom** Ⓐ, Ⓕ, Ⓖ
Water at the Surface Ⓑ, Ⓔ

马里亚纳海沟

海沟是长长的洞。当一个板块滑动到另一个板块之下，海沟就形成了。海底有二十二个大海沟。三个在大西洋，一个在印度洋，还有十八个在太平洋。最大的海沟被称为马里亚纳海沟，位于日本附近的太平洋中。

马里亚纳海沟是地球上最深的地方。它长 542 公里，宽 69 公里，深度为 11033 米。即使是将地球上最高的山放在里面也无法触及其最高点，要达到顶峰还有大约 2 公里的水深。

海沟的底部与表面不同。深处的压力是表面的一千倍。没有潜水艇，人无法到达。人类无法相信在这种条件下会有任何生命存在。但事实上，海沟的底部确实存在鱼和虾。

海沟底部的水不会被阳光加热，其不结冻的原因是深切入地壳的裂缝，从中散发出的热量达到 300 摄氏度。在表面，水比较清澈。在深处，水中到处都是动物的骨骸碎片和皮肤，还有细菌。这种混合形成了一个厚厚的混层。

Building Summary Skills

A & B

1. Man's Perception of the Universe

Man has tried to understand the [1] night sky for a long time, and he has created many [2] stories about it. For years, it was believed that man was the [3] center of the universe. [4] Copernicus and [5] Galileo showed us information to the contrary. [6] Newton came upon the idea of [7] gravity. This helped explain the [8] motion of all the objects in our universe.

2. Lewis and Clark and the Louisiana Purchase

The [1] Louisiana Purchase was a great addition to the United States, but it posed a few [2] challenges. Politically, many people did not [3] like the idea. Some were concerned about [4] relations with other countries, and others were concerned about how it would affect [5] political power in the US. After [6] buying the land, information about the people, the [7] resources, and the rivers was needed to [8] make use of it.

3. The Opossum

Opossums are the only [1] marsupials in [2] North America. They are mostly [3] nocturnal and, despite having many teeth, are very [4] gentle. They are adaptable in that they are [5] omnivores and can find a home in lots of places. Opossums have a number of [6] defenses. They are mostly [7] immune to rabies and snake poison, and they can also [8] play dead.

4. The Mariana Trench

The Mariana Trench is a long [1] hole at the [2] bottom of the sea. It is the [3] deepest place on earth. The pressure is huge at the bottom, but [4] animals still manage to live there. The water has unique [5] qualities: it does not [6] freeze because of [7] heat vents in the earth, and the water is a thick mix of [8] bacteria and animal particles.

Mini TOEFL iBT

1. Ⓓ   **2.** Ⓐ   **3.** Ⓑ   **4.** Ⓑ   **5.** Ⓒ
6. Planets Ⓐ, Ⓒ, Ⓔ / **Asteroids** Ⓓ, Ⓖ
7. Ⓑ   **8.** Ⓐ   **9.** Ⓒ   **10.** Ⓒ   **11.** Ⓓ
12. Convergent Ⓑ, Ⓓ, Ⓔ / **Transform** Ⓒ /
Divergent Ⓕ

太阳系

太阳系是由按照一定规律围绕太阳轨道运行的天体构成的。但情况并非总是如此。在最初，太阳与围绕它运动的天体以一种非常不同的形式运动。

人们认为太阳系最初是一个由气体和尘埃形成的巨大云层。云层呈圆形并缓慢旋转。旋转使气体和尘埃平摊成一个大盘。中心的气体和尘埃形成了太阳。气体和尘埃被重力牵引到一起，进一步开始了核反应。外部的气体和尘埃运动缓慢，它们逐渐在某处聚合。最终，当一定体积的物质聚集在一起后，便形成了行星。

太阳系中存在许多不同的天体。当然，也有行星。每一颗行星都与众不同。一些行星由岩石或金属物质构成，比如水星、金星、地球和火星。其他的行星更像是气体和冰，如木星、土星和其他一些行星。行星都有卫星，有的还有不止一个。

太阳系有一个主要的小行星带。小行星基本上是一块岩石，最大的直径大约 10 公里。大量的岩石在火星和木星之间围绕太阳运动。有时小行星相互撞击，逐渐靠近地球。在靠近的过程中，它们会被加热，燃烧。于是我们就看到了流星。

最后，还有冰和气体形成的彗星。它们以不规则的路径围绕太阳运动。当靠近太阳时，它们开始融化并形成一条尾巴。在远离太阳的寒冷宇宙中，它们始终是冰冻的固体。

板块构造学说

板块构造学说是一个地质学理论。该理论解释了地球表面是如何运动的。它表明地球表面是由可移动的漂浮板块构成的。

地球是由不同的层次构成的。最上面的一层是坚固的，但是分裂成十个左右不同的板块。它们大约有 100 公里厚。这些板块在地表漂移，下面是水。下层的高温推动板块移动。随着板块的移动，地震、火山、山脉和沿板块边缘存在于海底的海沟就形成了。

板块可以以三种不同形式移动。它们可以分散移动，这被称为发散边界。在海床上有一些这样的地方。当板块以此方式移动时，地心的液体上涌填入被称为裂缝的空隙。裂缝附近的岩石比远处的岩石年轻，大约每年向外发展 2 厘米。转换边界在两个板块并行运动时形成。这在美国加州非常常见。太平洋板块和北美板块之间的摩擦处大约有 1300 公里。它们每年移动 0.6 厘米，形成了圣安德烈亚斯断层，这个断层导致了很多地震的发生。当两个板块相对移动时，汇聚边界便形成了。通常，一个板块滑到另一个板块下。在这种情况下，上层的板块升起，山脉因此形成。喜马拉雅山脉就是这样形成的，它是全世界最年轻的山脉之一。在印度下面的板块不断滑入西藏下面的板块。这些高大的山脉每年上升大约 5 毫米。

Vocabulary Review

1. Ⓒ 2. Ⓓ 3. Ⓒ 4. Ⓑ 5. Ⓓ
6. Ⓒ 7. Ⓓ 8. Ⓑ 9. Ⓐ 10. Ⓓ

Actual Test

1. Ⓒ 2. Ⓓ 3. Ⓒ 4. Ⓓ 5. Ⓐ
6. Ⓒ 7. Ⓑ 8. Ⓒ 9. Ⓓ 10. Ⓑ, Ⓓ, Ⓔ
11. Ⓐ 12. Ⓐ 13. Ⓐ 14. Ⓒ 15. Ⓑ
16. Ⓓ 17. Ⓒ 18. Ⓐ 19. Ⓒ
20. Ⓑ, Ⓒ, Ⓕ   21. Ⓑ 22. Ⓑ
23. Ⓒ 24. Ⓓ 25. Ⓓ 26. Ⓓ 27. Ⓐ
28. Ⓒ 29. Ⓐ
30. **Problem** Ⓒ, Ⓔ / **Solution** Ⓑ, Ⓕ, Ⓖ

白尾鹿和黑尾鹿

在所有北美洲的大型动物中，数量最多的当属白尾鹿。这个鹿种的习惯是提尾，并用尾巴拍打后背，露出白色的下腹和臀部。在它们跑开时，人们经常可以看到这种标志性动作。尾巴放下时呈棕色，但带有一个白边。随着季节的变化，白尾鹿的颜色在夏季变成微红，而在冬季变成微灰。一头成年雄鹿一般能长到肩高 1 米以上，体重超过 110 公斤。雄性有鹿角，偶尔会和其他雄鹿的角缠在一起，这使得双方只能等死。

白尾鹿也被称为弗吉尼亚鹿，居住在美国的绝大多数大陆地区，同时也存在于加拿大南部、墨西哥、中美洲以及南美洲的北部国家。而且，它们还被引入北欧，特别是芬兰。

白尾鹿的适应能力非常强。虽然绝大多数情况下住在密林地区，但它们也能够适应热带（或亚热带）稀树大草原的气候，比如得克萨斯的平原或委内瑞拉的大草原等地区。白尾鹿的交配季节是在秋季，雄鹿会与尽可能多的雌鹿交配。在晚春时节，雌鹿就会产下一或两头小鹿。雌鹿有时会离开它的小鹿几个小时，因为小鹿的天然伪装——有斑点的外皮和没有任何的体味——使得绝大多数捕食者无法发现它们。母鹿会阶段性地返回来哺育小鹿。

有了充足的食物和庇护，白尾鹿的数量迅速增加，这种增长有时会超出地区的承受能力。以农作物为食的它们常常给农民惹麻烦。同时，它们也常在跳跃地穿越公路时与汽车相撞，致使自身死亡以及汽车驾驶员受伤或死亡。为了控制白尾鹿的数量，人们定期组织狩猎。事实上，猎鹿在许多地区都是一种重要的文化仪式，在一些地区猎鹿甚至有提升地方经济的重要作用。为了经济发展而砍伐森林的行为剥夺了许多鹿群的天然聚居地，这导致鹿群的饥饿，增加了高速公路交通事故的可能性。

黑尾鹿是几百万年前由白尾鹿演变而来的。科学家认为白尾鹿从北美大陆的东海岸穿越墨西哥到达加利福尼亚海岸的北部，最终它们在那里进化成了黑尾鹿。它们共同的祖先揭示了为什么两个物种在外在特征和心理特点上非常相似。确实，两种鹿常常很难辨别。虽然黑尾鹿的尾巴是黑的，但它们与白尾鹿的习性相同，喜欢翘起尾巴，露出白色的下腹。而且，两个种类的雄鹿有相似的鹿角。但是黑尾鹿只存在于美洲大陆西岸沿线——从加拿大的英属哥伦比亚到加利福尼亚南部。此外，黑尾鹿比它们的亲戚白尾鹿要小一些。

直到最近，科学家们相信黑尾鹿是长耳鹿的一个亚种。但是 DNA 测试证明两者没有什么联系。长耳鹿是通过与白尾鹿和黑尾鹿交配而进化出来的一个不同的物种。

有经验的猎手说黑尾鹿是最难捕获的。其中的一个原因是黑尾鹿居住在更炎热的气候环境中，在夏天，白天气温高达华氏 100 度，而这时正是加州的射箭季节。在这种温度下，黑尾雄鹿在白天很少活动，而只在夜色的保护下出没。雨季，黑尾鹿在白天非常活跃，但是没有猎人愿意在恶劣的天气中外出冒险。西部各州的捕猎季节在雄鹿活跃地寻找雌鹿的交配季节之前结束，因此，对黑尾鹿的猎捕就变得更加困难。所以，它们在很难进行捕猎的时节反倒更容易见到。

尽管猎捕黑尾鹿相对困难，但猎人还是能够成功捕捉到它们。事实上，加州每年大约有 20 万捕鹿猎手，这为当地经济贡献了 45 万美元的收入。

古代洞穴壁画

史前洞穴壁画始于公元前四万年到公元前一万年的旧石器时代晚期，但直到 1879 年，它们才在西班牙的一个洞穴中被再次发现。最初，它们被怀疑是一个骗局。但是其真实性随着洞穴艺术在全球其他地区被发现而得以证明。现代的碳测年技术已经证明了它们起源于远古。在法国、意大利、非洲、澳大利亚和东南亚的洞穴墙壁上同样发现了让人印象深刻的画作。

1879 年的发现是马格德林时期的作品，这个时期以附近的西班牙小镇马格德林命名。这里的人们生活在公元前一万八千年到公元前一万年。马格德林时期的艺术非常有特色，以不断重复的主题和风格为特点。最流行的主题是动物，特别是野牛、鹿、马和已经灭绝的猛犸象。现实的人类主题很少见，仅限于人体的抽象表达。但是，起到艺术家"签名"作用的手的形象还是偶尔出现在画作之中。

洞穴壁画始终被掩藏有两个原因。首先，画家选择在洞穴深处进行绘画，而洞穴深处的石墙"画布"可以免遭天气侵蚀。这些地方对于寻找古代文明印记的现代寻访者来说是不容易发现的。第二，一旦一个洞穴的壁画被发现且被好奇的公众知晓，发掘工作就会展开，将这些被保护了几千年的画作公之于众。因此，一批在第一次世界大战期间在法国被发现的宝贵壁画在对大众开放六个月后就消失了。空调可以保护一些用于参观的壁画遗址，但是绝大多数都不对旅游者开放。学者们需要申请才能与壁画近距离接触，而且研究的时间非常有限。

尽管洞穴壁画的信息难以获取，但科学家还是得以推测出古代画家所使用的方法和颜料。最早的画作是在岩石表面的软粘土上的手指画，主要用来描绘动物的爪痕。后来，画家们使用了雕刻的方法，用石质工具在石墙上刻画。将自身的绘画技巧和专门的工具结合，画家们可以改变一个场景的色调、颜色和深度。

最后得以发展的技术是墙壁绘画。当时使用的颜色很少，因为石器时代的人只能在自然环境中寻找材料。他们使用各种各样的矿物和树木来生产颜料。例如，红色是从氧化铁中提取的，而白色是从云母中提取的。他们还从烧过的树木中获取碳来制作黑色颜料。

即使是靠如此原始的手段，画家们也表现出了混合和使用色彩的天赋。人们已经在藤壶壳中发现了近两百种制造颜色的矿物碎片，这些颜色都是混合而成的。一个画家使用人的颅骨来混合颜料。洞穴中含钙的水被用来调配色彩，而动物和植物油被用来粘合颜色。虽然没有发现画笔，但完成的画作有明显的画笔印记。有时，他们将吹管作为喷绘画作的主要工具，将颜料喷到蜡板覆盖的墙壁表面。

绘画是一种职业。对于那些要用大量时间打猎并寻找生存方式的业余绘画者来说，绘画是困难而且昂贵的。其中的一个难题是如何照亮黑暗的洞穴墙壁。科学家认为古代画家是将动物油脂制成火把照明的。另一个问题是一些洞穴墙壁难以触及。有些地方非常狭窄，只有躺着才能作画；还有一些很高的地方则需要特别的脚手架。

当地人绘画的场所为人类学家研究旧石器时代晚期人们的生活方式提供了重要线索。虽然洞穴绘画是他们的一个标志，但古代绘画者们并不住在洞穴中。他们将洞穴的墙壁作为画板是因为露天的画作很容易消失，而洞穴保护了画作。他们想要画作永远流传下去，并不仅仅因为供自己娱乐之用，还因为画作有重要的文化功能。画作是史前文明传承历史并对传统和祖先表示敬意的媒介。

时区的历史

地球在围绕太阳公转时也发生自转，所以时区的划分显得尤为必要。地球每转一周需要二十四小时，其受太阳照射的地区形成白昼，其他地区形成黑夜，如此反复。如果人们向西方不断行进，在每一个地区，太阳到达最高点——即正午十二点——的时间都不一样。因此，一个城市是正午十二点，而仅仅向东一百英里的另一个城市由于太阳已经移过最高点而处于不同的时间。

在科技使得长距离即时交流成为可能之前的前工业时代，这并不是问题。计时仅仅是地方现象。每一个城市都自行设定钟表，因此正午十二点就是太阳在某处到达最高点的时间。一个到其他城市的旅行者必须调整自己的钟表以适应当地的时间。

19 世纪，铁路开始铺设，电报通讯也开始发展。在整个历史上，人类得以第一次一天内穿越数英里，并通过电报进行跨国贸易。旧的不规律时间体系使商业和通讯变得非常困难和混乱。由于车站遵循不同的时间，所以无法制订统一的火车时刻表。每一个铁路公司都使用自己的时间标准，常常是公司总部或一个重要站点的时间。有的火车站有其站内每一条铁路使用的显示不同时间的钟表。例如，到达一个主要城市的旅行者会看到车站墙上挂有六个钟表，分别显示不同的时间。铁路的有效运营需要时间的标准化。

1878年，加拿大铁路工程师斯坦福·弗莱明爵士提出了一个解决方法。他提议根据地球的经线将地球划分为不同的时区，每一个时区的宽度是十五度。按照他的计算，地球的三百六十度就可以被划分为以十五度为单位的二十四个分区。依此划分体系，地球每旋转一个十五度或地球的二十四分之一就是一个小时。

美国铁路在1883年使用了弗莱明的体系，但要想在全球有效使用该体系还需要指定一条经线作为基准。1884年，一个为了这一目的而召开的国际子午线会议在华盛顿特区举行，最终决定将穿越英国格林威治的经线确定为"本初子午线"或零度经线。在这条经线上的时间被称为格林威治时间，简称GMT。每条经线都是从北极穿至南极，与赤道垂直。虽然在理论上经线是直的，但实际上许多都呈曲线以满足当地人民的需要。

并不是所有的国家都立即采用了这一体系。美国的绝大部分地区直到1895年才采用这一体系，并且直到1918年国会才通过《标准时间法案》。即使是今天，有些国家也并不完全依照这一标准。以色列一天的开始是在下午六点而不是中午十二点。虽然中国应该有五个时区，但事实上，政府规定全国统一使用一个时区。还有一些国家则采用半小时时区制。

另一种通行的时区管理方法是日光节能时制，在一些国家也被称为夏令时。这些国家在春天时将钟表调快一小时并一直持续到秋季，将工作日的白天增加了一个小时，主要目的是节能。如果黑夜晚一个小时到达，那就意味着人们会少消耗一个小时的电能。另一个好处是人们可以利用延长的时间在温暖的月份到外面活动。

格林威治时间依据地球自转的速度，而地球转速并不守恒，因此随着时间的推移，时间标准会有误差。因此，在1972年，格林威治时间与超级精准的原子钟同步，使用"闰秒"这一概念，解决了时间与地球转动一致的问题。这一新的计时体系被称为"协调世界时"，简称UTC。